'The centenary of the UK's Co-operative
opportunity for reflection on the legacy a
education. Drawing on examples from the
in this book demonstrate rich diversity
education, ranging from practical tra.
co-operative principles to schools and universities. The book offers
stimulating contributions to debates about education, management,
democracy and the role of co-operatives in our society.'

**Professor Mary Hilson, School of Culture and Society,
Aarhus University**

'This book clearly demonstrates the powerful contribution that
co-operative education can make to addressing the major challenges facing
the world today. It is a treasury of exciting ideas, historical examples and
emerging possibilities and should be read by everyone with an interest in
developing education that is adequate to our present interesting times.'

**Keri Facer, Professor of Educational and Social Futures,
University of Bristol, and Zennström Chair in
Climate Change Leadership, University of Uppsala**

Learning for a Co-operative World

Learning for a Co-operative World

Education, social change and the Co-operative College

Edited by
Tom Woodin and Linda Shaw

 is an imprint of

First published in 2019 by the UCL Institute of Education Press, 20 Bedford Way, London WC1H 0AL

www.ucl-ioe-press.com

British Library Cataloguing in Publication Data:
A catalogue record for this publication is available from the British Library

ISBNs
978-1-85856-680-1 (paperback)
978-1-85856-699-3 (PDF eBook)
978-1-85856-901-7 (ePub eBook)
978-1-85856-902-4 (Kindle eBook)

Typeset by Quadrant Infotech (India) Pvt Ltd
Printed by CPI Group (UK) Ltd, Croydon, CR0 4YY
Cover design by emc design ltd

Contents

Part Three: Learning from new practices

About the contributors

Tom Woodin

Dr Tom Woodin is a reader in the social history of education at the UCL Institute of Education. He has researched and published widely on co-operatives and learning, including *Community and Mutual Ownership: A historical review* for the Joseph Rowntree Foundation and the edited book *Co-operation, Learning and Co-operative Values* published by Routledge. He also works on the history of education and is currently co-writing a history of the Co-operative College for Palgrave Macmillan, and, with Gary McCulloch and Steven Cowan, he wrote *Secondary Education and the Raising of the School Leaving Age – Coming of Age?*. His most recent book is on workers' writing and community publishing, *Working-Class Writing and Publishing in the Late-Twentieth Century: Literature, culture and community*, published by Manchester University Press. Tom co-edits the journal *History of Education*.

Linda Shaw

Dr Linda Shaw was formerly vice principal at the Co-operative College in Manchester where she was responsible for research and international programmes. She has worked with co-operatives internationally and published widely on co-operative development and history for both academic and wider audiences. Linda has also worked at the University of Manchester and for the Open University. Most recently she has been working in the field of business and human rights.

Michael L. Cook

Michael L. Cook is the Robert D. Partridge Endowed Professor in Organization Economics in the Division of Applied Social Sciences at the University of Missouri, Columbia (MU). His research activities include work in more than 60 countries and 100 published works. His primary research addresses the ownership costs of vaguely defined property rights in patron-owned and controlled enterprises. His research and outreach work is embedded into Graduate Institute of Cooperative Leadership (GICL) programmes. Professor Cook is executive director of GICL. He served for 12 years in senior management positions with three global enterprises, two of them co-operatives, and has occupied board positions with numerous co-operatives, subsidiaries and associations. In May 2012, he was inducted into the Cooperative Hall of Fame at the National Press Club, Washington, DC. In 2015, Michael received the Frederick B. Mumford Outstanding Faculty Award at MU, which recognizes a faculty member with a sustained record of excellence in teaching, research and/or extension/outreach who is viewed as an exemplary educator by both students and faculty.

Keith Crome

Dr Keith Crome is principal lecturer in philosophy at Manchester Metropolitan University, and he leads the Manchester Metropolitan University Co-operative Network. Together with Patrick O'Connor, he has published several articles on the philosophy of education. He is currently researching a monography on the history of the concept of character.

Richard Hall

Richard Hall is professor of education and technology at De Montfort University, Leicester, and a UK National Teaching Fellow. He has been a director of Leicester Vaughan College and a co-operator at the Social Science Centre in Lincoln. Richard is a Trustee of the Open Library of Humanities and a member of the Management Committee for Leicester's Primary Pupil Referral Unit. His most recent monograph is *The Alienated Academic: The struggle for autonomy inside the university*, published by Palgrave Macmillan. Richard writes about life in academia at: http://richard-hall.org

Liz McIvor

Liz McIvor is the manager of the Co-operative Heritage Trust and works to engage with audiences for the National Co-operative Archive and the Rochdale Pioneers Museum. Her background is in museums and heritage and, over the past two decades, she has worked as a curator of social and industrial history, including at local authority museums and textile mills in the North West and Yorkshire. She has collaborated with writers, researchers and media organizations to increase and promote access to museum and archive collections, as well as historic buildings, places and stories in the UK. She decided to train for this profession following a life-changing museum visit made as a primary schoolchild in Manchester. Her main area of specialism relates to the ways in which ordinary people have made their living, their experiences and influences, particularly in the context of industry, trade and transport in the urbanized areas of the nineteenth and twentieth centuries. She has published widely in popular magazines and blogs, and presented a number of programmes on TV.

Mike Neary

Mike Neary is professor of sociology at the University of Lincoln. His main research interest is the future of higher education. He is a founder member of the Social Science Centre, a co-operative organizing no-fee higher education in Lincoln, and a member of the Co-operative University Working Group, co-ordinated by the Co-operative College.

Patrick O'Connor

Dr Patrick O'Connor is a senior lecturer in philosophy at Nottingham Trent University. He researches European philosophy, with special reference to phenomenology, nineteenth- and twentieth-century European philosophy, early to mid-twentieth-century French philosophy, and the philosophy of education. He has published two books, one entitled *Atheism Reclaimed* on atheism and existentialism, the other on phenomenology, ethics and the work of Jacques Derrida entitled *Derrida: Profanations*. He is currently working on a project that investigates the intersection between philosophy and literature in the work of Cormac McCarthy.

Deborah Ralls

Deborah Ralls is a Leverhulme Early Career Research Fellow at the University of Manchester with particular interests in social justice issues in education and the potential to develop more equitable relationships between schools and their students, parents and community members. She is currently at the start of a three-year international research project, Redefining Education for a Social Solidarity Urban Economy: Becoming Relational, which explores the way in which four different cities (Barcelona, Berlin, New York and Rio de Janeiro) engage with their locality through various relational mechanisms and infrastructures, such as governance, curriculum and pedagogy. The research focuses on how education interventions could build stronger relationships with urban communities and help to lay the foundations for more inclusive social solidarity economies. She has published articles in the *Journal of Co-operative Studies* (2016) and *Forum for Promoting 3–19 Comprehensive Education* (2016). Prior to beginning her research career, Deborah worked as a teacher and teacher educator in both further and higher education, developing and teaching literacy, ESOL (English for speakers of other languages) and postgraduate certificate in education programmes as well as managing an alternative education provision for 13–19 year olds.

Rory Ridley-Duff

Rory Ridley-Duff is Professor of Cooperative Social Entrepreneurship, at Sheffield Business School, Sheffield Hallam University. He entered academia after working at Computercraft Ltd, a London-based worker co-operative, for 12 years. Since then, he has contributed to establishing social enterprise as a new academic field and supported co-operative development through multi-stakeholder 'FairShares' co-operatives. He is associate editor of the *Journal of Social Entrepreneurship* and is author of *Understanding Social Enterprise: Theory and practice* (co-authored with Dr Mike Bull) and *The Case for FairShares*. His articles on co-operative governance, community development, industrial relations, entrepreneurship and ethics have appeared in top management journals and he has been recognized for research excellence through awards from Emerald Publishing, the Institute for Small Business and Entrepreneurship, and the International Social Innovation Research Conference.

Cilla Ross

Dr Cilla Ross is an educator, historian and sociologist with a background in higher, labour and adult education. At the Co-operative College she has overall responsibility for co-operative education, research and future thinking. Decent work, livelihood building and co-operative placemaking are current priorities alongside popular and co-operative education methodologies. She is currently co-editing and co-authoring *Reclaiming the*

University for the Public Good: Experiments and futures in co-operative higher education (with Malcolm Noble, Palgrave) and recent publications include research on the degradation of work (T. Isidorsson and J. Kubisa (eds) (2018) *Job Quality in an Era of Flexibility: Experiences in a European context,* London: Routledge); and on union co-operatives and precarity (Co-operatives UK and the Co-operative College (2017) *Organising Precarious Workers: Trade union and co-operative strategies,* London: TUC). Most recently she has been working on designing the first Co-operative University in the UK and devising a project that celebrates the Ministry of Reconstruction's 1919 Report on Adult Education. Cilla is a visiting fellow of the Institute of Place Management at Manchester Metropolitan University and works closely with co-operative councils, such as Rochdale, on ways to rebuild and remake co-operative identity and place.

Joss Winn

Joss Winn works at the University of Lincoln, where he is responsible for the School of Education's doctoral programmes. He has written extensively on co-operative and alternative forms of higher education. Most recently he has turned his attention to the education and training of luthiers (makers of stringed instruments) and the associated social, institutional and individual challenges related to the transmission of knowledge and skills in this craft tradition.

List of tables and figures

List of tables

List of figures

Acknowledgements

We would like to thank Gillian Lonergan and Sophie McCulloch from the National Co-operative Archive as well as Co-operative College staff, particularly Simon Parkinson, Cilla Ross, Steve Kingman and Nina Eastwood, who all gave their backing for this project. The College project team in Malawi, especially John Mulangeni, provided important support. We thank all those who have organized and contributed to the regular co-operative education research conferences in Manchester for their discussion and feedback. We would also like to thank Gillian Klein, Jonathan Dore and Sally Sigmund from Trentham Books / UCL IOE Press for supporting this book. Thanks also to Ella and Eva.

Foreword

Simon Parkinson, Chief Executive and
Principal at the Co-operative College

As the Co-operative College reaches its centenary, I feel an equal sense of privilege and responsibility to be leading the team at the College. Together with our board of trustees, under the stewardship of Nigel Todd, we are well placed to continue the work of the College across the UK and internationally. Beyond this we are keen to work with like-minded individuals and organizations to explore new areas of work. We are committed to ensuring the relevance of co-operative education to the international co-operative movement and society at large.

This is an important moment, not only in the Co-operative College's history but also in its future and in the future of co-operative education across the globe. We see many examples of people seeking alternative solutions that address the pressing issues facing the world today. Be it the changing, and often more precarious, nature of work or the increasing problem of youth loneliness in the UK, or the advancement of the Sustainable Development Goals in the Global South, co-operation, co-operators and co-operative enterprises all have a vital role to play.

What does it mean to co-operate, to be a co-operator or to lead in a co-operative enterprise? These are important questions and the key to answering them is co-operative education. From traditional, in the best sense of the word, approaches to community-based adult education – learning to be and learning to do – to harnessing the wealth of knowledge and information in the commons, society at large needs education to understand the co-operative advantage and how to implement it.

This book is unique as it sets out for the reader the frameworks within which co-operative education exists. It moves on to appraise different themes relating to co-operative education that highlight its continued relevance and importance. It critically assesses real practices of co-operative education, from around the world, and the difference they make.

I would like to thank all of the contributors for both their work here and the important contribution each of them continues to make to the international co-operative movement. Special thanks to the editors, Tom Woodin and Linda Shaw, for their hard work in pulling all of this together as well as for their important individual contributions.

Thank you to you, the reader, for your continued interest in co-operative education. Here at the Co-operative College we remain convinced that great things happen when people co-operate and, in that spirit, I look forward to hearing your views both on the book and how we can work together to ensure that co-operative education thrives over the next hundred years.

Introduction

Tom Woodin and Linda Shaw

Co-operative education encompasses a rich set of ideas and practices that help us to rethink rapidly changing social worlds. In recent decades, the concept and practice of co-operation has attracted co-operators, academics and educators, from inside and outside the co-operative movement, who are keen to explore alternatives to dominant educational ideas. The codification of co-operative values and principles by the International Co-operative Alliance (ICA) in 1995 stimulated original thinking and action about the role of values in educational and co-operative endeavours. Co-operative values are democracy, equality, equity, self-help, self-responsibility and solidarity. The fifth principle refers explicitly to 'education, training and information' and avows that:

> Co-operatives provide education and training for their members, elected representatives, managers, and employees so they can contribute effectively to the development of their co-operatives. They inform the general public – particularly young people and opinion leaders – about the nature and benefits of co-operation. (ICA, 2018)

This broad approach can be identified in new understandings of how leaders, managers and members learn: in co-operative history and heritage; in the development of co-operative schools and plans for a co-operative university; in co-operative and mutual development in the provision of other public services; in the expanding range of related non-profit organizations, including social enterprise; in the renewed importance of co-operatives in international development; in the growing significance of co-operative themes in research; and in the attempts to value co-operative studies in higher education as well as co-operation within the school curriculum. This fissiparous range of initiatives, which are expanding in new directions yet remain connected to a set of common reference points, highlight a potential moment of historical change.

Education and learning have themselves moved centre stage in international discourses on economic, social, political and cultural matters. With the ending of the Cold War, the onset of globalization, the rapid spread of digital technologies and the forceful reassertion of human capital theories, education and training could no longer be demoted to a minor position. Jacques Delors' UNESCO report, *Learning: The treasure within* (1996) recognized and made visible the manifold aspects of learning in the new world order and these were to be continued in UNESCO Global Reports on Adult Learning and Education. Yet the story has not been one of uninterrupted expansion, and the new regimes of learning have been contested from a number of quarters. In fact, the recognition of multiple aspects of learning was to some extent undermined by the cutting of adult education programmes for general, liberal and leisure learning because they were viewed as wasteful public expenditure that did not fit with a narrow skills-based agenda or make a direct economic contribution. Moreover, public scrutiny of education has led to the demand for simplified forms of accountability delivered through the technology of the league table, championed by national and international agencies such as the OECD, which skews educational activity in particular directions. Schools have been accused of being 'exam factories' in their pursuit of results (Fielding and Moss, 2011). This is a tricky area to navigate, as results and standards are clearly important, and it is an agenda that was once dominated by those who advocated common schooling for all. These reservations received a further shock in the wake of the 2007–8 financial crisis and the prolonged era of austerity when alternative visions were being restricted. Yet the UN Sustainable Development Goals did seem to offer some hope, for instance:

> By 2030, ensure that all learners acquire the knowledge and skills needed to promote sustainable development, including, among others, through education for sustainable development and sustainable lifestyles, human rights, gender equality, promotion of a culture of peace and non-violence, global citizenship and appreciation of cultural diversity and of culture's contribution to sustainable development. (United Nations Sustainable Development Goals (n.d.), Goal 4.7)

At this historical moment, co-operative education started to attract people who wanted to pursue such visions. This book articulates these concerns and evaluates co-operative responses to our current predicament. In attempting to understand co-operative education and its place within co-operative and educational settings, it engages with wider debates about the future.

Co-operative education is a category that needs to be examined further (Woodin, 2015: 1–4). We have purposefully left its meaning open as we view it as a space that is being actively reworked at the current historical juncture. At the centre of it are the ways in which co-operative values and principles are applied and adapted to education and learning. This includes learning to work within co-operatives, for co-operative development as well as in support of co-operative values and principles more generally (Facer *et al.*, 2012). The concept may refer to the education and training needs of co-operatives as well as the potential that co-operative practices, values and principles can play in diverse social areas, from education to care, sport, shopping and production. Public services have been reconceptualized through the lens of co-operation. More intangibly, the process of participating in co-operatives is an educative one, in terms of skills and working together: what Ian MacPherson, in a phrase reminiscent of Robert Owen, referred to as 'associative intelligence' (MacPherson, 2002: 14). Co-operatives are based on meeting the needs of members. This means they are dependent on those members for their success, an educational process that involves both informal and formal learning. Thus, co-operators have for a long time embraced a version of the knowledge economy, recognizing that the progress of co-operation is dependent on the skills, education and understanding of members. Yet in the UK, the squeezing of traditional forms of education and training within the consumer co-operative movement has caused co-operators to ruminate on the future. Co-operative education cannot be easily contained within any one organization or movement and does not fit into existing categories and divisions, in part because its very purpose is to break some of them down. Indeed, the rich tapestry of co-operative activity extends across disciplinary boundaries, including management training, social science and the humanities. Its ambiguous location is one reason why it has not been straightforward in developing a coherent area of 'co-operative studies' (MacPherson and McLaughlin-Jenkins, 2008), which in any case would be hard to incorporate in the academy without a full awareness of pedagogy and learning.

However, the scope and importance of education within co-operation is visible in certain national and international arenas. Mondragon University, which has emerged from the Mondragon complex of co-operatives, has provided an important example of how education and learning at a high level can be both integrated into higher education and organized on a democratic co-operative basis (Wright *et al.*, 2011). Recently, two African university co-operatives have been established: the Moshi Co-operative University in Tanzania and the Co-operative University of Kenya (see Woodin, 2018). The Association of Cooperative Educators (ACE) lists a number of centres for co-operative studies in Ireland and North America (ACE, 2016–17). Other educational agencies fostering co-operation include the Italian Federazione Trentina della Cooperazione, the Academia José Moreira da Silva in Portugal, and the Unión de Cooperativas de Enseñanza de Trabajo Asociado de Madrid. On a broader level, many countries support co-operatives in education where co-operation may be taught as a subject, where co-operative structures are introduced into schooling and where co-operative enterprises form part of the learning process, for instance in France (Office Central de la Coopération à l'École (OCCE)) or Poland and Croatia, where school co-operatives have proliferated. In addition, co-operative organizations are emerging in educational arenas, including in childcare, early years education and compulsory schooling. Co-operatives have provided solutions to new problems such as the redundancies of music teachers that have led to the formation of successful co-operative structures enabling educators to self-organize (Musicians' Union, n.d.). The Co-operative College itself is involved in various international networks looking at development and leadership across countries that nurture mutual learning (see Cooperatives Europe, n.d.; Sheffield Hallam University, 2018).

It is a paradox that during a period of neoliberal dominance and even triumphalism, co-operatives have grown on the international stage. The global co-operative movement itself had, since the early 1990s, actively responded to the dominance of what became known as neoliberal ideas, which lauded the shareholder corporate model of democracy as the only way of doing business. In 2012, the UN recognized this significance in declaring it the International Year of Cooperatives and the then Secretary-General, Kofi Annan, affirmed that half of the world's population had benefited from co-operatives. The World Co-operative Monitor tracks the progress of the 300 largest co-operatives, which have a turnover exceeding $2.1 trillion. Co-operation embraces both the large-scale enterprise as well as the small informal co-operative run directly by members. It has developed secondary co-operatives and federal structures that represent and promote their members. At least 12 per cent of the world population are members of up to 3 million co-operatives that provide work for 10 per cent of the population (ICA/EURICSE, 2018).

The growing interest in co-operative education builds upon deep historical roots. By the late nineteenth century, the co-op in Britain had become a major industrial and commercial enterprise with a membership that would later peak at over 10 million and occupy about a third of the grocery market. These achievements had been built gradually from the savings and enterprise of working-class people. The long history of co-operation stretched back to the late eighteenth century and beyond. Co-operative action can be identified in agriculture and industry in the Middle Ages or even in ancient Rome, although specifically co-operative organizations are creations of the past 250 years. Their impact on social, economic and political life has been profound. Co-operatives have represented an important way in which working people took control of their lives, redistributed wealth and then kept it within their own communities (recent examples include Robertson, 2016; Wilson *et al.*, 2013; see also Cole, 1944). They offered important avenues of educational and cultural expression. By organizing themselves for mutual benefit, co-operators learnt by participating in co-operatives. Co-operatives provided the proof about the responsibility and respectability of the working class to justify extending the franchise. The power of working people to organize their lives democratically also fed into debates favouring the introduction of compulsory schooling.

Over the past century, the Co-operative College has been at the heart of co-operative education. It was established in 1919 to co-ordinate the varied educational programmes and initiatives organized by the consumer co-operative movement. It offered long-term training courses for managers and secretaries alongside courses in social science and humanities. Training for members and directors would be arranged as well as shorter modules targeting specific issues and problems facing the movement (see Woodin, 2017). In doing so, it extended the work of the Co-operative Union under whose umbrella the College sat. Yet the new institution also had an impact in other ways. As the first college of its type, it was to have significant repercussions internationally. The College provided a model that other countries emulated in establishing their own colleges across the globe. It attracted students from around the world – Australia, Europe and the Indian sub-continent in particular. For forty years after the Second World War, it was funded by the UK government Colonial Office to train co-operative leaders who came for a year to the College and then went on to occupy high-level positions in co-operatives, co-operative development and policy. College staff and students played a key role in the emerging field of international development in both policy and practice from the 1950s.

Celebrating the centenary of the College is certainly important and its history over the past century is currently being written. Its longevity is testament to the validity of its vision, the important role it has played in education as well as the way it has adapted to changing circumstances. But standing still is not an option and current social and political crises pose considerable challenges. It has recently moved to become more independent of the Co-operative Union, and the movement as a whole, as a member-led charity. This provides many opportunities for the College but also reflects the decline of the educational spaces in which the College traditionally circulated. This has been most marked with the reduction in the number of co-operative societies, while those that have survived have tended to organize their own training and education programmes. However, the College is actively responding to contemporary developments and is looking outwards to plan co-operative futures. Indeed, the wide focus and potential of co-operative education is a major justification for this collection of articles that uniquely addresses co-operative education from multiple angles. Our purpose is to open up a discussion about the many directions in which co-operative education is developing. Co-operatives and co-operative education are an under-explored field of study. We hope this book will encourage dialogue about further potential areas in which co-operative values and principles may have an impact – pedagogy and youth to mention two topics. For instance, co-operatives could make a significant contribution to learning theory, given the recognition of how learning takes place in situated places but involves holistic change in individuals and groups. The notion of 'community of practice' is one that would be interesting to investigate further in terms of the co-operative learning networks (Lave and Wenger, 1991; Jarvis and Parker, 2005).

Researching and understanding the broad arena of co-operative education is both topical and urgent. Despite the considerable significance of co-operative education for co-operatives and co-operative development, there is a limited amount of work on the topic despite the potential connections to recent intellectual currents and social and economic changes (Fairbairn, 2003, 2008). This book takes as a starting point the fact that co-operative education is more than just a discrete set of activities, upgrading of skills or acknowledgement of values and principles. It is all these things but must also be conceived as the motor of co-operative change, the agency that holds members and their co-operatives together as well as the force that extends co-operative practices into wider areas. It operates with traditional forms of liberal education but articulates them in new directions, also requiring specific and targeted forms of learning that are moulded to the co-operative contexts.

Part One highlights the potential for learning from the past. Keith Crome and Patrick O'Connor develop philosophical perspectives on the importance of character by analysing the work of Robert Owen. They warn us of the dangers of simply adopting the language of character without an awareness of its contested history. Co-operation is understood as a virtue worth pursuing in terms of productive human relationships, mutual interests and collective purposes that eclipse technical assumptions and goals. The historical framework offered by Tom Woodin provides an overview of key traditions of co-operative education that have been built over the past two centuries. His analysis points to the complexity of co-operatives, which relate not only to liberal education but also vocational training, the building of character, citizenship and education for social change. Many of these themes are scrutinized in the following chapters.

Linda Shaw examines the role of the Co-operative College in international work as well as the development of co-operative colleges across the globe. In doing so, she provides an important account of how co-operative education mutated in colonial and post-colonial contexts. She focuses on Africa where co-operative colleges remain important and where the state often plays a strong role in funding and recruitment. Finally, Liz McIvor analyses the development of archives of the National Co-operative Archive and the Rochdale Pioneers Museum as part of an important shift towards recognizing the everyday experiences, struggles and visions of those who formed and sustained co-operatives in the past. Making this heritage available to current and future generations has been the source of interesting dialogue and new understanding about the past.

Part Two delves into key examples of learning from contemporary practice. Michael L. Cook returns us to a core understanding of co-operative education, that of leadership and management education. He deliberates over the tension between traditional forms of management education via full-time courses and the more analytical and theoretical bespoke training demanded today for which it is not possible to meet demand fully. Resolving this issue is a vital one for the expansion of co-operation through various stages of development. He emphasizes the importance of a co-operative life cycle in which process and an awareness of history play an important role. Cilla Ross takes up education and training for new co-operative enterprises and their members who operate in a rapidly changing world that has undermined many assumptions about work and welfare. Indeed, she characterizes the modern world as one in which 'disruption' is dominant. For her interviewees, values were an important foundation, although the link to co-operation and co-operative movements was not always clear. As practical co-operators with limited time, they tended to value solidaristic and participative pedagogies. Linda Shaw then examines the role of co-operatives in building sustainable development in the Global South, which often face problematic legacies including weak infrastructures and capacity issues among members. The capability approach, linked to an awareness of the life cycle of co-operatives, allows Shaw to argue productively that pedagogies, values and capacity building, as well as the connection to the broader co-operative movement, play an essential role in effective international development.

Part Three looks at the ways that co-operative education has extended into new areas. Richard Hall addresses the ubiquitous issue of technology in relation to co-operatives and the commons. His primary concern is how knowledge production, which has been enclosed within the university, might become a resource for the development of autonomous communities. In doing so, he views actually existing co-operatives and their platforms as important in themselves, but also points to an expansive conceptualization of the commons and the potential for social change. Rory Ridley-Duff surveys the contested territory of social enterprise that has entered global discourse and practice. He underlines the radical potential of social enterprise that should be articulated in collective ways rather than depending on the individual entrepreneur. Indeed, he argues that co-operators were fundamental in bringing social enterprise into being on terms that challenge neoliberal assumptions. The final two chapters investigate new co-operative structures in schools and higher education. Deborah Ralls looks into the role of education and schooling in the development of solidarity economics and inclusion. Using relational forms of democratic engagement, she considers the experience of co-operative schools in England in helping to redefine a democratic education system. The potential for 'thick' models of democratic engagement based on collective well-being are prioritised over thin relationships that pay lip service to democracy. Mike Neary and Joss Winn appraise the journey towards a co-operative university in the UK. They point to the historical desire to establish a co-operative university in the consumer movement and juxtapose this to contemporary work in this area. Multi-stakeholder models of governance, models of finance as well as co-operative curriculum and pedagogy are discussed in relation to the potential for a co-operative university.

Taken together, these chapters scope out and critically analyse an under-studied area of social life. Overall, we hope this book will make an important contribution to the related fields of co-operation and education, as well as contributing to a democratic future. It provides resources to understand the connections between the past, present and future of an area that is rapidly changing, while being tied to an enduring set of values and principles.

References

ACE (Association of Cooperative Educators) (2016–17) 'Resources'. Online. http://ace.coop/resources (accessed 10 November 2018).

Cole, G.D.H. (1944) *A Century of Co-operation, 1844–1944*. Manchester: Co-operative Union.

Cooperatives Europe (n.d.) 'Cooperatives in development'. Online. https://tinyurl.com/y9jgn6ow (accessed 25 January 2019).

Delors, J. (1996) *Learning: The treasure within: Report to UNESCO of the International Commission on Education for the Twenty-First Century*. Paris: UNESCO Publishing.

Facer, K., Thorpe, J. and Shaw, L. (2012) 'Co-operative education and schools: An old idea for new times?'. *Power and Education*, 4 (3), 327–41.

Fairbairn, B. (2003) *Three Strategic Concepts for the Guidance of Co-operatives: Linkage, transparency, and cognition*. Saskatoon, SK: Centre for the Study of Co-operatives.

Fairbairn, B. (2008) 'Communications, culture and co-operatives: Liminal organizations in a liminal age'. In MacPherson, I. and McLaughlin-Jenkins, E. (eds) *Integrating Diversities within a Complex Heritage: Essays in the field of co-operative studies*. Victoria, BC: New Rochdale Press, 179–222.

Fielding, M. and Moss, P. (2011) *Radical Education and the Common School: A democratic alternative*. London: Routledge.

ICA (International Co-operative Alliance) (2018) 'Cooperative identity, values and principles'. Online. www.ica.coop/en/cooperatives/cooperative-identity (accessed 20 November 2018).

ICA (International Co-operative Alliance)/EURICSE (European Research Institute on Cooperative and Social Enterprises) (2018) *Exploring the Cooperative Economy*. World Cooperative Monitor. Online. www.monitor.coop (accessed 20 November 2018).

Jarvis, P. and Parker, S. (eds) (2005) *Human Learning: An holistic approach*. London: Routledge.

Lave, J. and Wenger, E. (1991) *Situated Learning: Legitimate peripheral participation*. Cambridge: Cambridge University Press.

MacPherson, I. (2002) 'Encouraging associative intelligence: Co-operatives, shared learning and responsible citizenship'. In *Co-operative College Co-operative Learning and Responsible Citizenship in the 21st Century*. Manchester: Co-operative College, 11–19.

MacPherson, I. and McLaughlin-Jenkins, E. (eds) (2008) *Integrating Diversities within a Complex Heritage: Essays in the field of co-operative studies*. Victoria, BC: New Rochdale Press.

Musicians' Union (n.d.) 'Co-operatives'. Online. https://tinyurl.com/ybbtd8qv (accessed 25 January 2019).

Robertson, N. (2016) *The Co-operative Movement and Communities in Britain, 1914–1960: Minding their own business*. London: Routledge.

Sheffield Hallam University (2018) 'PGCert Cooperative Leadership and Social Entrepreneurship'. Online. www.shu.ac.uk/courses/mba/pgcert-cooperative-leadership-and-social-entrepreneurship/part-time (accessed 30 October 2018).

United Nations Sustainable Development Goals (n.d.) '4 Quality Education – Goal 4 targets'. Online. www.un.org/sustainabledevelopment/education/ (accessed 12 February 2019).

Wilson, J.F., Webster, A. and Vorberg-Rugh, R. (2013) *Building Co-operation: A business history of the Co-operative Group, 1863–2013*. Oxford: Oxford University Press.

Woodin, T. (ed.) (2015) *Co-operation, Learning and Co-operative Values: Contemporary issues in education*. London: Routledge.

Woodin, T. (2017) 'Co-operation, leadership and learning: Fred Hall and the Co-operative College before 1939'. In Hall, R. and Winn, J. (eds) *Mass Intellectuality and Democratic Leadership in Higher Education*. London: Bloomsbury Academic, 27–40.

Woodin, T. (2018) 'Co-operative approaches to leading and learning: Ideas for democratic innovation from the UK and beyond'. In Gornall, L., Thomas, B. and Sweetman, L. (eds) *Exploring Consensual Leadership in Higher Education: Co-operation, collaboration and partnership*. London: Bloomsbury Academic, 71–88.

Wright, S., Greenwood, D. and Boden, R. (2011) 'Report on a field visit to Mondragón University: A cooperative experience/experiment'. *Learning and Teaching*, 4 (3), 38–56.

Part One

Learning from the past

1

The character of co-operation: Reflections on education and co-operative learning[1]

Keith Crome and Patrick O'Connor

Introduction

The last few years have seen a renewed interest among educationalists in the connection between education and the formation of character.[2] The link between character and education is long-standing, weakened only by the historically more recent focus on education as a means for the transmission of knowledge and the teaching of skills.[3] However, notwithstanding frequent observations about the etymological provenance of the term 'character',[4] the same educationalists have largely avoided any sustained historical reflection on the role of the idea of character in thinking about education. Perhaps this is because there is a lingering suspicion that, despite the rehabilitation of character in current pedagogical theories, in the past it had a less positive function, amounting to nothing more than 'an ideological device for imposing middle-class values upon a potentially disruptive working class' (Collini, 1985: 30). There is some truth to such a view, but as Stefan Collini has argued, the idea of character is much richer in meaning and function than this allows. Is it necessary to recall that like all our ways of talking, the vocabulary of character is enriched by a constant contestation of meanings, and that if we invoke the idea of character without an awareness of these contestations, it is our own voices that grow strident and monotonous? Certainly, given the richness of the history of the idea of character, there is much that can be learnt from it, particularly in terms of criticizing the current instrumentalization of education – its identification with the goal of producing wealth – and the consequent reduction of relationships between people to relationships of utility.[5] Because of its principled concern with the virtues of self-help and mutuality, and its aim to provide education and training to its members, the history of co-operative education and learning is a vital resource for furthering our understanding of this connection.

What follows is not intended to be a systematic clarification of the idea of character. An idea does not exist independently of its use in a particular context, in relation to other ideas with which it is associated, or which it displaces or replaces. The idea of character is no different. It was not an invention of the nineteenth century, but in that century it came to have a broad range of application: it existed amidst a cluster or cloud of psychological, social and political assumptions that were loosely coherent. Consequently, its meanings and uses were many and varied, lending it a somewhat elusive quality, both within and without the co-operative movement. For this reason, our aim is simply to suggest how a retrieval of the connection between co-operation and character could be useful in reflecting on the current predicament of education and on the future development of the co-operative movement.

However, there is a critical ambiguity in how we think about co-operation, and we think that that ambiguity has not been without some practical impact on the co-operative movement. There is scarcely an activity that we can perform alone – Aristotle defined humans as political animals for just this reason, and Adam Smith, the political economist whose work, *The Wealth of Nations*, laid the foundations for economic liberalism, and which has continuing impact on neoliberal ideas, knew that all economic activity involved co-operation. But there is a world of difference between Aristotle and Smith: Aristotle would have seen co-operation as a foundational political virtue – a way of being; while for Smith, or seen in the light of Smith as a necessary facet of economic behaviour, it is a way of doing something. This distinction, nascent in Smith, has hardened, and we now see co-operation more as a skill and less as a virtue, and that is perhaps true of the way in which co-operators think about co-operation, and in particular about the teaching of co-operation, which is imparted as a skill, or at least judged as a skill might be judged – by its results. In truth, however, the early co-operators recognized that co-operation was a moral as much as a practical issue, and that means it was not to be valued solely for its economic outcomes but also for how it enriched people's lives and characters. It was for this reason that in his *The History of Co-operation*, George Jacob Holyoake was moved to observe that co-operation is no social novelty, having existed since 'the commencement of human society' (Holyoake, 1875: 2); and that, following the practices of Robert Owen and the Rochdale Pioneers, the word has come to acquire a novel meaning, signifying 'a new power of industry, constituted by the combination of worker, capitalist, and consumer, and a new means of commercial morality, by which honesty is rendered productive' (Holyoake, 1875: 2).

We think that it is necessary to think of co-operation in this way – as a virtue, and that when we teach co-operation, we should teach people not just how to co-operate effectively, but how to co-operate well, that is to say, that we should teach people to *be* co-operative. To explain why, it is worth considering a common argument about the origins of co-operation, an argument that finds an influential formulation in Adam Smith's *The Wealth of Nations*.

It is often said that natural co-operation begins with the fact that we cannot survive alone – we must work together – and that our individual insufficiencies are made good by the division of labour, which multiplies our powers. Adam Smith makes this observation in the opening chapter of *The Wealth of Nations,* where he remarks that, 'the greatest improvement in the productive powers of labour, and the greater part of the skill, dexterity, and judgement with which it is anywhere directed, or applied, seem to have been the effects of the division of labour' (Smith, 1991: 4). On this account, co-operation is co-ordinate with the division of labour. If we are not only to endure, but also to prosper, then it is necessary that we observe the principle of the specialization of labour. However, by doing so we rely on others to produce for us that which we do not make ourselves. Mankind stands in need of the co-operation and assistance of others, and in civilized societies that need extends to great multitudes – and in order to underscore this requirement, Smith famously points to the multitude of workmen whose joint labour is required to produce even a coarse and rough woollen coat (the shepherd, the sorter of wool, the comber or carder, the dyer, the scribbler, the spinner, the weaver, the fuller, the dresser, etc.).

Now, for Smith, the division of labour does not arise from the wisdom of the human being, it is not the product of intellection, foresight or intention. It arises from 'a certain propensity in human nature ... the propensity to truck, barter and exchange one thing for another' (Smith, 1991: 12). It is this propensity that properly distinguishes the human from all other animals: 'nobody ever', Smith observes, 'saw a dog make a fair and deliberate exchange of one bone for another with another dog' (Smith, 1991: 12). Of course, a dog that wants something, either from another dog or from a person, can fawn and beg, abasing itself and throwing itself upon the compassion of another creature, as can one person of another, 'using every servile and fawning attention to obtain their good will' (Smith, 1991: 12–13). But one person has almost constant need of the assistance and help of others, both those whom he knows and those whom he does not, and he relies not on their benevolence in order to obtain it. Instead he prevails upon them by appealing to their self-love, showing that it is for their own advantage to do for him as he requires of them. It is not from the benevolence of the butcher that we expect our dinner, Smith argues, but from their regard for their own interest.

Since what governs the practice of exchange is the principle of self-love, co-operation is an expression of that principle. Ultimately, we co-operate not out of regard for others, but from self-regard. Every act of co-operation becomes a transaction, which ultimately can only be rooted in self-interest, and the co-operator is essentially an economic agent. Conceived and practised in this way, co-operation can doubtless be carried out more or less effectively, at least when effectiveness is reckoned in terms of productivity and profit. However, its deleterious effects were well noted by the first co-operators, who, as Beatrice Potter observed in her short study *The Co-operative Movement in Great Britain*, saw in it the dehumanization of all human relationships, reducing men, women and children to commodities 'to be bought at the cheapest rate, and to be consumed, like the coke with which they stoke their furnace' (Potter, 1904: 10).

The co-operation that is practised in the co-operative movement is different. Even if it is not entirely exempt from economic motivations, it involves something else, and co-operators are moved by different motives to mere economic agents. For this reason, we should consider co-operation as a way of life, a fundamental disposition, one that allows us to negotiate our individual interests and desires with the reciprocal benefits of engaging in collective actions.

This is very much a preliminary contribution to such an undertaking in the sense that we examine Robert Owen's observations on the formation of character. Owen is widely seen as the intellectual and practical forefather of the co-operative movement.[6] Despite his esteemed place in the movement, the ambiguity of Owen's proposals for reform has long been recognized: they are at once liberal and illiberal – both paternalistic and authoritarian, and generous and humanitarian. We will show that this ambiguity is an inheritance, a product of the antitheses that structure an extensive debate over the role of education and the reform of character from the latter half of the eighteenth century and first half of the nineteenth century. In doing this, our aim is threefold: (1) to uncover the conceptual terms of the debate on character that informs and limits current thinking about character and education; (2) to present and evaluate the relative merits of Owen's arguments for the type of character necessary in the new moral world; and

(3) to retrieve the positive elements of Owen's account of character as social disposition.

The making of character

> In taking a calm retrospect of my life from the earliest remembered period of it to the present hour, there appears to me to have been a succession of extraordinary ... events, forming connected links of a chain, to compel me to proceed onward to complete a mission, of which I have been an impelled agent, without merit or demerit of any kind on my part. (Owen, 1920: xii)

The term 'character' is usually supposed to refer to a distinctive quality of something, and we speak of both things and people as having a particular quality or characteristic. The word and the idea have a long history, stretching back at least as far as Ancient Greece, and it has consequently enjoyed some notable inflections in its meaning, reflecting some of the critical shifts in our ways of life and ways of thinking about our ways of life. Aristotle thought of character as related to our habitual desires and preferences that are manifest in our choices and behaviour. Character was for him the sum of our virtues and vices (Aristotle, 2002). St Augustine of Hippo (AD 354–430) used it in this sense to refer to the quality that baptism, or confirmation or holy orders, impressed upon the soul. In the late seventeenth and early eighteenth centuries, a vogue for character writing, the 'character study', emerged in English court society – short, satirical, portraits of character types, written to satirize distinctive vices (Aldington, 1924). As a result of its concern with the self, the individual, and in particular the development or growth of the person, the modern age – at least from the late eighteenth century through to the end of the nineteenth century – lent a decisive impetus to the concern with character and education.

With its emphasis on self-scrutiny and self-revelation, autobiography became an increasingly popular and important mode of writing in the eighteenth and nineteenth centuries. In opposition to some instances of twentieth- and early twenty-first century reflexiveness, which reflect the contemporary overvaluation of opinion, and obsession with shameless self-promotion, nineteenth-century autobiography is distinguished by its tone of sober self-reflection, where an emphasis is placed on self-interrogation rather than self-assertion. Of course, irrespective of the century in which it was written, an autobiography is often an individual's attempt to write something like their own epitaph, to fix for posterity the sense of who they were and what they were about, to sum themselves up, so to speak.

An autobiography is the story of the sense of a life and the shaping of character by the one who, by dint of having been present through all of its episodes, knows their life best – at least if they can view it dispassionately and objectively, that is to say, with the requisite rationality. There is for that reason an intimate connection between autobiography and education.

Robert Owen's autobiography, *The Life of Robert Owen, by Himself*, sits firmly within this tradition, and so, given our concerns, it is an instructive read. Owen dedicated his *Life* to the exhibition of one proposition which, in the preface to the first, and only, volume of this autobiography, he proclaims 'the greatest discovery that man has made for the universal happiness of his race through all future time' (Owen, 1920: ix). What is discovered is the idea that, 'the made receives all its qualities from its maker, and that the created receives all its qualities and powers from its creator' (Owen, 1920: ix). To a lesser person than Owen,[7] this idea may seem unremarkable, merely echoing, in a diminished form, the philosophical commonplace that nothing is without cause. Yet, it animated Owen's entire existence. In a tone that exhibits his powerful millennial enthusiasm, Owen goes on to explain the greatness of this discovery: by realizing the ultimate aim of all knowledge – self-knowledge – it opens 'a new book of life to man' (Owen, 1920: x), for it will enable him to 'perceive more clearly ... that [he] is formed by a double creation – the one previous to birth, a mysterious and divine organization of wonderful powers ... the other a secondary or new creation, superadded, to bring the first to its earthly maturity' (Owen, 1920: x). In short, this discovery reveals to us how our characters are created. In so doing it makes possible the improvement of mankind, 'by creating entirely new surroundings in which to place all through life, and in which a new human nature would appear to arise from the new surroundings' (Owen, 1920: xii).

As contemporary critics were quick to point out, his own declarations concerning the originality of his discovery notwithstanding, Owen was not alone in arguing that character was created. Certainly, Owen's position must be set against the view, more prevalent in the eighteenth century than the nineteenth, but still current in the later century, that character was fixed. However, what Owen was essentially arguing against was the view that we ourselves make our characters by proposing the diametrically opposed principle that 'our characters are made *for* us, not *by* us'. As Harold Silver has suggested (Silver, 1965: 85ff), his most immediate influence was most likely William Godwin, who first adopted Helvétius' view of character being completely moulded by environment, and then modified it to admit of some innate differences – these being Owen's 'mysterious and divine organization of wonderful powers' (Owen, 1920: x).

Owen himself was not forthcoming when it came to attributing the source of his discovery to others. Instead, he located its sources in his own experience. But his reticence in this regard was not motivated by the desire to gain credit, or inflate his reputation – since the extent that what we acquire through circumstance is so little due to ourselves that we can neither be praised nor blamed. Rather, in attributing his discovery to experience, Owen was appealing to what he would have understood as his empirical and experimental bent of mind, an inclination that was part and parcel of the *habitus* of the late eighteenth- and early nineteenth-century scientist. Still, it is worth attending closely to Owen's own account of what led him to his discovery, for the narrative he gives is not simply its documentation; it is also its corroboration, demonstrating in its discovery the truth it purports to tell. His discovery was, he implies, neither an entirely chance one, nor a wholly intellectual one. Instead, as befits a moral principle, it was a discovery that owed much to his natural constitution, and the framing of his character during his formative years by a series of significant events.

Noting his fondness for reading, cultivated from a young age, Owen tells of how three local 'maiden ladies', who were Methodists, and anxious to convert him 'to their peculiar faith' (Owen, 1920: 4), lent him many of their books. However, as he read he grew surprised to learn of the deadly hatred between the various faiths, and between them and the Pagans and Infidels, and this nurtured in him the suspicion that 'there must be something fundamentally wrong in all religions' (Owen, 1920: 4). The early awakening of a sceptical cast of mind meant that Owen could not enjoy the same intellectual diet as others his own age, that he could not 'eat and drink' as they did, and was consequently more discerning, more 'temperate', in his likes and dislikes. Still, Owen did not suffer an enforced solitude because of his intellectual fastidiousness and nascent religious scepticism. Rather, he 'entered into the amusements of those of [his] own standing' (Owen, 1920: 5) and followed the games played by boys at that time – marbles, handball and football – and attended dancing classes for some time. In fact, he excelled at sports and music and learning. According to his own report, he was a favourite among the townsfolk, and in the kind of competitive games that took place in towns and villages at the time, he was often 'pitted against [his] equals, and sometimes [his] superiors in age – sometimes for one thing and sometimes for another' (Owen, 1920: 6). However, far from delighting in his superiority and the attendant acclaim that followed from it, Owen quickly perceived the injustice of competition. This was a lesson learnt when he was made to compete against his elder brother, John, in a writing competition. Upon it being decided that his writing was better than his brother's, it became apparent to Owen that John no longer had 'as strong an affection for me as he had before' (Owen, 1920: 6). According to Owen, the unwisdom of the affair lay in the principle of competition itself, for there can be no just comparison between the efforts of individuals whose capacities and powers, or whose 'organization' as Owen would have it, are different by nature. Consequently, he says, no one wins from competition; all it provokes is 'vanity' in the successful, and jealousy and hatred in the unsuccessful.

These two events have an exemplary value for the man that Owen was to become. On the one hand, Owen is first induced by his awareness of the conflict of faiths to suspect his own faith, and then to reject the fundamental, but absurd, tenet of all religions, namely 'that each one [of us] formed [his or her] own qualities, – determined [his or her] own thoughts, will, and action, – and was responsible for them to God and to [his or her] fellow-men' (Owen, 1920: 22). By contrast, through rational reflection on his own nature and experiences, Owen is taught the very opposite:

> That he could not have made one of his own qualities – they were forced upon [him] by Nature; – that [his] language, religion and habits, were forced upon [him] by Society; and that [he] was entirely the child of Nature and Society; – that Nature gave the qualities, and Society directed them. (Owen, 1920: 22)

On the other hand, from the incident with his brother, Owen learnt to replace his religious feelings with the 'spirit of universal charity' (Owen, 1920: 22) – a care for the human race, transcending all sects and creeds and classes, and for that reason fundamentally opposed to the principle of competition, the seed of all contention and division among people.

Thus we can see that how Owen's pursuance of the conventions of Victorian autobiography explains the beginning of his notion of character. Character is not something self-inaugurated, made present by the will. Rather, it is something responsive, emerging from the activities and practices of its times. Character allows us to mediate between self and other, moving us from local practices, dispositions and habits to a more universal form of care for the human race.

On the reform of dangerous characters

Owen was indefatigable in his affirmation that character was made *for* us, not *by* us. He was equally steadfast in his denunciation of the doctrine of free will, a doctrine that is used, Owen tells us, to hold men responsible for their convictions and feelings, the two motive forces that impel us to act. However, Owen argues that not only do we have no power to choose freely what we like and dislike, what we believe and disbelieve, but that the will itself emanates from the feelings and convictions that are formed for us by our instincts and environment.[8] Collini has seen in this polemic an inflection of the debate between 'voluntarism and determinism' (Collini, 1985: 35). Collini is right to say that John Stuart Mill's insistence that our characters are not simply formed by external circumstances is a nuanced, even ambiguous, appeal to the idea that we have the capacity to mould our own characters, and make ourselves different from how we actually are. But by inflecting the polemic in this way, giving it a decidedly metaphysical cast, Collini makes the same mistake that Hazlitt did just over a century and a half earlier when he denounced Owen as a man of but one idea.[9] It was a denunciation to which Owen quite justly replied, 'had he said that I was a man of one fundamental principle and its practical consequences – he would have been nearer the truth' (Owen, 1920: 105). For Owen, while not always disinclined to speculative grandiloquence, was nevertheless overwhelmingly concerned with social reform, envisaging a new moral world created through the reform of character, itself brought about by the agency of government according to rational principles and a national system of education.

To be properly appreciated, Owen's concern with character must be viewed in terms of his ambition to correct the damage that human character had endured in recent times. The rapid growth of industrial manufacturing, the reckless pursuit of profit by factory owners, facilitated by the exclusion of all moral considerations from a political economy operating solely on the principle of maximizing profit by buying cheap and selling dear, and governments either convinced of the inalterability of human nature, or holding the individual alone responsible for their actions, had contributed to a deterioration of character.

In itself, Owen's anxiety over the deterioration of character was not peculiar; it was a long-standing staple of political and moral philosophy to observe the enervation of character under contemporary conditions. Still, in the nineteenth century this anxiety was underpinned by an explanatory framework that came to give it a decisive inflection. For Owen, the creation of character through the action of external circumstances on the original animal organization of the individual was a chemical process, rather than a mechanical change, each change producing new powers of action in the individual. It is, for all that, a process that has a decidedly utilitarian bent, since such changes to the character are most 'frequently effected by the sudden appearance of a new, disagreeable, or lovely object, producing very powerful effects on the feelings, thoughts and actions' (Owen, 1840: 3). The agreeable and disagreeable sentiments aroused by an object are the expression of a power of attraction or repulsion that sets our spirits in motion, binding our behaviour much as chemical atoms, having a certain affinity to each other, are able to form links and bonds that create novel substances.

As insightful as is this observation about the compound nature of character, we might be inclined to regard it as a metaphor transposed from the field of scientific study of the action of chemical elements to the behaviour of the animal spirits, a metaphor perhaps suggested to Owen by way of his association with John Dalton. Yet, to regard this simply as a metaphor of Owen's inventing, or a mere flight of fancy or poetic conceit, would be to miss its true significance: it is a way of seeing, a view of human nature, that galvanized an age and that has guided and governed social and political thought from the eighteenth century onwards. A little later, Thomas Laycock, Henry Maudsley, William Benjamin Carpenter, Alexander Bain, George Croom Robertson and Herbert Spencer were to deepen the comparison: developing the study of the mind as a 'nervous' phenomenon, and entertaining the supposition that character was chemically altered by way of physiological changes, and thus that new capacities and powers of mind or character were excited by real changes to the body, while any enervation of the character would be occasioned by a counterpart physiological degeneration. One might suppose that both the speculations of the physiological psychologists and Owen's theories on the nature of character were expressions of a more general historical tendency towards the scientific (or pseudo-scientific) explanation of human character or behaviour. Nevertheless, if they were that, they were also the manifestation of a more or less rationalized strategy of action, of intervention, upon the vital characteristics of individuals and populations – their health, their behaviours, their productive capacities, their morbidity, their rates of reproduction and mortality. This strategy, more or less common to the political powers of Europe since the eighteenth century, is what Michel Foucault (1998) has call bio-politics. It operates through a nexus of power and knowledge, aiming to exert a positive influence on life, to control and shape its forces, to make it grow, expand and multiply, thereby turning human character into a resource.

Against this background, Owen is constrained to think of the injury to character as a social phenomenon – it is not just that its causes are social: the injury is a social one too. In the first of the essays in his *A New View of Society*, he observes that the dissolute and delinquent poor and working class of the British Isles, who at the time of his writing amounted to three-quarters of the population, are a danger not only to themselves but to the nation too. In fact they are, he says, raising the spectre of revolt, 'the worst and most dangerous subjects in the Empire' (Owen, 1991: 10). Despite being of a dangerous and delinquent character, the poor and working classes should not themselves be held accountable, for they are not responsible for their characters, and for that reason they are not responsible for their actions. Their character is attributable to their upbringing, their lack of education, and the miserable poverty that they must endure, and which, ultimately but essentially, is a result of poor government.

Owen's account effects a transfer of responsibility and, implicitly, of criminality from the vicious and uneducated poor and profligate working classes, to those who 'govern and control the affairs of men' (Owen, 1991: 12), particularly since by the nineteenth century crime was distinguished from transgression, being defined as what is injurious to society. Hence, since the condition of the working class was the consequence of their social situation, and since as a result of their condition they were made dangerous subjects, the real crime lay with those who bore responsibility for creating that condition. Nevertheless, the remedy, while social, targets the individual, aiming at the amelioration of the character of the working classes through the civic reform of education. In this sense, it is a philanthropic mode of the disciplinary power identified by Foucault as emerging in eighteenth- and nineteenth-century Europe, which aimed not so much to punish individuals for what they did, but to exercise control over 'what they might do, what they were capable of doing, what they were liable to do, what they were immanently about to do' (Foucault, 2002: 57). Education – and this is not specific to Owen, although he uses this particular idea of education in a quite specific way – becomes disciplinary; it aims to shape character in the sense of controlling behaviour through the imposition of a pedagogic orthopaedics.

Conclusion

Informing Owen's *A New Vision of Society* is an idea of education as the power to shape through discipline the disposition and behaviour of the individual. The legacy of this idea of education as creating and controlling potentialities of character is problematic. Fundamentally, education has two functions. On the one hand, it has to prepare individuals for work, inculcating the skills that are required in order to work. On the other hand, it has to prepare people for life, which is not the same thing at all (although it would not be possible without teaching skills). For the latter is a matter of endowing them with the capacity to respond creatively to the challenges of living together in the world. And insofar as that is a matter of taking on the responsibility of renewing the world by acting together to change it (and not merely reproducing the existing state of things, which is the equivalent to regression), it is a matter of character. However, the disciplinary formation of character acts upon behavioural capacities, creating and shaping aptitudes and inclinations. Operationalized in institutions characteristic of modernity – schools, hospitals, prisons – it treats such aptitudes and inclinations as analogous to skills. In other words, it treats the shaping and improvement of character as a technical operation, and ultimately this is damaging to both our idea of education and our idea of character.

One historical consequence of this reduction of the formation of character to a technical operation is the wholesale identification of co-operation as a skill. Certainly, co-operation is, as the word 'operation' suggests, a matter of doing, and in that respect co-operating well is something like a skill; but, as the prefix 'co' indicates, co-operation is a matter of relationships, of *being with* and *acting with* one another, and in that sense, it is a virtue, or something like a virtue. Regarding co-operation as if it were a skill, teaching as if it were such, means treating it as a transactional activity judged in terms of its productive utility. Co-operation is valuable only inasmuch as it realizes a specific goal. However, there is a virtue to co-operation beyond its productive outcome, a virtue in co-operation for its own sake. For that reason, co-operation cannot be taught simply as if it were a skill, for by doing so at best one runs the risk of teaching people to co-operate effectively but not to *be* good co-operators. Additionally, it should be noted that the very essence of co-operation is that it is not a mindless pursuit of what has instrumental value, of what works irrespective of the outcome, but that the very activity and process of co-operation are crucial for ensuring the democratic dimension of co-operative character.

Ultimately, when we lose or abandon the vocabulary of virtues and the language of character, we impoverish our thinking about education and our educational practices, and our thinking about co-operation and our co-operative activities. Without doubt, given its history and its historical uses, any invocation of character is not without risk – as our analysis of Owen's own treatment of character shows. Still, it is important to remember that, like all our ways of talking, the vocabulary of character is informed by a vigorously contested history. Certainly, if we invoke the language of character without an awareness of those past contests and its continual contestation, then our voices will inevitably become shrill and monotonous. The current return to character in education is a case in point. It comes following a recognition of the recent pedagogic and political exhaustion of the instrumentalization of education, alongside the diminishment of state welfare responsibilities for education, in the most developed nations. However, that recognition was only in part motivated by an acknowledgement of the problem of yoking education exclusively to the pursuit of individual and national economic gain. In part it has been motivated by a recognition that 'character' itself is now the only truly saleable commodity, the only viable capacity that labour power has, in the era of flexible capitalism, where, for ordinary workers, there are no jobs for life. For under this mode of capitalism, what is utile and profitable for employers are not fixed skills but 'virtues' such as resilience and adaptability. As such, capitalism is now colonizing the virtue of co-operation, offering its own version of the traditional virtues: what once was resilience is now flexibility, adaptiveness and grit, what was once co-operation is now competition and efficiency. Capital curtails the fullest expression of the virtues, since virtues are purely productive devoted to the pursuit of immediate ends. If we think of co-operation as a virtue, then we can consider co-operation as something that, as we have mentioned, helps negotiate mutual interests and collective purposes, while forming enduring rather than fleeting identities.

Nevertheless, as we suggested in our introduction, character was significant for the first co-operators, as a response to the inequities of capitalism. They saw co-operation not only as a specific type of commercial relationship between worker, capitalist and consumer, but also as a distinctively moral practice. As George Jacob Holyoake observed, co-operation, 'In the sense of two or more persons uniting to attain an end which each was unable to effect singly' (Holyoake, 1875: 7) may indeed have been common since the commencement of society, but only with 'the benefit … always accruing to the stronger' (Holyoake, 1875: 7). However, co-operation that 'begins in mutual help, with a view to end in a common competence' (Holyoake, 1875: 7) requires the sustained cultivation of the virtues of mutuality, solidarity and fellow-feeling. In themselves, these are positive attributes of character – they are virtues because they intend sociality.

Notes

[1] We would like to thank Gillian Lonergan of the National Co-operative Archive for her invaluable advice and assistance in the research for this article.

[2] In the UK, particular impetus has been lent to exploring this link by the Jubilee Centre for Character and Virtues, University of Birmingham. Full details of the

Centre's work and publications can be found at: www.jubileecentre.ac.uk/432/character-education

[3] The link between education and the formation of character goes back at least to Ancient Greece, as Werner Jaeger's monumental *Paideia* testifies. However, more recently, in the post-war period, and in particular from the 1960s, the association was strained by an increasing emphasis on the development of intelligence and the cultivation of skills. Thinkers working at the intersection of philosophy and sociology such as Richard Sennett (1999), Pierre Bourdieu (1999), André Gorz (1999), and Turner and Stets (2005) have all attempted to contextualize the function of character development in education in the context of the ill-effects of neoliberal capitalism. Sennett (2009, 2012), in particular, has shown that educationalists find it increasingly difficult to instil a durable sense of meaning and identity due to the unthinking and relentless innovation and change that characterizes contemporary educational work practices. That is not to say that a concern with what is variously called 'character-building' or 'character formation' was entirely lost. Schools and colleges still sought to produce pupils with good morals, and universities have looked beyond the confines of a discipline in order to cultivate among their students the so-called 'soft skills' – the personal attributes that enable a person to interact successfully with others. However, as critics of educational policy in the most developed nations have pointed out, there was a decisive shift of focus in the post-war period, and education became increasingly instrumentalized, yoked to the purpose of increasing individual and national economic gain through the cultivation of skills and technical proficiencies. To what extent the renaissance of an interest in character can be set against that is a moot point, but one that we take up at the end of this essay.

[4] See, for example, Mark Steed, who, in an article on the importance of character-building in schools, in *Independent Education Today* on 24 December 2014, observes the derivation of the word 'character' from the Ancient Greek *kharassō* (χαράσσω), which means 'I engrave'. Steed is the Principal of Berkhamsted School; the reference to classical Greek is doubtless deployed as a signifier of both a certain kind of education and a certain type of character.

[5] See Martha Nussbaum (2010: 2), who has argued that 'radical changes are occurring in what democratic societies teach the young [...] Thirsty for national profit, nations, and their systems of education, are heedlessly discarding skills that are needed to keep democracies alive. If this trend continues, nations all over the world will soon be producing generations of useful machines rather than complete citizens who can think for themselves, criticise tradition, and understand the significance of another person's suffering and achievements.' In particular, she draws attention to the disregard of the 'faculties of thought and imagination that make us human and make our relationships rich human relationships, rather than relationships of mere use and manipulation' (ibid.: 6).

[6] Irrespective of its merits and faults – which we do not intend to assess here – the view that Owen is the forefather of the modern co-operative movement is deeply rooted in the history and development of the movement. Not only is it found in the writings of many of the leading figures of the British co-operative movement such as G. J. Holyoake (see, for example, Holyoake, 1875, 1879), but it was also promulgated in the educational programme of the Co-operative Union, which produced syllabuses, examinations and textbooks for the use of local co-operative societies to support the education of their members in the principles and history of co-operation. It is powerfully expressed in Potter's seminal history of the movement. Potter claims that in observing the immiseration of the working classes in the industrial revolution of the late eighteenth and early nineteenth centuries, Owen 'became a Socialist, and conceived the idea of a co-operative system of industry to replace the unrestrained competition of modern trade' (Potter, 1904: 12). For Potter, Owen was significant as a visionary enthusiast of co-operation and as 'a man of action', successful in the application of socialist principles to secure the betterment

of the working classes. For a more nuanced assessment of Owen's role in the history of the development of the English working class, see E. P. Thompson's *The Making of the English Working Class* (2013).

[7] Owen is listed by George Jacob Holyoake in his *The History of Co-operation in England* alongside Napoleon, Wellington, Goethe and Fourier, who were all born within four years of each other. 'Nature,' Holyoake says, 'was in one of her adventurous moods at that period', for they were all 'historic men [...] world destroyers and world makers' (1875: 52). 'World makers' he tell us elsewhere is a term he prefers to 'utopianist', for the former is a literal description of their ambitious and insurgent schemes (see ibid.: 22).

[8] See Owen (1840), in particular Chapter IV, 'Explanation of the Third Fundamental Fact: "That man's feelings or convictions or both united, form the motive to action called the will, which stimulates him to act, and decides his actions"', 7–11.

[9] Hazlitt, quoted in Williams (1963), 46.

References

Aldington, R. (ed.) (1924) *A Book of "Characters"*. Trans. Aldington, R. London: George Routledge and Sons.

Aristotle (2002) *Nicomachean Ethics*. Trans. Sachs, J. Newburyport, MA.: Focus Publishing.

Bourdieu, P. (ed.) (1999) *The Weight of the World: Social suffering in contemporary society*. Cambridge: Polity Press.

Collini, S. (1985) 'The idea of "character" in Victorian political thought'. *Transactions of the Royal Historical Society*, 35, 29–50.

Foucault, M. (1998) *The History of Sexuality: Volume 1: The will to knowledge*. Trans. Hurley, R. London: Penguin.

Foucault, M. (2002) 'Truth and juridical forms'. In Faubion, J.D. (ed.) *The Essential Works of Foucault, 1954–1984: Volume 3: Power*. Trans. Hurley, R. London: Penguin, 1–89.

Gorz, A. (1999) *Reclaiming Work: Beyond the wage-based society*. Trans. Turner, C. Cambridge: Polity Press.

Holyoake, G.J. (1875) *The History of Co-operation in England: Its literature and its advocates: Volume 1: The Pioneer Period – 1812 to 1844*. London: Trübner and Co.

Holyoake, G.J. (1879) *The History of Co-operation in England: Its literature and its advocates: Volume 2: The Constructive Period – 1845 to 1878*. London: Trübner and Co.

Jaeger, W. (1939–44) *Paideia: The ideals of Greek culture*. 3 vols. Trans. Higher, G. New York: Oxford University Press.

Nussbaum, M.C. (2010) *Not for Profit: Why democracy needs the humanities*. Princeton: Princeton University Press.

Owen, R. (1840) *The Book of the New Moral World; containing The Rational System of Society, Founded on Demonstrable Facts, Developing the Constitution and Laws of Human Nature and of Society*. Glasgow: H. Robinson and Co.

Owen, R. (1920) *The Life of Robert Owen, by Himself, with an Introduction by M. Beer*. London: G. Bell and Sons.

Owen, R. (1991) *A New View of Society and Other Writings.* Ed. Claeys, G. London: Penguin.

Potter, B. (1904) *The Co-operative Movement in Great Britain.* London: Swan Sonnenschein and Co.

Sennett, R. (1999) *The Corrosion of Character: The personal consequences of work in the new capitalism.* New York: W.W. Norton and Company.

Sennett, R. (2009) *The Craftsman.* London: Penguin.

Sennett, R. (2012) *Together: The rituals, pleasures and politics of cooperation.* London: Penguin.

Silver, H. (1965) *The Concept of Popular Education: A study of ideas and social movements in the early nineteenth century.* London: MacGibbon and Kee.

Smith, A. (1991) *The Wealth of Nations.* New York: Alfred A. Knopf.

Thompson, E.P. (2013) *The Making of the English Working Class.* London: Penguin.

Turner, J.H. and Stets, J.E. (2005) *The Sociology of Emotions.* Cambridge: Cambridge University Press.

Williams, R. (1963) *Culture and Society, 1780–1950.* Harmondsworth: Penguin.

Chapter 2

Recovering histories of co-operative education and training: Character, culture and citizenship

Tom Woodin

The histories of co-operative education offer new insights into our understanding of learning and social change. In Britain, since the early nineteenth century, co-operators have actively educated themselves, fashioned education for their own purposes and campaigned for educational change. The size, scale and longevity of the consumer co-operative movement, which has retained a continuing interest in education, has made it a considerable yet undervalued educational force that has impacted on the development of educational systems and institutions for two centuries. Today, co-operatives and co-operative values and principles are helping to unlock social and public innovation. Ideas for a co-operative university have built upon a groundswell of dissatisfaction that has grown over the last decade, especially since the 2007–8 financial crisis and the ensuing period of austerity.

Simultaneously, the consumer movement itself faces a new educational crisis in the early twenty-first century, which makes this an apposite time to review its history. The reduction in the number of consumer societies has depleted the range and depth of co-operative education. While the Co-operative College began in 1919 as the headpiece of a complex educational structure, today it is more of a stand-alone structure and its raison d'être is harder to justify solely in terms of the actually existing consumer movement. In addition, the decimation of funded adult education provision since the 1990s has left co-operative education isolated (Co-operative College, 2019). Evaluating the history of co-operative education thus provides a means of reflecting on key contradictions while thinking about the future.

Ironically, the centrality of education to contemporary economic and political thinking has squeezed marginal practices. The assumption of some human capital theories – that everyone is educable – contrasts sharply with earlier historical phases when it was commonly believed that there was a 'pool of ability' and only a small percentage of the population were capable of educational achievement (Simon, 1991). Yet today, the narrowing of compulsory education in terms of curriculum and assessment has aroused concerns about educating the whole person. These changes relate directly to notions of a democratic deficit and low levels of social well-being. Indeed, the current historical moment is characterized by a surfeit of individualism and a reluctance to address head-on issues of belonging, mutuality and collective welfare.

The relevance of co-operative education is not always apparent. Co-operation and education are both contested practices that have varied considerably over time. At the heart of co-operative education is the belief that education is a vital force underpinning the success of co-operative democratic ventures, and a basis for its expansion. It connects to vocational learning, liberal education and education for social change. There is also a constant tension over whether co-operative education is distinctive or merely makes use of generic forms of learning. Examining the different pasts of co-operative education may provide the groundwork for understanding our present predicament and, in turn, fashioning the future. What follows is a partly chronological account of the primary developments in co-operative education, predominantly within the consumer movement in Britain from the early nineteenth century to the mid-twentieth century. It outlines the positive embrace of education by the movement, the ways in which it advanced new ideas and made use of education, while also having to respond to broader changes, notably the expansion of state funding and provision.

Knowledge is power

The British co-operative movement arose out of the political, social and economic ferment of the early nineteenth century when new forms of industrial capitalism were being imposed. For radicals, the transformatory potential of education was encapsulated in the popular idea that 'knowledge is power', a phrase commonly attributed to Francis Bacon. They took forward enlightenment traditions of learning while also critiquing the nature of power and inequality (compare Simon, 1960 and Johnson, 1979). Robert Owen was an influential figure in the development of the co-operative movement and an important educational thinker. He believed that a harsh environment imprisoned the minds and bodies of working people, a predicament that his infant schools at New Lanark were intended to ameliorate. Indeed, Owenites believed that education was to provide the means to overcome difficult circumstances and the principal force underlying all useful and social behaviour, which might ultimately make government unnecessary (Claeys, 1989: 71, 75, 120–1). The power of education struck a chord across various radical movements. But Owen was also a paternalist and could be wary about small-scale attempts by the 'lower classes' to build the 'New Moral World' through co-operatives:

> The working classes never did direct any permanently successful operations ... Whenever the working classes have attempted any complicated important measure that required unity, patience and perseverance to bring it to a successful issue they have failed in every instance as soon as they have taken the direction of it. (Mercer, 1947: 183)

Owen would come to appreciate the significance of small-scale self-help projects that, at first sight, had appeared trifling in comparison with his community experiments (Lovett, 1920: 44). In fact, many of the problems and obstacles to creating co-operatives also beset Owenite communities. It exposed a dilemma about agency of the working class that was to remain central to co-operative education over the coming two centuries. Owen's critique recognized the severe practical limitations on co-operative action from below. In order to fathom a successful example in practice, many experiments had to be tried out first and working-class co-operators realized that these had to be small-scale to get off the ground.

However, co-operators were also motivated by utopian ideas about the future state of society and these were a motor for social change. Owen advanced a crucial insight – that education was a vital force in transforming society and the conditions under which people laboured. Indeed, human agency was to be the basis for a revolutionary conception of learning and social change, the foundation for a new humanity. The New Moral World was to be constructed from 'that material of humanity which contains within itself the germs of every kind of human excellence and of high attainments; – germs which, when they shall be rationally cultivated, will insure high intellectual, healthy and joyous happiness to each individual, and to every association of men' (Owen, 1968: 121). Through education, new circumstances would be moulded in order to 'regenerate the human race from its gross irrationalities' (ibid.:122). In addition, education was conceived in terms of everyday experience. It was not to be stored away in discrete institutions but rather the 'rational character ... must be formed in the great school, academy, college and university, of actual life, amidst men and things (ibid.: 123). Thus, despite Owen's paternalism, the democratic impulse implicit in his thought and action rapidly spread among radical movements.

The Rochdale Society of Equitable Pioneers operated within this milieu and is credited with creating the first successful consumer co-operative in 1844. Education was a central part not only of the Pioneers' vision, but also of the way in which they viewed the world: they were to 'arrange' their powers of production, distribution, government and education, which were understood to be the four key departments of society. This revolutionary vision helped to generate enthusiasm for building a co-operative. In 1877, when reflecting on the educational work of the Pioneers, Abraham Greenwood coupled prosaic and utopian elements in noting that the Pioneers were sentimentalists who desired revolutionary change yet had the 'common sense to curb that sentiment within the bounds of reason and what was practical'. They formed newsrooms, a bookshop and a library, disarming the critics who complained of wasteful expenditure, and it was agreed that 2½ per cent of profits would be devoted to education. By 1858, the newsroom was made free to all members and a year later the library had over 1,000 volumes (Greenwood, 1877: 6). New reading rooms spread across the town and atlases, globes, telescopes and opera glasses were acquired, as well as, in 1862, a full-time librarian. By 1867, there were 6,000 volumes and ten newsrooms (ibid.: 7). The collection included works on theology and morals, arts, science, history, poetry, geography and fiction. The instrument department made available magnetic batteries, opera glasses, telescopes, microscopes and a cosmoscope, all of which could be rented at a relatively low cost.

The demand for general transformation found expression in the fascination with diverse forms of learning among members of the Society. From 1870–3, as part of the nascent university extension movement, the Pioneers organized a series of free lectures that stimulated many other organizations to follow suit, until the town became 'surfeited' with lectures. New initiatives proliferated. Classes were organized through the Science and Art Department from 1873 with courses on mechanical and architectural drawing, applied mathematics, geometry and perspective, and French, which attracted 30 students a year (ibid.: 10). Moreover, blending scholarship, moral action and practical skills was to hasten the arrival of a new society and the independence of working people – this was the basis for 'social science' as opposed to the dismal science of political economy (Janes Yeo, 1996).

According to Greenwood, improvement had resulted from two factors. First, higher levels of human happiness accrued from the advancement in science and arts, increased productive powers of industry and the abundance of things. The second was a notion of what would later be called equal educability, that everyone could participate in the new intellectual universe, which linked into radical ideas:

> Some approximation to intellectual equality, by the extension to the many of the knowledge and tastes developed amongst the comparatively few, so that a co-operation for common purposes has been rendered possible, and the utmost result for the good of all extracted from the knowledge and skill which is and shall be attained. (Greenwood, 1877: 16)

Greenwood expresses a sense of equality in arguing that education should be available to all classes of the community, including 'he who follows the plough or wields the trowel'. Across the country, co-operative libraries became places where working-class people found an education. They would open up new possibilities and many labour movement leaders experienced the power of learning in them (Mansbridge, 1944: 14).

The expansion of co-operative education also had an impact on mainstream developments. Co-operatives did much to ensure the 'spread of education and diffusion of knowledge among those of the labouring classes' that supported the development of state education, and in some areas co-operative societies for a time became an essential educational agency (Mansbridge, 1944: 15–16). Although many societies did not devote a lot of resources to education, the movement as a whole served as a seedbed for new practices, such as the Workers' Educational Association, established in 1903 (Woodin, 2019). However, generic educational provision by co-operative societies went into decline around the turn of the twentieth century in response to the expansion of state provision. Local authorities took over libraries and adult education classes that had outlived their usefulness or were becoming harder to justify (Rae, 1904). W.R. Rae, from the Co-operative Union, wrote that 'Our duty is plain … to see that … [local authorities] do theirs', meaning that co-operatives were to cede control to local government (Rae, 1904: 6). While the wariness about state action among many co-operators was evident, even co-operative stalwarts such as George Jacob Holyoake had recognized the need for state elementary schools. In fact, fear of state education softened in the face of municipalization and, later, nationalization. This development could of course leave a bitter aftertaste and Rae noted how co-operative libraries had been 'managed out of existence' by local authorities. Nonetheless, he argued that the movement should concern itself with distinctively co-operative education across the age range, inculcating the history and principles of the movement, including classes for children, young people and adults; specialized libraries; and classes on co-operation that might involve the Women's Co-operative Guild. He also wanted to refocus scholarships on secondary education, technical colleges and workers' colleges with direct links to the movement as he felt that general educational scholarships to Oxbridge colleges had done the movement little good (Rae, 1904: 7).

Through the nineteenth and twentieth centuries, different approaches to the state can be discerned within the history of co-operative education that are not necessarily polar opposites but existed in a creative tension (see Vernon, 2013). Co-operators were often aware of the limitations of the state and fiercely guarded their autonomous democratic societies. At times they hoped to form a new co-operative state, the co-operative commonwealth. Yet co-operative action had always been curtailed by the state and legal system, most notably when, at one point in the 1850s, the registrar of friendly societies had ruled that contributions to education were not legal. Although this was to be temporary, it pointed to a contradiction, that co-operatives were independent and autonomous but often came up against state regulation and provision, not least in education. This was apparent to Joseph Reeves, the educational secretary of the Royal Arsenal Co-operative Society (RACS), who noted that the 1918 Education Act created an opportunity to sustain and safeguard 'full autonomy':

> That the workers have to develop their own culture no sympathetic observer can possibly deny, and the more they use the educational funds of the State for the purpose of developing their own system of education, the greater will be their chances of building a new system of society. (Reeves, 1921: 4)

A further approach was to make advances in new areas such as managerial education and higher education. In 1912, R.H. Tawney was actively encouraging co-operators, having played an important role in the development of compulsory education, to make their influence felt in the arena of higher education, particularly concerning the availability of scholarships (Tawney, 1912). As ever, the movement's strategy was to influence wider developments while establishing their own alternatives. The Co-operative College was to come into being in 1919 as a form of 'higher education' for the movement. It would provide specialist and tailored courses for co-operative leaders who had already received a certain level of general education (Woodin, 2017; Woodin et al., 2019).

In the post-war period, further opportunities were opened up by the 1944 Education Act and its promise of 'secondary education for all' that offered escape routes for a small section of the working class who might previously have been funnelled into the labour movement. Innovation proved harder in a system dominated by the state and where co-operatives struggled to connect their members to new business models. It would be some time before co-operatives started to once again emphasize their unique character as member organizations.

The spirit of association and co-operative character

From the turn of the twentieth century, as the general educational presence came to be seen as unnecessary, there was a reassessment of co-operative education. From 1896 to 1898, the movement actively debated education and this process drew upon a definition of education that relied on specifically co-operative purposes and meanings. The main aim of co-operative education was:

> primarily the formation of co-operative character and opinions and secondarily, though not necessarily of less import, the training of men and women to take part in industrial and social reforms and civic life generally. (Hall and Watkins, 1948: 168)

These twin perspectives represented two forms of specialization out of the broad assault upon education that stretched back to the Owenite period.

The idea of 'co-operative character' made visible a hidden history of informal learning. From the inception of the movement, it had been acknowledged that co-operatives had a significant effect on individuals and communities. By marrying self and collective interest, they supported the individual, the co-operative and the society. Indeed, the movement claimed to be:

> a valuable means of education in the widest sense of the term. Through their membership of the Movement a number of men and women are being trained to exercise tolerance, forethought, and self-restraint, are being trained in the general conduct of business, are learning to trust men and women of sterling character, and are discovering the power and value of united action and organization. Many working men and women have gained a great deal of moral and intellectual power through their interest in the practical and varied work of their societies and by

attendance at the annual Co-operative Congress and at local and other conferences. (Acland and Jones, 1884: 8)

Holyoake distilled these thoughts and practices in his injunction to foster the 'spirit of association', which would help co-operators to work together in solidarity:

> to prepare members for companionship. They did not require classical, scientific, and historical knowledge in order to sell oatmeal and candles. It was the social education which goes before and after which they had primary need.
>
> Education is not co-operative, because it is given by co-operators to co-operators, unless it is conducive to the formation of the co-operative mind ...
>
> The education of the schools is of supreme service in public citizenship, but co-operation is a school of social citizenship, which erudition does not supply. (Holyoake, 1898: 7)

Holyoake drew a direct comparison with the attempt to promote 'associative character' among the Owenites.

Character could of course be an elusive term that was difficult to categorize and act upon but was part and parcel of working together in a democratic co-operative. Writing in 1914, the Plymouth co-operator W.H. Watkins drew lessons from a historical analysis of the previous century in arguing that training, education and character were indispensable if people were to 'avail themselves of such improved social and industrial conditions' (Watkins, 1914: 4). Co-operative character was a prerequisite for the new state that was to be brought into being:

> We are ... building up a State within a State, a State in which ... people are arranging the business of life on harmonious and co-operative lines, rather than on the competitive and discordant lines we find in the competitive world. (ibid.: 8)

Watkins noted that something more than 'intellectual assent ... outwardly conforming to co-operative principle' was necessary. Rather, in line with Holyoake, he asserted the need for the 'spirit of co-operation':

> We may have co-operative students; we may have numbers of people joining co-operative societies and taking part in the work of the co-operative movement; but unless these people hold within themselves the true ideal of co-operation, and endeavour

strenuously day by day to act it outwardly, we shall not have
co-operators, and there will be in them no force of co-operative
character. (ibid.: 10)

The religious inflection was apparent in the requirement to know thyself
and develop the 'inner state of condition' that was necessary for outward
co-operative expansion.

Co-operative character pointed in different directions. It was to
cultivate committed co-operators who would put visions into practice
yet it could also concentrate the mind on purity of purpose, which might
be best attained in small groups. This related to a puritan leaning that
favoured purposeful learning over more amorphous social participation or
entertainment. But activists were also troubled by their need to influence all
co-operators:

> ... a few people can determine the rate and course of development
> of the whole co-operative movement. We, however, do not
> desire it shall be a few people; we desire to make the whole of
> those within the movement true co-operators, and develop the
> co-operative character; and so we must be unflagging in our
> efforts at co-operative education. (ibid.: 14; see Woodin, 2011)

One answer to this conundrum was to expand the explicitly educative aspects
of co-operation. The urgency to acquire knowledge, metaphorically on the
same basis as cheese or bread, helped co-operators to access education as
an everyday resource but it also created problems in terms of co-operative
growth beyond certain groups. In later years, one aspect of this strand of
co-operation would connect with training for committee members and
lay directors of societies that became a staple of the Co-operative College.
However, during the post-war period, with the onset of the welfare state,
the informal and intangible nature of co-operative character was harder to
access and became less sought after in any case.

Co-operatives and citizenship – schools of democracy?

The second area of specialism mentioned in the definition of co-operative
education related to citizenship and civic participation. During the late
nineteenth and early twentieth centuries, the seemingly inexorable rise of
democracy was a potentially explosive force that splintered off in multiple
directions and generated varying class responses. The notions of progress
and improvement were palpable and propped up by growing prosperity
coupled with advances in education, welfare and the built environment.

On the eve of the 1867 Reform Act, co-operatives themselves provided compelling evidence of the 'progress of the working classes' and were a vital conduit through which the new ideas of citizenship were funnelled (Ludlow and Jones, 1973). The spread of democracy created a concern to bring the working classes into the nation and empire and to align their interests in a common project. The most publicized introduction of the concept of citizenship to co-operators was that of Arnold Toynbee at the 1882 Co-operative Congress where he argued for 'the education of the citizen. By this I mean the education of each member of the community, as regards the relation in which he stands to other individual citizens, and to the community as a whole' (Toynbee, 1882: 60). He specified the need for political, industrial and sanitary education. Similarly, Arthur Dyke Acland, who was appointed to the Central Co-operative Board in the early 1880s, argued that co-operative societies were in a unique position to enlarge the scope of citizenship. He addressed working-class co-operators as members of the nation:

> ... your own daily lives as part of the great body of working people – as English citizens of a great country, as fathers and mothers, as neighbours of the suffering and the poor. We want you to think about your daily lives in your homes and cities, and also your lives as citizens of England, to remember that we are always thinking about things connected with these lives of ours. (Acland, 1883: 11)

Systematic knowledge, aided by university men, was to support the development of English citizens, 'to apply common sense and sober judgment to the many problems of our lives as English citizens ...' (ibid.: 18–19). The approach wedded the practical nature of citizenship and attendant responsibilities to an appreciation of the history and literature of the nation. For instance, the writings of Thomas Carlyle, Charles Kingsley, Elizabeth Gaskell, Charles Dickens, George Eliot, Thomas Macaulay, Robert Owen and William Cobbett were all recommended.

Working-class co-operators were supportive of citizenship and higher learning but many were not content with what they perceived to be an attempt to divert the movement from its core purpose. Indeed, citizenship was interpreted in terms of the practical and long-term needs of co-operatives and revealed simmering class distrust within the movement. The nation was not construed as a finished product but rather as a space in which co-operative ideals could be used to reconstruct social arrangements. As a result, there was a need for practical forms of citizenship that encouraged the growth of co-operation through what Ben Jones described as 'a careful and systematic teaching of the principles and practice of co-operation' (Jones, 1882: 61). Indeed, one practical outcome of this discussion was the production of a handbook, *Working Men Co-operators*, jointly authored by Acland and Jones (1884).

In the coming generations, co-operators would embrace Toynbee's talk but interpret their responsibilities as citizens in co-operative ways. They occupied public spaces as teachers, magistrates and school board members as well as local and national political representatives who supported co-operative ideals. In addition, the importance of this work was not lost on the Women's Co-operative Guild, which worked hard to get women into civic positions as well as elected posts within the co-operative movement itself. The Guild's educational schemes would also challenge both the movement and society at large, on issues relating to poverty, maternity and the lives of working-class women. The needs of members brought them into close contact with the state and extending welfare services along co-operative lines became a priority (for instance, Scott, 1998).

The emphasis on citizenship could also spill over into cultural activities in changing contexts. At the Royal Arsenal Society, Reeves was a great proponent of cultural activity, which had expanded from the late nineteenth century, especially the National Co-operative Festivals held at Crystal Palace (Magnanie, 1988). In the 1930s, Reeves' conception of 'education for social change' fused radical citizenship with cultural action and reflected his disenchantment with the state as a representative of capitalist economics. He was influenced by the Labour College movement as well as the ideas of the Popular Front, expressed in various cultural productions such as the London Co-operative Societies' film *Advance Democracy* (Reeves, 1936).

Culture, progressivism and standards

Cultural participation became a significant feature of co-operative education during the early and mid-twentieth centuries. It was one way of responding to the burgeoning membership, which officially grew from 3 to 8 million between 1914 and 1939. Cultural groups were given a fillip with additional funding for adult educational classes in the 1918 Education Act. Choirs, drama groups, pageants, bands and dance groups were all organized. Cultural activity was conceived in democratic and co-operative terms so that co-operatives were merely reclaiming a social activity that was theirs by right. For example, in 1937, 74 dramatic groups were counted in the movement and this was highlighted as a positive development:

> Drama ... implies very practical co-operation between different groups of people – dramatists, actors, producers and stage craftsmen. Drama originally belonged to the people ... at the market place or in the churchyard, and the whole community attended. (Co-operative Review, 1936)

However, co-operatives were not simply receiving and passing on cultural practices; they did so in rapidly changing circumstances. Mounting technological and business challenges combined with the need to represent co-operatives in the best possible light while also ensuring popular participation by members themselves. Co-operatives were to aspire to the best in culture just as they did with standards of food. This was a difficult set of contradictions to manage. One commentator noted that 'If drama is worth organizing on a co-operative basis through amateur societies then it is worth organizing properly, and co-operative societies should see to it that drama is presented at its best' (Co-operative Review, 1936). The desire for outward-facing provision, which might appeal to new audiences, aroused political anxieties. For example, the *Co-operative Review* observed that cultural provision might help to attract a 'vast middle class public ... on grounds of commercial merit ... not ... social revolution' (Co-operative Review, 1939: 108).

Co-operative culture also blended participation and business. One educational committee developed the notion of 'co-opera' and 'made a considerable financial gain by transferring its show from a school room to a super cinema' (Co-operative Review, 1937: 182). Indeed, scale impressed co-operators and was implicit in the idea of a co-operative commonwealth that was being supported across the labour movement and beyond. RACS put on Handel's *Belshazzar* at the Scala Theatre, which told a story of liberation of the Jews from Babylon. London societies also used the Royal Albert Hall on occasions, which represented a continuation of the visible celebrations of co-operative power in the public displays at the opening of new premises and the co-operative parades through city centres on International Co-operative Day. Perhaps one of the most symbolic of these events was the 1938 Wembley Stadium pageant, Towards Tomorrow, which was attended by over 60,000 people. Each of these events involved hiring professional conductors and specialist advisers to help celebrate and co-ordinate the immense voluntary activity of co-operative singers, dancers and performers. Alan Bush, Benjamin Britten, Michael Tippett, L. du Garde Peach, André van Gyseghem and Montagu Slater were some of the luminaries who supported co-operative societies to represent their cultural and artistic skills on a public stage.

The interest in culture also related to the broadening curriculum in compulsory elementary schooling. By the early twentieth century, the reaction against a restrictive basic curriculum had become visible and a new set of ideas began to have an influence among teachers, school inspectors and others (Holmes, 1911). Educators involved with the Co-operative Union and College were influenced by progressive educational ideas that emphasized the need for the all-rounded education of the whole person. The first principal of the College, Fred Hall, wrote about the possibility that young people might be engaged through:

> new methods of teaching juniors through action ... Singing, dancing, drawing, modelling, and other activities are employed, so that the children may play themselves into knowledge. (Hall, 1918: 9)

Similarly, Reeves explicitly compared the restrictive elementary school to the open possibilities of co-operative education and argued for:

> a broad humanistic system of education for the children, so helping to rectify the narrow and utilitarian methods now adopted in our elementary schools ... inculcating knowledge of human progress ... We should not set too much store on whether the child knows where and when Robert Owen was born, but upon the interest the child takes in the beauty of a noble life. (Reeves, 1921: 6)

These pedagogical interventions must be placed alongside the structured examinations system of the co-op itself, which Reeves may have been criticizing indirectly. However, under the growing influence of developmental psychology, progressive ideas also distinguished between levels and abilities. The tendency helped co-operators to structure their provision accordingly with classes targeting different ages and, to some extent, abilities. It could also have the unintended consequence of undermining the earlier espousal of equal educability. The onset of levels, exams and pedagogy all induced a reluctant acceptance of different abilities – a tendency also visible in vocational education.

Vocational education

The origins of the co-operative movement had been based on finding solutions to the industrial and social chaos of the early nineteenth century.

Co-operative stores, workshops and communities, which were to bring about working-class independence, gave prominence to learning practical skills. Into the 1870s, the veteran Owenite William Pare would speak and write about the need for 'co-operative industrial colleges'. This aspect of co-operation set the co-operative movement apart from radical and adult education movements, which often kept their distance from 'useful knowledge' or vocational learning, assuming it was a way of diverting the working class from power (Johnson, 1979; Harrison, 1961).

The remarkable growth of consumer co-operation rapidly highlighted the need for effective training of staff, managers and leaders, not only in technical skills but also in democratic processes that were essential to the effective functioning of a co-operative. For instance, *The Co-operative Managers' Text Book*, documented the complex internal workings of the society: 'The relationship between a manager and the committee, a manager and the employés, and of the latter to a society'. The textbook was a recognition that 'store-management by committee' had become outdated and that the manager's technical skills were pivotal in the success of a co-operative store (Wilson, 1915: xi). Indeed, the general manager was to be:

> so sympathetically disposed towards the theory and practice of co-operation as to impress his staff with the importance of understanding the primal features of co-operative service, such as loyalty to a society's trading departments, and the necessity of taking advantage of educational facilities for the better understanding of one's business tend very materially to promote efficiency within the movement. (ibid.: 13)

Managers were not solely to focus on the 'commercial aspect' but also 'schemes with an educational character' (ibid.: 16–17). The Co-operative Union developed a system of training for employees comprising training and examinations as well as on-the-job experience. Examination pass rates could be quite low as the movement demanded high standards (Vernon, 2011).

However, while the movement had its own impressive range of training courses, it was not entirely independent of the state. In political and policy circles, less priority was accorded to non-academic educational routes in comparison with the raising of the school leaving age. Fewer resources were devoted to vocational and part-time training. A number of co-operative societies did take advantage of the day continuation schools that were supported for a time under the 1918 Education Act but funding would be curtailed in the 1920s. In addition, after the 1944 Education Act, co-operatives looked forward to working with the vocationally oriented 'county colleges' that were on the statute book but were never implemented, again considered less important than the school leaving age (Woodin *et al.*, 2013).

Nevertheless, the Co-operative College would develop a range of management training and, after the Second World War, a faculty of management that trained staff full-time for a year. This represented a rich educational experience from which many co-operative leaders emerged, but it could only cater to a small number of people. In the post-war years, the habit of recruiting from within the movement persisted and the anachronistic image of co-operatives made it hard to draw in graduate staff. As the movement went into decline, which was particularly sharp from the 1960s, managers and leaders tended to hold on to their positions, which engendered further stasis. In addition, in the 1970s and 1980s, societies became less willing to release staff for such long periods of time. As societies merged, they often moved training in-house which could ironically lessen the influence of co-operative values. Universities also entered the field of business studies and management training but tended to marginalise co-operatives. Yet, during the 1990s, the importance of co-operative values was again reasserted and co-operatives saw business opportunities in values, for example, through fair trade. Following the problems that beset the movement in 2013, the evaluation reports made implicit criticisms of co-operative leaders and their skills. It is a challenge faced by the proponents of the co-operative university in 2019 who are attempting to blend skills-based education with social purpose and general education.

Conclusions

The British co-operative movement built and sustained these educational strands of activity that help to illuminate historical changes in capitalism and the state. Each of them changed over time and were not always fully developed in a movement that was not able or willing to financially support them. They also overlapped considerably. Indeed, one of the attractions of co-operative education has been that, when it attempted to prefigure a co-operative commonwealth, it blended management with social science, co-operative play with statistics, citizenship with liberal education. The curious mix made for distinctive co-operative activists whose lives cut across prevailing educational distinctions. Co-operative education has also for long had an international aspect and mutual two-way learning took place as British co-operation was exported to many other countries. For instance, the Co-operative College became a model for emulation as colleges were formed across Europe during the inter-war years and, after 1945, in Africa and Asia. More recently, an awareness of multiple co-operative traditions is rich with potential to understand how new futures may be moulded (see Shaw, Chapter 3, in this volume).

Co-operative education grew out of a democratic movement and was highly inventive in meeting the needs of members. It certainly went into decline in the post-war years when membership and the unique qualities of co-operatives were downplayed in a declining business faced by incomprehension and ridicule from without. However, co-operative education, in all of its diverse incarnations, has not died out completely and can potentially be redefined and reworked for the present. Since the Statement on Co-operative Identity was agreed in 1995 and the Co-operative Commission of 2001, there have been attempts to apply values and principles to mainstream institutions, asserting confidence in the co-operative message, particularly in terms of co-operative schools and a co-operative university (see Ralls (Chapter 10) and Neary and Winn (Chapter 11) in this volume). Once again, the tension between distinctiveness and working with the mainstream has resurfaced. We should not jettison either of these perspectives. Co-operators attempted to embrace the mainstream and develop an impact while maintaining a unique identity and remaining accountable to their members. The interconnections between liberal education, citizenship and specific co-operative learning has been at the heart of the movement. It is a dilemma faced by democratic institutions that necessarily have to engage with the world where state regulations and the 'needs of the economy' make co-operative and democratic working difficult but not impossible.

References

Acland, A.H.D. (1883) *The Education of Citizens*. Manchester: Central Co-operative Board.

Acland, A.H.D. and Jones, B. (1926 [1884]) *Working Men Co-operators: An account of the co-operative movement in Great Britain*. Manchester: Co-operative Union.

Claeys, G. (1989) *Citizens and Saints: Politics and anti-politics in early British socialism*. Cambridge: Cambridge University Press.

Co-operative College (2019) 'Adult education revisited 100 years on'. Online. https://tinyurl.com/y75bojzd (accessed 1 March 2019).

Co-operative Review (1936) 'British Drama League'. *Co-operative Review*, X (4), 119.

Co-operative Review (1937) 'Co-opera'. *Co-operative Review*, XI (6), June 1937, 182–3.

Co-operative Review (1939) 'Amateur v. professional'. *Co-operative Review*, 14 (4), 108–9.

Greenwood, A. (1877) *The Educational Department of the Rochdale Equitable Pioneers' Society Limited: Its origin and development*. Manchester: Central Co-operative Board.

Hall, F. (1918) *Further Prospective Developments of Co-operative Education*. Manchester: Co-operative Union.

Hall, F. and Watkins, W.P. (1948) *Co-operation: A survey of the history, principles and organisation of the co-operative movement in Great Britain and Ireland*. Manchester: Co-operative Union.

Harrison, J.F.C. (1961) *Learning and Living, 1790–1960: A study in the history of the English adult education movement*. London: Routledge and Kegan Paul.

Holmes, E. (1911) *What is and What Might Be: A study of education in general and elementary education in particular*. London: Constable and Co.

Holyoake, G.J. (1898) *Essentials of Co-operative Education*. London: Labour Association.

Janes Yeo, E. (1996) *The Contest for Social Science: Relations and representations of gender and class*. London: Rivers Oram Press.

Johnson, R. (1979) '"Really useful knowledge": Radical education and working-class culture, 1790–1848'. In Clarke, J., Critcher, C. and Johnson, R. (eds) *Working-Class Culture: Studies in history and theory*. London: Hutchinson, 75–102.

Jones, B. (1882) 'Education of co-operators'. In *14th Annual Co-operative Congress*. Manchester: Co-operative Union, 61–2.

Lovett, W. (1920) *Life and Struggles of William Lovett in His Pursuit of Bread, Knowledge and Freedom*. New York: Alfred A. Knopf.

Ludlow, J.M. and Jones, L. (1973) *The Progress of the Working Class, 1832–1867*. Clifton, NJ: Augustus M. Kelley.

Magnanie, L. (1988) 'An event in the culture of co-operation: National co-operative festivals at Crystal Palace'. In Yeo, S. (ed.) *New Views of Co-operation*. London: Routledge, 174–86.

Mansbridge, A. (1944) *The Kingdom of the Mind: Essays and addresses, 1903–37, of Albert Mansbridge*. London: J.M. Dent and Sons.

Mercer, T.W. (1947) *Co-operation's Prophet: The life and letters of Dr. William King of Brighton*. Manchester: Co-operative Union.

Owen, R. (1968) 'Rational education for the new moral world'. In Harrison, J.F.C. (ed.) *Utopianism and Education: Robert Owen and the Owenites*. New York: Teachers College Press, 118–28.

Rae, W.R. (1904) *How Best Can Co-operative Societies Utilise their Educational Funds in View of the Educational Facilities Now Provided by Municipal and Local Authorities*. Manchester: Co-operative Union.

Reeves, J. (1921) *Educational Organisation*. Manchester: Co-operative Union.

Reeves, J. (1936) *Education for Social Change: A demand that co-operative education should prepare men, women and children for the new world*. Manchester: Co-operative Union.

Scott, G. (1998) *Feminism and the Politics of Working Women: The Women's Co-operative Guild, 1880s to the Second World War*. Hoboken: Routledge.

Simon, B. (1960) *The Two Nations and the Educational Structure, 1780–1870*. London: Lawrence and Wishart.

Simon, B. (1991) *Education and the Social Order, 1940–1990*. London: Lawrence and Wishart.

Tawney, R.H. (1912) *Education and Social Progress*. Manchester: Co-operative Union.

Toynbee, A. (1882) 'The education of the citizen'. In *14th Annual Co-operative Congress*. Manchester: Co-operative Union, 60.

Vernon, K. (2011) 'Values and vocation: Educating the co-operative workforce, 1918–1939'. In Webster, A., Brown, A., Stewart, D., Walton, J.K. and Shaw, L. (eds) *The Hidden Alternative: Co-operative values, past, present and future*. Manchester: Manchester University Press, 37–58.

Vernon, K. (2013) 'Co-operative education and the state, c.1895–1935'. *Forum*, 55 (2), 293–308.

Watkins, W.H. (1914) *The Formation of Co-operative Character*. Manchester: Co-operative Union.

Wilson, R.J. (ed.) (1915) *The Co-operative Managers' Text Book*. Rev. ed. Manchester: Co-operative Union.

Woodin, T. (2011) 'Co-operative education in the nineteenth and early twentieth centuries: Context, identity and learning'. In Webster, A., Brown, A., Stewart, D., Walton, J. K. and Shaw, L. (eds) *The Hidden Alternative: Co-operative values, past, present and future*. Manchester: Manchester University Press and United Nations University Press, 78–95.

Woodin, T. (2017) 'Co-operation, leadership and learning: Fred Hall and the Co-operative College before 1939'. In Hall, R. and Winn, J. (eds) *Mass Intellectuality and Democratic Leadership in Higher Education*. London: Bloomsbury Academic, 27–40.

Woodin, T. (2019, in press) 'Usable pasts for a co-operative university: As different as light from darkness?' In Noble., M. and Ross, C. (eds) *Reclaiming the University for the Public Good: Experiments and futures*. London: Palgrave.

Woodin, T., McCulloch, G. and Cowan, S. (2013) *Secondary Education and the Raising of the School-Leaving Age: Coming of age?* New York: Palgrave Macmillan.

Woodin, T., Vernon, K. and Shaw, L. (2019) *The Co-operative College and a Century of Social Change*. London: Palgrave.

Chapter 3

The Co-operative College and co-operative education internationally

Linda Shaw

Shortly after his arrival at the Co-operative College as Principal in 1946, R.L. Marshall commented that 'the international quality of the College' was 'one of its outstanding values' (Marshall, 1947: 3). He was to continue to highlight the international dimensions of the College throughout his time there. He was right to do so. The College's international influence on co-operative education has been a widespread and enduring one.

This chapter will explore the nature of this influence and its evolution throughout the century of the College's existence. There have been three main dimensions to its international work. First, since its inception, the College has been characterized by strong international ties and the presence of overseas students. Second, it has also provided inspiration for the formation of national centres as well as an institutional model for co-operative education that has been widely adopted. Finally, and not the least, the College has been a source of technical expertise on co-operative education within the international development policies and programmes of the UK government as well as international agencies such as the United Nations.

It is telling that, from the first intake, students came not only from the UK but also from Europe and even further afield. Contemporary commentators on College life clearly viewed this as an important feature and one that reflected its co-operative character. In July 1921, for example, an article in the *Co-operative Educator* proudly claimed that 'There are already ex-students of the college in Australia, Egypt, Iceland, Finland and Sweden.'[1] The College's 'College Herald' news bulletin in the *Co-operative Educator* magazine regularly reported on activities such as international summer schools and listed the arrivals and departures of the College's own overseas students. Several are listed as coming from British colonies and protectorates such as India and Egypt as well as from Europe. In 1926, an annual exchange of two students was established with the People's College at Elsinore in Denmark.[2] In March 1926, it was reported that 'some of these students have rendered excellent service in lecturing for the Educational

Fellowship, for branches of the Guilds, and for societies, on the co-op movements in their respective countries'.[3]

The numbers of residential students attending the College were relatively low during the 1920s and there are no records of a separate syllabus being provided for them so it must be assumed they took the same courses as the other students. Subjects taught included co-operation, British history, economics, citizenship, education, public speaking, and technical subjects such as management, bookkeeping, auditing and law.

All the residential students shared the same lodgings at the College hostel in Kersal, north Manchester, and the communal life there was often reported on in *Stokehole*, the student magazine. There were also articles by the overseas students describing co-operatives in their own country or commenting on life in Britain. An editorial in *Stokehole* in 1932 commented that the presence of overseas students at the College 'accentuates its co-operative character'.[4] In 1928, five students came from Manchuria, Egypt, Denmark and France. As the overall numbers of College students rose, reaching around 40 in the late 1930s, so did the numbers of overseas students. They tended to make up around a quarter of the student body throughout the inter-war period.

Occasional mentions in the 'College Herald' section of the *Co-operative Educator* magazine provide some clues as to what happened to students following their studies at the College. Some went on to distinguished careers in the movement internationally. Will Watkins came as a student in 1920, was then appointed lecturer and later left to join the International Co-operative Alliance in 1929, becoming its Director in 1951 (Watkins, 1986). It was reported that other international students went back as 'editors of national co-operative journals, as business advisers, as auditors, as principals or lecturers in co-operative schools' (Hall, 1928: 7). Colonial students often went back to assume senior government positions as registrars and inspectors of co-operatives. One former student, for example, went back to head up a regional co-operative training institute in Madras in 1927.[5] Another became Chief Inspector of Co-operatives in Egypt. In 1938, out of 37 students in total, 11 were from overseas coming from the USA, South Africa, Iceland, China, Ceylon, Estonia, Czechoslovakia, Egypt and Denmark. The chairman of the students' association reported that the 'exchange of ideas with foreign students has, as in former years, been one of the highlights of our stay here'.[6]

Although the UK College appears to have been the first to be formally established, it was part of a first wave of national college formation and development in Europe and North America during the inter-war period.

Unfortunately, we lack international comparative studies of these institutions, although there may well be some histories published locally. All appear to have been founded and supported by local co-operative movements rather than by the government. Although they may have been inspired by the UK example, there was undoubtedly much diversity in the approaches adopted. Several were focused on the acquisition of more technical and retail skills by retail staff. Some colleges certainly survived well into the post-war period and at least until the 1970s.

In the UK, teaching took place in the premises of the Co-operative Union although there was separate residential provision. In other countries, colleges enjoyed dedicated teaching and residential premises. For example, in Sweden, Vår Gård was founded in 1924 and catered for the needs of employees with short courses and with some longer courses aimed at future leaders. There was an emphasis on acquiring practical skills and the college was equipped with the latest store and office equipment (Potter, 1952: 18–19).

Writing in 1952 in the UK College's magazine as Director-General of the International Co-operative Alliance, and as a former student and staff member, Watkins commented that:

> The example of the college has been influential internationally.
> The idea that the national Co-operative Union should have a
> permanent school either at, or easily accessible to its headquarters,
> was swiftly appreciated and applied. Within a very few years
> Finland, Germany, France and Switzerland had emulated Britain
> or surpassed her in the provision made for co-operative teaching
> institutions. Somewhat later, but before the Second World War,
> the USA, Denmark, Austria, and Holland followed suit. (Watkins,
> 1952: 10)

Their emergence did not go unnoticed in the UK. In 1944, the 25th anniversary appeal leaflet for a new College fund pointed out that 'little countries like Denmark and Sweden have built National Colleges' while Switzerland had built a 'palatial' Central College and provided photographs of them. The message was clearly that Britain lagged behind. Even the Dutch, it was reported, had decided to set up a national centre for co-operative education and training while 'under the Nazi heel of occupation'.[7]

We know little about how much these colleges interacted with each other although biennial meetings of college principals from across Europe are mentioned in the *Co-operative College Review*. The report of the Oslo meeting of 1967 mentions participants from Austria, Denmark, Finland, Germany, Sweden, Switzerland and the UK.[8] The histories of these colleges clearly provide fertile grounds for further research although in the long term, however, most of these long-established European colleges do not appear to have survived beyond the 1980s. Today, only the UK College now seems to have survived from this first wave of college development. The reasons for the demise of the other colleges are undoubtedly diverse but, in some cases, are likely to be associated with the collapse of consumer movements in the case of Germany and Austria (Birchall, 1997).

However, the College model did not disappear. A second wave of colleges was founded from the 1960s onwards in the British colonial, and later Commonwealth, countries in the Caribbean, Africa and Asia. These colleges, in contrast to the first wave, did not originate from the co-operative movement but rather they were government-supported institutions often funded, at least initially, from international aid programmes. This reflected both the widespread use of the co-operative model in international development and the fact that education figured largely in development assistance programmes (Unger, 2018). More broadly, co-operatives featured in the international development programmes of many governments, including those of the UK and the USA, as well as the multilateral agencies such as the United Nations. In the mid-1980s, for example, over half of World Bank agricultural programmes in Africa involved co-operatives (Develtere *et al.*, 2008: 20). Post independence, co-operatives continued to be important development tools for the new governments.

Despite their key role, there are few studies of the histories of co-operatives in developing countries, let alone histories of co-operative education and its institutions (Shaw, 2014; Hilson *et al.*, 2017). In part, this also reflects the fact that international development is a relatively new field for historians, albeit one that is growing rapidly. There is now a growing literature on the history of development and a recognition that much more needs to be done to examine how development played out on the ground (Hodge, 2016; Unger, 2018). Much of this literature emphasizes themes of complexity, connection and reciprocity. These 'entangled histories' analyse the complex and multi-level connections that have operated between people, movements and institutions beyond national boundaries. The global co-operative movement clearly presents rich possibilities in this respect for historians. As Hilson has pointed out, the transfer of co-operative ideas was often reciprocal rather than a simple one-way imposition (Hilson, 2017: 47). She identifies education as an important area of exchange for the co-operative movement, especially in relation to national and international congresses. The College clearly provided an important such vehicle for the transmission and exchange of ideas and experiences internationally about co-operative education both via its international students and through the wider medium of development assistance programmes (ibid.: 8).

Many of the second-wave colleges have had strong connections with the UK College and most still operate today. However, as with the first-wave colleges, we lack histories and any comparative studies of them. In addition, there are further challenges such as the lack of archive repositories across Africa with a declared specialism in co-operatives. Existing national repositories may include relevant materials but to date their co-operative content remains unknown. In 2010–11 a survey of co-operative societies in Tanzania revealed the existence of many of their records, but these were housed in damaging and insecure environments.[9] Fortunately, the National Co-operative Archive in Manchester contains not only UK-based materials but also materials from the African colleges.[10] These collections, together with unpublished research carried out under the ILO CoopAfrica progamme,[11] have been used to outline the following overview of the evolution of co-operative colleges with a focus on the histories of those in East and Southern Africa.

Table 3.1: Second-wave co-operative colleges

Country	Year established	Original name of institution
Sri Lanka	1943	School of Co-operation
India	1947	Co-operative Training College
Uganda	1954	Co-operative College
Malaysia	1956	Co-operative College
East Africa	1952	Jeans training school
Pakistan/ Bangladesh	1960	East Pakistan Co-operative College
Tanzania	1963	Moshi Co-operative College
Egypt	1964	Higher Institute
Kenya	1967	Co-operative College
Ghana	1971	Co-operative College
Botswana	1972	Co-operative Training Centre
Trinidad & Tobago	1972	Cipriani College of Co-operative and Labour Studies
Nigeria (3)	1957	Federal Co-operative College - Ibadan
Swaziland	1976	Co-operative College
Zambia	1979	Co-operative Management Training Institution
Lesotho	1984	Co-operative College

As Table 3.1 illustrates, compiled from various sources at the National Co-operative Archive, colleges were set up in at least 16 countries.

The connections between the UK College and these second-wave colleges have been complex and multi-layered. The international connections of the College were boosted in the immediate post-war period when the number of overseas students studying at the College increased considerably. At the same time, the College also became an important hub of expertise for co-operative development within the emerging field of international development from the 1950s onwards. Many staff and students were engaged with large-scale co-operative education and development projects in Africa and Asia.

The origins of this expanded international role originated with the post-war Labour Government's approach to colonial development, which involved support for trade unions, co-operatives and local government as a way of engendering wider social and economic development (Holford, 1998; Kelemen, 2007; Riley, 2017). Education played an important role in the new policy on co-operative development and there was an emphasis on ensuring the availability of appropriate training for the government staff responsible for managing the sector. There was a considerable internal debate within the Colonial Office over the nature and the location of the training to be provided. In 1946, following an inspection of the new premises at Stanford Hall, Loughborough, the Co-operative College was chosen to provide a training programme for 'junior' co-operative officials, that is, local and native staff from the colonies.[12] Funds were made available by the Colonial Office (and successors) for the development and provision of a residential programme on co-operation (Shaw, 2009). Students received bursaries to attend.

The first students arrived at the College in the autumn of 1947 for the new Course on Colonial Co-operation.[13] This course, later renamed the Course on Co-operation Overseas in the early 1960s, continued to be delivered at the College for many years until the early 1990s. Up to 40 students a year were recruited from over 40 countries although the majority came from the British colonies. Even after independence for the colonies, places at the College for Commonwealth students continued to be funded by the UK government. Over the years, the numbers were not inconsiderable. During the years from 1947 to 1969, for example, over 600 students attended the courses.[14]

The College course for overseas students had dedicated staff and a syllabus that was initially approved by the Colonial Office. The syllabus focused on co-operative law, economics, bookkeeping and auditing, the UK co-operative movement and the 'art of teaching'. In the early years, parts of the course were not much adapted to the needs of colonial students. Those dealing with finance, for example, were based on the system of accounting used in UK consumer societies.[15] Later on, in the 1970s, the programmes were adapted to try to meet the needs of the students coming from the developing world better. There were both certificate and diploma programmes, which gained formal accreditation with the University of Nottingham in 1962.[16] In 1980, a postgraduate diploma was started and a programme of short specialist modules developed. Off-site visits were arranged to UK consumer co-operatives and work placements were arranged as well. The latter were largely with agricultural co-operatives.

These courses recruited students who were intended to work at a high level in the government. In 1951, the College prospectus reported that:

> These courses are designed primarily for Assistant Registrars and Inspectors and for the Officers of Co-operative Unions in the countries of the British Commonwealth and in other countries with similar conditions and problems of Co-operative development. They have also been of value for other students who wish to examine Co-operative progress in the developing countries or who are considering seeking appointments there.[17]

Students who had studied on these programmes then returned home and went on to form a (co-operative) elite in their own country (ILO, 1964: 49). Newly independent Tanzania, for example, had three cabinet ministers who had studied at the UK College. And the College Principal was invited and went out to join the country's independence celebrations (Marshall, 1962). In 1964, the *Co-operative Review* claimed that the sessional courses had made a 'substantial contribution' to overseas co-operative development 'including that of the Government Ministers, senior co-operative officials, principals of Co-operative Colleges and other responsible co-operative workers who have attended the College.'[18]

The College was not alone in this type of provision as UK-based training for overseas civil servants was an important feature of UK aid provision to developing countries during this post-war period. After the Second World War, British probationers for more senior positions in the Colonial Administrative Service attended the Devonshire training programmes at Oxbridge and LSE, which slowly opened up to local recruits until they too became wholly for overseas civil servants. Stockwell has argued that this reflected a 'distinctively British understanding' of the influential role that an elite administrative cadre could play' (Stockwell, 2018: 94). This was the case for the co-operative administrators graduating from the College.

It is striking, however, how few women benefited from these programmes. If the College's student body had a low number of women students, then their presence was even lower among the overseas students. Only 12 women overseas students are recorded on a list of all students compiled on the 50th anniversary of the College in 1969.[19] This was hardly remarkable in the early days of the programme as women were not allowed into the Colonial Administrative Service until the 1950s. However, this gender imbalance continued throughout much of the post-war period in the overseas courses and was also evident in domestic students.

These College programmes undoubtedly represented a powerful vehicle for the international transmission of ideas about co-operative education and the role of a college. Contemporaries claimed this was a two-way process. There are many references in College publications to the beneficial effect of the presence of overseas students on the UK student cohorts and to the wider movement. As noted earlier, in the early days of the College, overseas students went out and delivered lectures to UK co-operatives on the co-operative situation in their home countries. For Watkins, this was a function of greater importance than the exposure of the overseas students to British co-operatives and their history. The College was a channel through which 'international influence can be brought to bear on the co-operative movement at home' (Watkins, 1952: 10).

It is difficult to assess the extent to which this was genuinely a two-way and equitable process, although it is clear that for the students attending the College it shaped their perspectives on co-operative education. Student articles in College publications provide some insights into their experiences. Writing in 1960, for example, Shamsul Huq from Pakistan indicates how, for many students, the College became the preferred model for co-operative education:

> The last dream should be the establishment of a high-grade co-operative college in every country. Such a college will not only train high ranking officials of the co-operative organisation but also leaders of co-operative thought and opinion who will carry the movement forwards to the goal of social betterment. (Huq, 1960–1: 206–7)

Huq, who received a scholarship from the International Labour Organization to attend the College, then went on to become the Principal of the East Pakistan Co-operative College in 1961. Even if not explicitly endorsed as the only model for co-operative education, a single national-level college became the institutional model most commonly adopted in Commonwealth countries and the UK College was regarded by many as the 'mother college'. Staff and expertise were provided by the College to facilitate the development of many of the new African colleges (Shaw, 2009: 31) together with funding through other international development programmes. A Nordic consortium, for example, funded the initial establishment costs of the Kenyan college as well as providing staff expertise.[20] The UK government funded the building of a college in Uganda. College staff assisted with the establishment of new colleges in Africa in countries such as Tanzania and Kenya, which often had large campuses (Spaull, 1968).

During this period, another important feature of international development was the prominence given to technical assistance and expertise. Indeed, the decades of the 1950s and 1960s have been characterized as the high point of the development expert (Sobocinska, 2017). In addition to the development of new colleges, the College also generated many such experts who provided technical assistance for co-operative development projects in the 1960s, 1970s and 1980s for UN agencies and others. College staff and students such as Bert Youngjohns, Trevor Bottomley and Peter Yeo acted as advisers, consultants and registrars in many countries, especially in Africa. A series of basic manuals providing guidance on matters such as finance, committee work, start-up, housing, etc. were written by College staff or associates and jointly published by the Intermediate Technology Development Group. Some were still for sale in 2018.[21]

Short courses were also put on at the request of the government, such as one at Stanford Hall for Latin American co-operators held in 1965 (Marshall, 1965: 347). College staff continued to sit on government advisory committees for co-operative development until the 1970s. Harold Wilson, writing in the College magazine *Spectrum* in 1964 while still leader of the Opposition, commented that the existence of a residential centre for co-operative teaching 'is essential to our plans for social and economic development'. This was, he argued, because co-operatives provided the best basis for economic and social activities in former colonies and newly independent colonies (Wilson, 1964: 6).

While co-operatives continued to play an important role in overseas aid into the 1970s, there were some notable failings in large-scale co-operative development projects. One notable example was the Comilla programme in East Pakistan (Unger, 2018: 105). Here, co-operatives were captured by local elites and did not meet the needs of the poorest. This became a common critique. A conference was held at the College in 1977, convened at the suggestion of the United Nations Secretary-General, where questions were raised about the role of governments and their effectiveness in tackling poverty (ICA, 1978). As co-operatives began to lose their presence in the mainstream of development from the 1970s onwards, this inevitably affected the College. Government funding for the College programme and for overseas students greatly decreased in the early 1990s. The course was finally closed in 1997 due to the low numbers attending.

Outside the UK, co-operative colleges continued to operate although they no longer sent staff to the UK for training and they continued to be funded by their own governments as part of the tertiary education system. Their focus remained unchanged, with the provision of long-term residential courses aimed at staff and leadership (with the exception of Botswana) rather than on outreach courses for members or directors. In Malaysia, for example, the college was set up in 1956 to provide courses for government officers, co-operative society staff and co-operative department staff (which it still does).[22] The emphasis for all of the colleges was on managing established co-operatives rather than on co-operative start-up or entrepreneurship. In many ways they appear to have continued the original emphasis of the UK course on training for an administrative elite. The aim of many of the co-operative college students in East and Southern Africa, for example, was to obtain a government job in the co-operatives or another department.

Evidence from the National Co-operative Archive records indicates there were considerable similarities in the syllabus offered by African colleges in their early years. As with the UK College, the curriculum was focused on the administration and business skills needed to run co-operatives with key areas being accounting and bookkeeping, legal matters, marketing and management. In 1980, for example, the core modules at the Zambian college were bookkeeping and accounts, management, economics, marketing, co-operative basics, retail management, business calculations, and agricultural savings and credit. The college in Kenya offered similar programmes together with correspondence courses that attracted large numbers of students. Most provided certificates or diplomas for their learners but not degrees. In Malaysia, the syllabus largely focused on legal ordinances, economics and marketing although there was coverage of 'History, Principles and Practice of Co-operation'.[23]

Several colleges did offer short courses for members delivered either at the college or via outreach programmes, but these declined gradually and there was a greater emphasis on campus-based provision. In Zambia, the national outreach teams from the college had disappeared by the 1990s.

The numbers of active co-operators attending the residential programmes also declined, with an increasing proportion of the student intake comprising younger students straight from school.

Government support also brought challenges for many colleges. Typically, the African colleges often had little control over recruitment in some countries with staff being mainstream civil servants rather than educationalists. They were sometimes subject to relocation to other government departments. Many colleges struggled to appoint staff with knowledge and expertise in co-operatives or indeed in education. The rollback of the state that occurred under the structural adjustment programmes of the 1980s also had a negative impact on colleges. Budget cutbacks badly affected the maintenance of the physical infrastructure of colleges. The thriving correspondence courses run by the Kenyan college, for example, were hit by a breakdown of the print machinery and subsequent lack of money for repairs. This meant that students did not receive their course materials in 1986, after which their numbers plummeted and never really recovered.[24]

The nadir for most of the African colleges appears to have been in the 1990s. Chronic under-resourcing had meant library stock was not replenished for many years and the condition of college buildings continued to deteriorate. The curriculum was not updated. More widely, there was a lack of confidence by governments and donors in the co-operative model, which was seen as old-fashioned and not fit for purpose. Many colleges were isolated and marginalized from the mainstream of education and development.

Remarkably, all of the colleges survived this period of retrenchment albeit with some in better shape than others. In many cases, this appears to have been due in part to the dedication of the older co-operators on the staff of the colleges. At the time of an unpublished survey in 2008–9, the colleges in East and Southern Africa continued to offer residential programmes. The majority of students were school-leavers who attended programmes in co-operative and generic business management with more emphasis on the latter. At this point, there were just under 4,000 students attending courses at the colleges (Shaw, 2011).There was a limited outreach provision for the wider movement with the exception of some programmes in Botswana and Tanzania. In most countries, national co-operative apex bodies were weak and not in a position to support the colleges or provide education themselves (the exception being Uganda). Thus, an obvious partner for colleges to provide wider educational provision for the movement was lacking. There was a lack of education for co-operative employees, directors and members as well as for the agencies that worked with them such as government co-operative promotion staff and non-governmental organizations (NGOs). A co-operative development officer in Zambia reported that the co-operative sector was 'crying out for education' (Shaw, 2009: 7) and this was a common theme in all the countries. Unfortunately, the destinations of college students were not being tracked by the colleges, so little is known about what graduates did after they left. It was thought that many did not go on to co-operative organizations and elected instead to work in conventional businesses if they could not gain a government post.

In the following decade, a more positive picture has begun to emerge with several colleges entering a new and expansionary phase. There has been more investment in college infrastructure, notably in Tanzania, Uganda, Kenya and Botswana. The number and type of courses on offer have expanded as well. Several colleges have adopted a strategy of moving into the higher education sector. This has brought with it more funding and autonomy from government as well as the opportunity to undertake research and attract more students. There has been an increase in student numbers to over 8,000 in total, with most of the growth coming from the two colleges in Tanzania and Kenya that have now acquired full university status.[25] Some of the smaller colleges have continued to struggle such as those in eSwatini (formerly Swaziland) and Lesotho.[26] There is a new national co-operative training institute set up in Rwanda,[27] while in Nigeria there are plans to increase the number of colleges, which is currently three.[28]

Co-operative colleges have been, and still are, important actors in co-operative education, especially in Africa. This brief overview highlights the huge scope for more research, particularly at the country level as college trajectories have been very different in each country and the model has evolved in response to a changing environment. In recent years, research and project links have helped to sustain connections between the UK College and its sister colleges.

The UK College has played an important role in both the first and second waves of college development and provided an influential model that has been both adopted and adapted in many countries. However, while the influence of the College on co-operative education internationally has been an important one, the nature of that engagement has changed. The College can no longer rely on the direct funding it once received for students and instead must compete for project funds in a very competitive environment. Nonetheless, the College has run several successful co-operative education projects in Africa and South Asia.

However, the older, first wave of co-operative education and training centres across Europe and North America has not survived. By contrast, the colleges in Africa and Asia are mostly still functioning, typically as part of the public education system, and receiving funding through that route. To this list of current providers can be added Mondragon University in the Basque Country of Spain and the ADG centre in Germany. Clearly, there is no single blueprint for national-level provision, which is inevitably shaped by local context and local movements. The UK College model of a single national college providing tertiary-level residential education focused on co-operatives has proved an enduring one, especially in Africa. There have, however, continued to be ongoing tensions between institutional autonomy and public funding. Co-operative movements have either been unable or unwilling to provide the core funding needed for large-scale colleges. This has been a challenge, of course, for the UK College over its century of existence. The legacy of a syllabus that has focused largely on knowledge and skills needed for existing co-operatives rather than on start-up or co-operative innovation is also one that may have hindered the development of new co-operative sectors.

The College has continued to provide expertise and advice on co-operative international development, but again the nature of this has changed. There has continued to be some work with the UK government on co-operative development (DFID, 2010) and more recently the College has worked with European partners to bring co-operatives into European Union development policies and aid programmes (Cooperatives Europe, 2015). There has also been collaboration with the International Labour Organization to produce guides for co-operative policy (Smith, 2004).

One of the enduring features of the College throughout its existence has undoubtedly been its 'international quality' fostered by its students, movement connections and wider linkages. It offers a remarkable case study of how an individual institution has been central to the exchange and transmission of ideas around co-operation and education throughout the century of its existence.

Notes
[1] *Co-operative Educator*, July 1921, p. 101.
[2] 'College Herald', June 1925, *Co-operative Educator*.
[3] 'College Herald', June 1926, *Co-operative Educator*.
[4] *Stokehole*, March 1932.
[5] *Co-operative Educator*, 1935, p. 2.
[6] *Stokehole*, 1937, Chairman's notes.
[7] *The British Co-operative College 1919–1944*, p. 11.

[8] *Co-operative Review*, 12 August 1967.

[9] The UK Co-operative College, in collaboration with the Moshi University of Co-operative and Business Studies, carried out a pilot survey of co-operative records in Tanzania in 2010–11 funded by the Endangered Archives Fund, project ref. EAP402.

[10] See www.archive.coop

[11] See www.ilo.org/public/english/employment/ent/coop/africa/index.htm (accessed 18 September 2018).

[12] Office Committee on Co-operation in the Colonies, Minutes of Meeting, 2 May 1946, National Archives CO 1007.

[13] Advisory Committee on Co-operation in the Colonies, Adviser's Notes, 11 December 1947, CO852/900/1.

[14] The International Co-operative Training Centre Programme of Courses, 1989.

[15] ibid.

[16] *Spectrum* [Co-operative College Magazine] 1961–2, p. 4.

[17] College prospectus, 1950/1.

[18] 'The British movement and overseas aid', *Co-operative Review*, March 1964, p. 20–7.

[19] *Co-operative College Long-term Students 1919–1969.*

[20] Annual Reports of Co-operative College of Kenya 1970–88 held at the National Co-operative Archive.

[21] See https://developmentbookshop.com/catalogsearch/result/?q=co-operatives+ (accessed 18 September 2018).

[22] See www.mkm.edu.my/en (accessed 18 September 2018).

[23] Evidence taken from annual report of these colleges held in the National Co-operative Archive.

[24] *Annual Report Co-operative College Kenya 1986.*

[25] See www.mocu.ac.tz and www.cuk.ac.ke (accessed 18 September 2018).

[26] See, for example, www.ambou.edu.et

[27] See www.poverty-action.org/organization/rwanda-institute-cooperatives-entrepreneurship-and-microfinance-ricemaccessed (accessed 18 September 2018).

[28] See dailypost.ng/2018/02/28/federal-co-operative-colleges-bill-scales-second-reading-senate (accessed 18 September 2018).

References

Birchall, J. (1997) *The International Co-operative Movement*. Manchester: Manchester University Press.

Cooperatives Europe (2015) *Building Strong Development Cooperation: Partnership opportunities between cooperatives and the EU*. Brussels: Cooperatives Europe.

Develtere, P., Pollet, I. and Wanyama, F. (eds) (2008) *Cooperating Out of Poverty: The renaissance of the African cooperative movement*. Geneva: International Labour Organization.

DFID (Department for International Development) (2010) *Working with Co-operatives for Poverty Reduction* (Briefing Note). London: Department for International Development.

Hall, F. (1928) *The Co-operative College and its Work*. Manchester: Co-operative Union.

Hilson, M. (2017) 'Co-operative history: Movements and businesses'. In Hilson, M., Neunsinger, S. and Patmore, G. (eds) *A Global History of Consumer Co-operation since 1850: Movements and businesses*. Leiden: Brill, 17–48.

Hilson, M., Neunsinger, S. and Patmore, G. (eds) (2017) *A Global History of Consumer Co-operation since 1850: Movements and businesses*. Leiden: Brill.

Hodge, J.M. (2016) 'Writing the history of development (Part 2: Longer, deeper, wider)'. *Humanity*, 7 (1), 125–74.

Holford, J. (1988) 'Mass education and community development in the British colonies, 1940–1960: A study in the politics of community education'. *International Journal of Lifelong Education*, 7 (3), 163–83.

Huq, S. (1960–1) 'Co-operative education in an under developed country'. *Spectrum* [Co-operative College Magazine].

ICA (International Co-operative Alliance) (1978) *Report of an Experts' Consultation on Co-operatives and the Poor* (ICA Studies and Reports 13). London: International Co-operative Alliance.

ILO (International Labour Organization) (1964) *The Role of Co-operatives in the Economic and Social Development of Developing Countries*. Geneva: International Labour Organization.

Kelemen, P. (2007) 'Planning for Africa: The British Labour Party's colonial development policy, 1920–1964'. *Journal of Agrarian Change*, 7 (1), 76–98.

Marshall, R. (1947) *College Magazine*, 3 (3).

Marshall, R. (1962) 'Tanganika impressions'. *Co-operative Review*, 29–30.

Marshall, R. (1965) 'Stanford Hall in Latin America'. *Co-operative Review*, 347.

Potter, G. (1952) 'Another co-operative college'. *Co-operative College Review*, 18–19.

Riley, C.L. (2017) '"The winds of change are blowing economically": The Labour Party and British overseas development, 1940s–1960s'. In Smith, A.W.M. and Jeppesen, C. (eds) *Britain, France and the Decolonization of Africa: Future imperfect?* London: UCL Press, 43–61.

Shaw, L. (2009) *Making Connections: Education for co-operatives* (Co-operative College Paper 15). Manchester: Co-operative College.

Shaw, L. (2011) 'International perspectives on co-operative education'. In Webster, A., Brown, A., Stewart, D., Walton, J.K. and Shaw, L. (eds) *The Hidden Alternative: Co-operative values, past, present and future*. Manchester: Manchester University Press, 59–77.

Shaw, L. (2014) *"Casualties Inevitable": Consumer co-operation in British Africa* (ARAB Working Paper 8). Huddinge: Arbetarrörelsens arkiv och bibliotek.

Smith, S. (2004) *Promoting Co-operatives: A guide to ILO Recommendation 193*. Manchester: Co-operative College.

Sobocinska, A. (2017) 'How to win friends and influence nations: The international history of development volunteering'. *Journal of Global History*, 12 (1), 49–73.

Spaull, H. (1968) 'Cooperative colleges in Britain and East Africa'. *Review of International Cooperation*, 61 (1), 29–40.

Stockwell, S. (2018) *The British End of the British Empire*. Cambridge: Cambridge University Press.

Unger, C.R. (2018) *International Development: A postwar history*. London: Bloomsbury Academic.

Watkins, W. (1952) 'The college and its international influences'. *Co-operative College Review*.

Watkins, W. (1986) *Co-operative Principles Today and Tomorrow*. Manchester: Holyoake Books.

Wilson, H. (1964) 'A message from Harold Wilson'. *Spectrum*, 64–5.

Chapter 4

'O Pioneers': Presentation and meaning in the work of the Co-operative Heritage Trust

Liz McIvor

The Co-operative Heritage Trust is closely linked to the recent history of the Co-operative College and both organizations share a concern with the preservation and presentation of co-operative heritage today. The Trust was born in 2007 out of a decision to create a separate and independently governed body to care for the physical heritage assets of its founder members – Co-operatives UK, The Co-operative Group and the Co-operative College – as well as other co-operatives in the UK. Before this, the buildings, collections and documents relating to the story of the Rochdale Equitable Pioneers Society and other co-operative societies were the responsibility of different organizations and no cohesive strategy was in place to ensure their survival. The creation of an independent body was to enable these to be brought together and understood in the context of an established narrative of how the British co-operative movement had grown and influenced the fabric of social, economic and political change.

At first glance, and to the external observer, the preservation of such a history might be perceived as that of societies seeking to tell a story in order to be understood by audiences outside their sphere better. The nature of the celebration of co-operative heritage within the movement, however, seems, from its earliest days, also to be a way in which the movement and its members came to understand their own story. The beginnings of co-operative manufacture, retail and trade were fundamentally different in nature from other business models in the country and this would be reflected in the way societies understood themselves and their collective past. Before examining this further, it is appropriate to discuss the meanings of co-operative heritage and how the preservation and representation of it fit into the understanding of 'public history'. In other words, how did we get here?

The preservation of records and material cultures of the past is associated in the public mind with museums and archives. The concept of special places in which to study and venerate objects and records has been with us as long as we have been capable of documenting ourselves. Although the modern form of museum was not established in Britain until the eighteenth century, the first documented use of the word was 'mouseion', a third-century BC institution in Alexandria, Egypt, which translates as the 'place of muses'. In Greek tradition, the Muses were the daughters of Zeus and Mnemosyne (goddess of memory), who inspired and supported innovation through learning.

Early museum and archive repositories were based on the sharing of an individual's 'private' collection. A wealthy or well-travelled scholar (or at least one seeking to be recognized as such) might gather objects associated with learning and build their own sense of identity by exhibiting them to others. By sharing their collections, individuals were aware that they were leaving a social and educational legacy for others to make sense of the world at the same time as developing themselves. In most cases, the devoted private collector was aware of the power of leaving a collection to posterity. Those who did so often agreed to part with their collections during their lifetime for token sums in exchange for the immortality of public philanthropy. Elias Ashmole gifted his collection, before his death, to the University of Oxford. This, with some of the University's own holdings, formed the basis of what is now the Ashmolean Museum and became a cultural reference point for academic institutions to establish scientific or study collections of their own in order to assist learning and development, which was the core principle for those attending such 'modern' institutions.

The spread of the influence of public educational institutions, and the idea that people would be able to learn through broadening their perspective, was an attractive one that would grow exponentially with increasing literacy levels in later nineteenth-century Europe.

While the university was the first repository of the documented, material past, this eventually extended to the development of learning initiatives aimed at the newly urbanized masses. Gradually, guidebooks and evening lectures would encourage middle-class audiences visiting museums to embrace the power of learning through experience, to reread old documents and to study objects that reflected different cultures and the 'exotic'. It would be some time before this material culture would be inclusive of the experiences of a nation from the 'home perspective' or the lives of working-class people, but the seed had been planted that all such activity was 'improving' and therefore a valuable form of learning (Bennett, 1995).

Collections in the early days represented archaeology, natural history specimens and ethnographic collections. Those objects that were related to local events or the development of industry and trade were, at best, relegated to 'folk history', and were much less a focus for research or documentation. All this would change in the latter years of the twentieth century, when the increasing education of and representation for working people in the UK led to a greater appreciation of the need to represent aspects of their material culture.

The previously 'unaesthetic' remnants of heritage associated with trade, the working class, consumerism and globalization began to be valued more as educational resources. Records that could illustrate 'ordinary' people were becoming crucial in giving a voice to those who had been, for so long, left unrecorded, partly because they did not have the agency to record themselves. The former lack of scholarly enquiry into the use and meaning of objects and records associated with the 'masses', and their relative invisibility, meant that academics have since applied a greater sense of importance to objects and buildings that help to interpret, contextualize and provide evidence for the 'real' world of everyday life, work and voice. Thus, in the late twentieth century these trends to establish or formalize the presentation of 'people's histories' expanded significantly. However, a question would remain about how to do it.

The establishment of 'social history' collections would initially draw heavily on a developing fashion for folk history and objects of antiquity that reflected traditional practices rather than everyday life, but gradually the representation of the prosaic began to dominate the cultural heritage agenda. From the 1970s, the interest in representing the 'ordinariness' of the past and the lives of workers, their homes, leisure activities, and places or events of significance increased. This was particularly the case in the context of local authority museums, to reflect the memories or nostalgia of the audiences visiting them as well as representing a generalized understanding of what had 'been and gone'. The representation of working-class lived experience through triggered memories elicited by emotional responses to key objects or images was based on the concept of creating a 'dream space' (Kavanagh, 2000) through which users could examine their emotional responses to a version of history presented to them of which they may not necessarily have had first-hand experience.

This theory is useful for understanding co-operative heritage. It is based on the ownership of a narrative or shared history through 'perceived truths'. Those accessing them take on the role of a 'witness' in understanding a place or an event in history that is shaped by their response and interpretation of what is offered. The need to interpret, to tell a story in the context of, the co-operative movement was evident by 2007 with the founding of the Co-operative Heritage Trust. A generation had grown up in the shadow of consolidation of co-operative societies in the face of a national loss of retail market share in Britain. A person recalling their childhood in the 1930s with reference to 'the co-op' would have a direct personal connection with the village society store, with the children's gala put on by members, and with the opportunity for poor families to save through dividends and acquire not only material goods but also education and promotion by association with co-operatives. The children of post-war 'baby boomers' would be the first to experience a personal 'disconnect' with the all-encompassing cultural impact of co-operative membership that was available to those who came before. Those born after 1970 would not be members of co-operative societies as their parents and grandparents had been, would not join leisure groups associated with the movement, would not hold a 'DIVI' check, or shop locally or independently. Their only personal experience of the co-op might be in association with the funeral service provision for those who had experienced this 'co-operative culture' in a different and holistic way before (Robertson, 2016). Heritage providers face a constant question about how to approach themes and stories of public interpretation. The decisions made about how to tell the co-operative story have evolved, and still evolve, in response to a changing climate for the potential visitor or user of the movement's heritage resources.

And yet, how did the co-operative movement come to recognize the need to do this? An official representation of this history was always going to be difficult due to the different agendas of various co-operative societies, each with its distinctive history. Societies themselves had recognized the need to understand themselves and celebrate key events in their history. From the mid- to late nineteenth century, they produced printed histories and memorabilia for anniversaries such as jubilees of the opening of a village society store. The commissioning of often cheaply printed plateware given to members on celebratory occasions testified to a sense of shared legacy in the movement as well as local pride and achievement. Such items, displayed at premises and on domestic mantelpieces, would later form part of the offering to museum collections. A sense of legacy featured heavily in society publications and, indeed, the histories of many co-operative societies, whether located in the North of England or elsewhere, would often make reference to the shared history of the Rochdale Pioneers. However, despite this common heritage among co-operators, there was no centralized attempt to bring objects, documents or stories together in a unified way until the later twentieth century.

When the Co-operative Union opened Holyoake House in 1911, it committed its use to learning. This would be the first step towards the establishment of a library and archive to house publications and significant records documenting how the movement had developed. The decision to provide access to books through a reading room and library service was linked to one of the founding values and principles of the movement: to support education. This remains a core principle for co-operators today.

Even before 1919 and the formation of the Co-operative College, the Co-operative Union had provided formal learning to members to allow them to benefit from a traditional university education. The establishment of the Co-operative College would be one way to promote not only the skills needed to run a successful co-operative venture, but also an improved understanding of what it meant to be co-operative in character. Formal education in Manchester, at Stanford Hall near Loughborough after the Second World War, and by correspondence courses would be imbued with learning about the origins of the movement through published works, histories and journals, and the co-operative press.

While the collection and preservation of documents, representing the seeds of an archive, were being gathered in Manchester, the site of the Pioneers' first shop on Toad Lane was beginning to gain a stronger significance for the education of the movement.

Following the initial success of the Rochdale Equitable Pioneers Society, its board had recognized that the store was too small and expansion was a necessary step. Although the store and terms of its lease are mentioned in the early minute books, no special reverence for the fabric of the building is evident from the Pioneers themselves. By the time the store was acquired by the Co-operative Union in 1925, however, this had changed. Enough time had elapsed to confer a special status on the physical remains of the original premises, in the context of what had by now become a truly global movement. During the working life of the building under the Pioneers' tenure, international visitors from Europe, America and Asia had read about the nature of the enterprise and endeavoured to make a personal visit to Rochdale to see the model of co-operation in practice. These visits are recorded in the extant visitor books dating to the 1860s at the point when the remaining Pioneers and extended membership were transferring operations to a new purpose-built Central Premises on Toad Lane (see Figure 4.1).

Figure 4.1: Toad Lane in the 1920s, the site of the original Rochdale Pioneers
Source: National Co-operative Archive collections

By the 1860s, the focus for visitors would have been on the ways in which decisions were made about trading as well as the approach taken by the members to issues of social action such as in relieving destitute members. The primary interest was in the operation of the 'Rochdale Principles' rather than the physical store itself, the bricks and mortar being of lesser importance than the values and expectations of the founders. Even in relation to the opening of the new Central Premises on Toad Lane, the minutes for 1862 and 1863 record a debate about whether to hold a ceremony to unveil the keystone. An entry in May 1872 briefly mentions the 'old grocer shop in Toad Lane, lately used for tobacco manufacture, be prepared for the tailor's shop' (Rochdale Pioneers, 1872). The nature of the store itself would become significant to the 'Pioneer legend', but only for later generations of co-operators.

International visitors came to see how the idea had taken hold and how the concept worked in practice, hoping to learn from experiences 'on the ground' in order to understand what exactly had been the origins of success for co-operation in Rochdale in the 1840s. One early visitor, Victor Aimé Huber, described his experiences of visiting the Rochdale Pioneers during the store's early years of operation in a letter in the *Rundshau* or German 'Co-operative Review' of 1864, a translation of which was published in

1933. The Prussian educator had been warned to expect a somewhat less than refined experience by co-operators in Holborn, London. Although Huber's experience was reflective of this in the abrupt conversations he had with several of the Pioneers themselves during his visit, the concept of the unique birthplace of co-operation was underlined in his writings. He was told by the London and Coventry societies that, 'Those North Lancashire men among their hills are rather rough fellows, but stout and honest, and have, in fact, the lead of our movement.' Huber found himself in disagreement with the Pioneers on matters of religion, class and the use of propaganda, although his letters were used later by the Co-operative Union, which was 'striving to effect a reconciliation of co-operative activity in the historic birthplace of the modern system of Consumer's Co-operation' (Downie, 1933).

Co-operators from around the world would read letters and articles about the prototype society and attend conferences, seeking to bring this learning home by extending co-operative enterprise in the Rochdale tradition. This would feed into the establishment of the International Co-operative Alliance (ICA) in 1895. That this extended to the practices and principles of a concept, a way of working as well as a way of being, rather than the material aspect of business alone, is extraordinary. Yet more extraordinary is the way in which this concept, and the 'culture' of co-operation, was to spread and to effect change in response to global economic developments starting in the late twentieth century and continuing into the twenty-first (Gurney, 1996). Perhaps as a direct result of this, the 'pilgrimage' visitor, until the 1990s, represented the majority of those interested in travelling to Toad Lane to view the original store site. However, for many years, there was nothing to see beyond the bricks and mortar that had once housed the society's commercial life, so little could be gleaned from the fabric about its part in the movement's development.

Despite the emphasis on 'being' and 'doing' according to values and principles, the interest in the tangible assets of the movement's heritage began to grow at the point when the UK movement had achieved a peak of commercial success. By now, the Pioneers themselves were long dead; what remained was their records and what had been said of them, as individuals and representatives of the founding society, by historians and journalists. As co-operative societies published and republished the 'founding story', interest in intellectual study and demand for research grew. More people sought to understand why co-operation had succeeded in Rochdale and how it had become a dominant force in the twentieth century. Now, a different generation of visitors, both home-grown and international, would be seeking out the Pioneers. Subsequently, the Co-operative Union wished to establish an 'official' museum to enable such visits to have more meaning and, after raising funds to do so by subscription from individual societies to purchase and renovate the building, an official 'reopening' was held in 1931 (see Figure 4.2). The store had housed different businesses and, by the time the Co-operative Union bought the site, nothing remained of its life as the prototype co-operative. The records relating to its business had mostly ended up in the hands of Rochdale Town Council and there was a concern that the civic interest in the 'birthplace of co-operation' was waning.

Figure 4.2: The symbolic reopening of 31 Toad Lane in Rochdale
Source: National Co-operative Archive collection

After 1931, in addition to trips organized by the Co-operative Union, visitors arriving in Rochdale could apply to the local co-operative society premises for a key to make an informal visit. By the 1970s, due to the post-war development of road networks and commercial districts in Rochdale, Toad Lane had been cut in two to construct a bypass. The remaining section of the street containing number 31 was now isolated both from the ring road and the town centre. It had also become clear that the building had some structural problems that would necessitate a temporary closure to stabilize what was, by this time, a 250-year-old working building. The building was relaunched in 1981 offering regular opening hours and guided tours to visitors as part of Rochdale Borough Council's newly established 'conservation area' of what remained of Toad Lane.

Gradually, the 'Co-operative Museum' began to be professionalized and the connection to what would become the Co-operative Archive was strengthened in 2001 with the relocation to Manchester of the Co-operative College from Stanford Hall, Loughborough. As the archive service developed within the management of the College, the museum achieved official registration. In the year 2000, the Co-operative Union reconstituted itself as the modern apex body Co-operatives UK by merging with the UK Co-operative Council and the Industrial Common Ownership Movement, and the existing archive records and management of the museum were transferred to the Co-operative College. The 2000s were a time of significant change and challenge for the consumer co-operative movement, and drastic changes to the business structure and governance of The Co-operative Group would mean that independence was seen as a way to protect heritage assets for the future.

In order to acquire accredited museum status and the necessary public funding that was needed to turn the building into a functioning visitor attraction for the years to come, plans were made to create an independent charitable trust. In May 2006, a fund was established to support and sustain the activities of the independent body and, by the time the Trust was established in September 2007, a donation of £3 million from The Co-operative Group to a restricted endowment fund allowed financial independence from the founding organizations. This independent status and a commitment to offering a public archive and museum service conferred the right to apply for transformational public funding as part of the phased Rochdale project. This resulted in the closure of the entry-fee model museum in 2010 and the building being reopened free to the public in 2012. The Heritage Lottery Fund supported the refurbishment and provision of increased physical access to the Toad Lane site, along with other funders including the J Paul Getty Jr General Charitable Trust. As a result, there was improved access to free research resources through the archive collection. Continuing professional relationships with the Co-operative College worked to enhance the experience for the traditional visitor base as well as develop new audiences for the Heritage Trust through community outreach and formal education offers.

Collections were professionally catalogued, digitized and conserved to demonstrate the diversity of co-operative business history in the UK as well as the track record of commitment to ethical trade and retailing, purity and quality control, and an ongoing commitment to community.

Collections now had a mandate to represent the wider interests of the co-operative movement in a variety of media representing leisure, governance, charitable giving and events as well as the recent histories of societies reflecting contemporary experiences of co-operators in the UK. The redesign incorporated public storytelling, not only the story of the Pioneers and Rochdale, but also of how the British co-operative movement influenced ideas and social reform. The development of the Trust reflected a growing commitment to follow public trends and reflect a mounting interest in social history by making collections meaningful and accessible to the general public. In 1934, archives and libraries belonging to businesses were supported by the Business Archives Council, established to ensure that their records of historical importance were preserved and recorded in a standardized way and used to raise the profile of this part of British history.

Throughout the twentieth century, businesses increasingly began to realize the wider historical significance of the records and materials in their keeping as well as their internal value as resources on which to build and develop brand loyalty and organizational culture. In consumer retail companies, in addition to contributing to institutional memory, access to records and materials charted approaches to advertising and marketing and shed light on the history of individuals for family and local historians, providing valuable information about major events as well as national social and cultural shifts. Companies in the UK had the choice either to conserve and allow access to their own materials through establishing 'in-house' offerings – primarily to facilitate the existing firm and its associates to make good use of records for future development – or to open up to allow public scholarly research. Offering a more public service requires custodians to make adequate provision for development and to expand holdings with the continued collecting of the company and associated partners as, inevitably, once there is public recognition of a collection, more potential donors come forward.

For example, in 2012, Marks and Spencer's archival collections were housed in a new facility in partnership with the University of Leeds in order to make its previously privately held collections more accessible. The collection remains part of Marks and Spencer plc, with commercial access and research its main priority. But, as a British firm since 1884, its history and heritage were able to represent a unique insight into the domestic lives of British people, especially in the city where the business was founded. Unilever, too, established an archive service at the historic Lever Brothers' model community 'Port Sunlight' on the Wirral. It was able to represent the history of the company prior to and following the major mergers and acquisitions that had created Unilever as a commercial giant in 1929 with brand names for hygiene, foods and speciality chemicals. Although not sharing the value systems underpinning co-operation, for firms seeking to explore and share their heritage the concept of uniqueness of place and special character attached to brand and corporate identity would become increasingly important, and collections would be subject to the ethical guidelines and best practice observed in the wider heritage industry.

In the light of this trend and the way archival holdings were being accumulated relating to the co-operative movement, the importance of physical objects and the stories they could tell were becoming a consideration. Before the formation of the Co-operative Heritage Trust, the primary focus had still been the building representing the movement's tangible heritage at 31 Toad Lane. The creation of a museum in Rochdale was dependent on the use of the building as a venerated object, the focus of the co-operators' pilgrimage. For the publicly compiled museum collections previously discussed, the buildings that have housed them over the years have been varied, modified, and sometimes purpose built or rebuilt during their histories. In the cases of the British Museum and the Victoria and Albert Museum, the buildings have played a secondary role to the collections. In recent years, the movement towards the telling of the 'stories of the people' and the approach to diversity of message in the heritage world have been matched by the desire to recognize the importance of *places* by association. The inclusion of industrial and trade sites in the lists of 'special places' compiled by public bodies serves to remind us about the need to consider history and experience of it through heritage in context. This situates industrial heritage sites in line with castles, palaces and the birthplaces of key figures in politics, literature and religion, and allows for the recognition of something less tangible. Number 31 Toad Lane fits into this picture as the physical representation of the birthplace, not of an individual, but of an idea: a place of veneration, a concept, and how its application might change the lives of those committed to it.

In 2018, the public body Historic England, responsible for the listing of significant structures in the landscape and built environment, chose 100 places that were considered integral to the story of how the country changed and developed to make it what it is today (see Figure 4.3). Among those places chosen for their part in the story of trade and commerce was the former Pioneers' store. The choice was made by Tristram Hunt who, at the time of writing, was serving as Director of the Victoria and Albert Museum. He recognized that the societies that had formed since 1844 had done so in 'conscious imitation' of the Rochdale Society and that, therefore, the Rochdale store must be considered influential for those home-grown co-operators as well as those in countries to which the movement had spread and had an impact on trade and culture. This influence had been redoubled in 1857, when George Jacob Holyoake published *Self-Help by the People: The history of the Rochdale Pioneers*. It was said that there were 332 co-operative societies in operation in 1863, 251 of which had started since the publication of Holyoake's book. What had begun in Rochdale had turned into a movement (Wilkinson, 2018).

Figure 4.3: Rochdale Pioneers Museum has received national recognition as part of the 100 Irreplaceable Places of Heritage in England
Source: Copyright permitted A. Hirst

As societies recorded themselves and their connection to the Rochdale story, they had a framework by which to do so owing to the work of George Jacob Holyoake who became known as the 'official historian of the co-operative movement' following the publication of his history only a dozen years after the Toad Lane store had begun trading. In 1857, the Co-operative Union had yet to be founded and it would be many decades before the history of the material culture of the movement would be recognized. Holyoake's contemporary history suggests the understanding of the power of legacy, and a need to inform and educate the readers of the future as well as those of the present. Holyoake's personal commitment to co-operation and self-help for working people prompted him to write in the vein of hagiography about a movement and a handful of established societies whose future was uncertain at that time. However, not everyone agreed with Holyoake's version of the story even then, as is clear from an article of 2017 which shows that the writings of John Kershaw, a former Pioneer, differ from Holyoake's description of how the business was initially formed (Mayo, 2017: 38). John Kershaw's manuscript, setting out his own account, *The origin of the Equitable Pioneers Society of Co-operators, Rochdale*, is held in the Trust's archive collection.

For Holyoake, the Pioneers and their followers, the veneration of 'things' and 'place' was certainly far less significant than the perceived success of co-operative practice and adherence to the principles themselves. The very fact that there was little attempt by the founding members to record or preserve the material story of the movement at its outset or that, by the time attention was paid to the movement's place in history, several of the original Pioneers had died, reveals an interest in the preservation of the concept or ideal over the physical. However, as the first generation of pioneers passed away, it provided an occasion for celebrating and commemorating their lives, as in the following poetic reflection at the Rochdale Co-operative Congress in 1892:

Pioneers, O Pioneers!

Suggested by hearing G.J. Holyoake at the graves of Smithies and Cooper, Rochdale Co-operative Congress, 1892:

WHAT memories hover round this hallowed spot,
    So long connected with these honoured names,
For Smithies, Cooper, ne'er can be forgot:
    These noble men with still more noble aims.
Men do not die, although their bones may rot —
    Their deeds live after them and show their worth;
The truths they teach and fearless do die not;
    The good remains which they have brought to birth.
O valiant soldiers on a bloodless field,
    Ye dauntless, true, heroic Pioneers,
What glorious harvests now your victories yield!
    Your fame shall brighter grow through coming years;
    For through the grand example you have shown,
    The masses everywhere have happier grown.

A voice has spoken from your graves to-day;
>A comrade lingers still to tell your worth,
>And keep your memory green upon the earth;
And hold your standard high amid the fray.
Nor shall that voice be lifted up for naught:
>True hearts still answer to the call of truth,
>And forward press, in spite of toil and ruth,
To carry out the principles ye taught.
Ere long those truths their world-wide way shall win,
>Cast out the demon Self, and end the strife.
E'en now we see that glorious day begin,
>The toilers enter into larger life:
>A foretaste of the Golden Age to be,
>When men shall all be truly good and free.

The tendency to glorify the Pioneers rapidly became embedded in the co-operative movement of the late nineteenth and early twentieth centuries. For example, David Lawton, writing as '*Th' Old Weighver of Saddleworth*' (Lawton, 1892), continued the trend to eulogize the personalities while extolling the positive message of the movement. This is an example of the cult of the 'saintly pioneers' who had by the late nineteenth century become beacons of light for the now much wider movement. It is telling that this particular missive entered Lawton's publication during a time of great economic uncertainty and depression in traditional textile manufacture and export:

Sow a thought, and you reap an act;
Sow an act, and you reap a habit;
Sow a habit, and you reap a character;
Sow a character, and you reap a destiny. (Samuel Smiles, 1889)

The influencing nature of the popular literature and journalism of the day would have made it difficult for commentators to avoid explaining the events of history without recourse to the deeds of those who would inspire the kind of hope in others to bring about lasting change.

Despite the writings of later generations, the death of Holyoake prompted an official recognition of his personal contribution with the establishment of Holyoake House. During his lifetime, Holyoake had worked to secure the influential papers and correspondence of Robert Owen, known widely in the movement as the 'Father of Co-operation' and, in 1903, some 3,500 letters were deposited with the Union. Holyoake's daughter Emilie Holyoake Marsh deposited his personal papers to join them in order that they might be accessed by co-operators after her father's death.

The formation of a charitable trust to bring together the resources of a National Co-operative Archive and Rochdale Pioneers Museum was a key development on the road to offering a more publicly fronted experience to wider audiences in addition to the traditional 'co-operator' seeking information about their own society or having developed a scholarly interest as a result of it. It was also considered an important step to formalize the way in which co-operative records, including those belonging to active societies and The Co-operative Group itself, could be preserved and used in the future. A key part of ensuring sustainability would be responding positively to change and being able to reflect this in programmes and policies.

In May 2016, a report funded through Arts Council England looking at 'resilience in heritage' examined the trends in the industry following the economic crisis of 2007–8 and the resulting cuts in both public and private funding to all aspects of cultural provision. The report examined the aims and ambitions of the Trust in using co-operative history and heritage to help connect the values and principles to change-making activity for modern audiences. The aim of the report, *Pioneering Funding through New Governance Models* (Rowe *et al.*, 2016), was to establish how resilient and sustainable the museum was following its reopening in 2012. The report recognized the need for the museum to do more than showcase the movement's history. It was suggested there was a need to be a place of meaning to the non-co-operator, to the diverse audiences in the Borough of Rochdale for whom the unique identity of co-operation would be key in the Borough Council's plans to regenerate the urban centre.

Resilience in cultural organizations is described as having a clear vision and using strong networks as well as intellectual assets to innovate and attract the interests of audiences in a way that is responsive to change (Royce, 2011). It was suggested that in order to achieve this the Pioneers Museum should play on its uniqueness of message and 'walk the talk', offering insight into the spirit of co-operation for local people where a need was perceived, by demonstrating the benefits of collaborative effort framed by the values and principles of the movement. Action should show that education, improvement, equity and community remained at the forefront. Suggestions were made to the board of trustees about how to allow archive and museum collections to become more integrated as well as create opportunities for heritage partnerships and concentrate efforts on community outreach to raise the profile of the Trust and its mission.

Doing this would seem natural, but not easy. The task would be to show co-operative practice and, by doing so, re-engage local citizens with the aspects of the town and borough that led to it being recognized as the birthplace of co-operation. To this end, the Co-operative Heritage Trust and the Co-operative College were well placed to work together in helping to build understanding of co-operation with the citizenry already acknowledged as those outside the framework of understanding.

To acquaint younger audiences with the idea of co-operation in a way they understand, the College approached young people in the care system about embedding some life skills around co-operative practice to engage the principles of working together in social enterprise. This is part of making what might just be seen as local history mean something useful for modern life and for those experiencing it with an unequal start. Co-operating to create project content, groups examined what co-operative practice might be harnessed for in the world of work, accessing housing and services as well as plugging gaps in the local economy such as tackling the increasing problem of youth loneliness and mental health support in an age of automation and digital communication.

In this climate of increased commitment to co-operation in Rochdale, the Co-operative College will open a co-operative enterprise hub in 2019 on Drake Street as part of the ongoing effort to breathe new life into historic spaces. The Co-operative Heritage Trust's work as a named partner with Historic England with the aim of creating a Heritage Action Zone for Rochdale will be to develop and deliver outreach programmes to engage with hard-to-reach audiences in urban and rural parts of the borough. It will engage with local schools through targeted sessions to embed pride in local heritage and will prioritize working with young people to grow the concept of co-operation locally in order to sustain the meaning of the heritage it exists to represent.

So why is this activity important, and why should heritage organizations prioritize activity with local audiences in this way? Based on the funding cuts affecting national and local government institutions, the trickle-down effect has revealed increasing competition for charitable funding among heritage organizations. In this climate, the way potential visitors and users spend their leisure time is reflected in the widening gap in social capital as a result of austerity and hegemony, especially in the context of deprived communities in the UK.

In his paper *Museums and Happiness* (2013), Daniel Fujiwara not only argued that access to heritage and cultural context of place would be beneficial for populations, but also that this could be measured to give a social and economic value. In view of the impact of heritage as social capital, the findings indicated that those who had a sense of local heritage and experienced direct engagement with it were more likely to score positively on well-being charts and rely less on core services. Although the report was commissioned for the Department for Culture, Media and Sport, it highlighted the importance of connection to heritage for forming a sense of identity, responsibility and pride. If this engagement and its effects on culture can be mapped and shown in this way, lessons can be learnt by other organizations in the heritage sector for proving that what they can offer is not only beneficial, but also sustainable.

The importance placed on embedding education and opportunity through positive experience within co-operative practice remains part of the commitment to the values and principles of the Co-operative Heritage Trust for the future beyond immediate projects. The Trust is committed to working with partners such as the Co-operative College to continue to offer formal and informal learning and outreach to ensure shared outcomes that will enable diverse audiences to develop their own meaningful connection to the past and its lessons for the future. As a form of modern co-operative action, it is an inherent part of the way both organizations were established almost a century apart and continues to be a key tenet of the way they work together and with others to fulfil their aims and objectives.

If the Pioneers themselves did not focus on the importance of bricks and mortar, the legacy of commemorative china produced by a long since wound-up village society, the whimsy of the 1920s Co-operative Wholesale Society advertising for tea or jam, or even the wisdom enshrined in their early minute books and records, they would have certainly recognized and promoted efforts to help local people to make a difference for themselves and their communities through co-operative practice.

References

Bennett, T. (1995) *The Birth of the Museum: History, theory, politics.* London: Routledge.

Downie, J. (1933) 'Contemporary views of Rochdale'. *Co-operative Review*, 7 (42), 269–72.

Fujiwara, D. (2013) *Museums and Happiness: The value of participating in museums and the arts.* London: Arts Council England.

Gurney, P. (1996) *Co-operative Culture and the Politics of Consumption in England, 1870–1930.* Manchester: Manchester University Press.

Holyoake, G.J. (1900) *Self-Help by the People: The history of the Rochdale Pioneers.* London: Swan Sonnenschein and Co.

Kavanagh, G. (2000) *Dream Spaces: Memory and the museum.* London: Leicester University Press.

Kershaw, J. (no date) The origin of the Equitable Pioneers Society of Co-operators Rochdale – In his own words (Manuscript). Collections of National Co-operative Archive, Manchester.

Lawton, D. (1892) *Webs from Fancy's Loom: Worthy tales for warty foaks and village co-operation*. Manchester: Co-operative Wholesale Society.

Mayo, E. (2017) *A Short History of Co-operation and Mutuality*. Manchester: Co-operatives UK.

Robertson, N. (2016) *The Co-operative Movement and Communities in Britain, 1914–1960: Minding their own business*. London: Routledge.

Rochdale Pioneers (1872) *Minute Book*. Rochdale: Local Studies.

Rowe, E., McDermott, V. and Ashley-Taylor, H. (2016) *Pioneering Funding through New Governance Models*. London: Arts Council England.

Royce, S.J. (2011) *Business Models in the Visual Arts: An investigation of organisational business models for the Turning Point Network and Arts Council England*. London: Arts Council England.

Smiles, S. (1889) *Happy Homes and the Hearts That Make Them; or, Thrifty People and Why They Thrive*. Chicago: US Publishing House.

Wilkinson, P. (2018) *Irreplaceable: A history of England in 100 places*. Swindon: Historic England.

Part Two

Learning from
contemporary practice

Chapter 5

Leadership in co-operatives

Michael L. Cook

Co-operative education in the USA is an activity that has experienced considerable variability in quality and intensity for the past 100 years. Contrary to the well-documented and historical professional histories of the major co-operative movements – agricultural, financial, utility and consumer – co-operative education history continues to await seminal discourses. This chapter takes a first step towards filling this void by initially presenting a brief introduction to the evolution of US agricultural co-operative education. In the USA, agricultural co-operatives account for approximately 30–35 per cent of the $950 billion food value chain. Producers, through ownership of co-operatives, control well-known national consumer brands such as Land O'Lakes, Ocean Spray, Blue Diamond, Sunkist, Florida Natural, Borden, Tillamook, Cabot and many others. Agricultural co-operatives are very prominent in commodity processing, storage and distribution of many bulk commodities including soybeans, wheat, corn, rice, fertilizer fuel, animal genetics and rural retail outlets generating between $250 million and $300 billion in revenues. Rural financial co-operatives are also very important as they manage more than $300 billion in operations and capital assets. Forty-five per cent of the spatial territory receives electrical service from an 800-co-operative rural electric system. Most agricultural producers in the USA belong to at least four rural and agricultural co-operatives. In many of the commodity sectors, co-operatives have important or dominating market shares including dairy, citrus, cotton, nuts and dried fruits, and many of the farm inputs. Outside agriculture, co-operatives have very prominent roles in the housing, credit union, food retailing, sporting goods and alternative energy sectors.

The second part of this chapter introduces a mini-case study/story of the emergence of a co-operative education programme. The emphasis of the story will concentrate on multiple organizational factors, financial and other resource constraints, and preferences of participants – shared by direct feedback from participants in this programme named the Graduate Institute of Cooperative Leadership (GICL) – to demonstrate the heterogeneity of challenges in an attempt to describe a small example of co-operative education in the USA. There are many players who deliver educational benefits to co-operative members, leaders and employees. Many apex organizations exist such as the National Council of Farmer Cooperatives (NCFC), the National Cooperative Business Association (NCBA), the National Rural Electric Cooperative Association, the Farm Credit System, the National Credit Union Association (CUNA) and many others who have co-operative training or education programmes.

Brief overview of US agricultural co-operative education

The US agricultural sector covers a broad expanse of land, ethnic groups, and more than three hundred crops and most livestock and fishery species. Since the significant waves of immigration commenced in the 1840s, groups arrived with varying philosophies and models of collective action. By the late 1800s, the British Rochdale principles were broadly accepted with pockets of German, French, Portuguese, Italian and Scandinavian co-operative philosophical influences. There are no federal co-operative incorporation statutes in the USA. All co-operatives are considered corporations and the co-operative statutes are subsets of state corporation laws. There are more than 110 co-operative incorporation statutes. Each of the states has a stock form of incorporation (capital contribution by patron, like the Rochdale system) and a non-stock form (complete service at cost entity). In addition, there are three major functional types: purchasing, selling/processing, and multipurpose – marketing producers' output, selling farm inputs/services to producers.

To add to the complexity, two uniquely American philosophical schools of thought emerged: the 'competitive yardstick' school advocated by Edwin Nourse and the 'single commodity monopoly' philosophy advocated by Aaron Sapiro. The competitive yardstick school of thought of Edwin Nourse, a Midwest economist, proposes that the role of a co-operative is to modify the behaviour of rivals in a similar industry, thus encouraging the market to produce fair prices. Most multipurpose co-operatives pursue this defensive philosophy. It is a very anti-monopoly approach to business. Nourse was very influential during the apex (1920s to 1935) period of co-operative formation in the USA. His philosophy still dominates the values and strategies of most supply and multipurpose co-operatives. Nourse became a very famous economist and in 1947 was named by President H.S. Truman as the first Chairman of the Council of Economic Advisers. Conversely, Aaron Sapiro, a California attorney, was active in starting marketing co-operatives during the 1920s. His California Plan advocated single-commodity co-operatives whereby farmers should organize centralized (tier one) commodity marketing entities using the monopolistic power granted by the 1922 Capper–Volstead Act. These two battled over their contrasting monopolistic versus anti-monopolistic platforms. Almost all US agricultural co-operatives are organized around the philosophy of one of these two very influential co-operative thinkers, yet 90 per cent of the co-operative leaders have no idea who they were. These schools demanded very different economic and sociological theoretical underpinnings, and this continues to complicate co-operative education and member understanding. They also differ from the co-operative sector approach more familiar in Europe and Eastern and Central Canada. To address these distinct schools, with their cultural backgrounds and spatial challenges, a centralized approach to co-operative education was initiated.

In the early 1920s, the American Institute of Cooperatives (AIC) was founded as a floating university with the objective of educating leaders, members and employees of rural co-operatives. After 80 years, AIC merged with the National Council of Farmer Cooperatives, one of the apex national organizations representing 2,500 farmer co-operatives and state and regional councils of co-operatives. This unification resulted in reduced centralized national co-operative education efforts but they were supported and complemented by state co-operative councils, Land Grant universities and agricultural co-operatives. The federal government entered co-operative education with the passage of the Cooperative Marketing Act of 1926 (Torgerson, 1996). In addition to expanding co-operatives' ability to share information, the Act created the Cooperative Research and Service Division of the USDA (United States Department of Agriculture), which conducted research, service and education for members of co-operative marketing, purchasing and service co-operatives. By the 1970s, the Division employed approximately 100 professionals. As resources have decreased so has the number of professionals in co-operative education.

Agricultural co-operative education became important in the early twentieth century after an explosion of interest in collective action surfaced after the First World War during the agricultural depression of the 1920s, followed by the Great Depression commencing in 1929. Simultaneously, the Credit Union Movement and the Cooperative Farm Credit System also had their roots in this period. These movements were facilitated and nurtured by a set of statutes and regulations starting with the federal Sherman Antitrust Act of 1890, the Clayton Act of 1914, the Capper–Volstead Act of 1922 and the state co-operative incorporation laws primarily enacted during the 1920s. Additionally, the 1914 passage of the Smith–Lever Act encouraged extension agents, which became the third leg of the US Land Grant University System.

The Land Grant University System was established as an institutional mechanism to influence and control the agenda of scientists within a revolutionary system of higher education. It was explicitly anti-elitist and seen as an experiment in democracy that contrasted with the British and European models of the 1900s. The Land Grant universities were to be better than Harvard and Yale in practising the values of democratic America. This uniquely American experiment was explicitly democratic by institutionalizing a three-pronged approach to raising the level of education in rural America through instruction, extension and research:

1. It created people's colleges offering formal classroom instruction.
2. It distributed knowledge to the field and to ordinary people through extension.
3. It conducted research and scientific enquiry on co-operative endeavour.

Previously, scholarship had been confined to theology, history, arts and letters, and law. Americans consider the character of Land Grant scholarship to be profoundly democratic (McDowell, 2003).

While it is a rich and complex topic, the history of US agricultural co-operative education is dispersed throughout articles and speeches found in the annual *American Cooperative Yearbook, Journal of Farm Economics, American Journal of Agricultural Economics*, USDA's *Rural Cooperatives* magazine, *Journal of Agricultural Cooperation*, and the *Journal of Cooperatives*, in addition to seminal works by Joseph Knapp, Henry Bakken and Marvin Schaars (Bakken and Schaars, 1937; Knapp, 1969, 1973).

Between 1862 and 1914, the Land Grant System was constructed through a number of stages and formalized by three major pieces of federal legislation, each intending to improve the lives of rural Americans. These three statutes include the 1862 Morrill–Wade Act that created the Land Grant System with the initial objective of funding a university in each state with the mission of instructing rural citizens in agricultural sciences and engineering. The 1887 Hatch Act created the Agricultural Experiment Stations that funded research conducted by the professors employed by the Land Grant universities. The 1914 Smith–Lever Act completed the Land Grant System with the Extension Service whose objective was to carry the research to the country and assist farmers and rural people to learn without having to come to a central location. Extension was very important in teaching farmers how to organize legally and formally, and played a major role in the proliferation of 12,500 agricultural co-operatives in the 1920s and 1930s. This system continues today albeit with significant changes in the role of co-operatives. Co-operatives have become so sophisticated and complex that they require a different level of training and education in order to maintain their value for farmer members (McDowell, 2003).

The evolution of the Graduate Institute of Cooperative Leadership

In the 1960s and 1970s, agricultural co-operatives and their educational initiatives were marginalized by dominant social and economic changes. Co-operative academics were noticing not only the resource reallocation shift away from co-operative education within the US Land Grant System, but also the structural change affecting the agricultural production sector and agribusiness supply chain firms. Helmberger (1966) observed that the future of traditional agricultural co-operatives was in jeopardy because technological scale economies would eliminate the small/medium-sized farms and, consequently, small/medium-sized agribusinesses. A key assumption in his analysis was that farmers could not govern economic entities that were not small. Simultaneously, a clairvoyant co-operative leader, Howard Cowden, who had risen to lead the largest agricultural co-operative in the USA at the time, Farmland Industries, had also observed the shift of public monies away from social and management sciences in the agricultural sector and particularly agricultural co-operatives. He convinced Farmland Foundation to contribute 'starter' monies to develop an institute at the University of Missouri in 1970. Thus was born the idea of the Graduate Institute of Cooperative Leadership (GICL) with the primary objective of starting the first executive education-styled programme in the USA for agricultural co-operative employees. The primary outputs of GICL programmes were initially directed towards middle and upper middle co-operative management with a focused emphasis on fostering, nurturing and embedding a culture of flexibility comfortable with the rapidly consolidating and globalizing agriculture sector (Cramer, 1994).

During the first twenty years of GICL, different programme formats, contents, curriculum designs and leadership portfolios were practised. Meanwhile, Cowden's endowment inspired other agricultural co-operatives to invest more heavily in co-operative education. Feedback from GICL training programmes inspired board chairs and CEOs to request an executive education programme be established for co-operative senior leadership and they funded the first endowed chair in co-operative leadership at the University of Missouri in the College of Agriculture, Food, and Natural Resources. It was named after Robert D. Partridge, the former CEO of the National Rural Electric Cooperative Association, and is currently occupied by Professor Michael L. Cook. At the same time, further named professor positions were established commemorating past co-operative leaders: William Hirth, the first CEO of MFA, a successful Missouri co-operative currently 105 years old; Fred Heinkel, the second CEO of MFA; Howard Cowden, the funder of a GICL endowment and founder of Farmland Industries; and, in 2016, a named and endowed co-operative chair was established at the University of Missouri, the MFA Professorship in Agribusiness.

In the early 1990s, the GICL board and the University of Missouri were determined to experiment with a more research-oriented and theoretical approach to co-operative education. This purpose and culture change started GICL on a new life cycle. The endowments and the net revenues generated enough cash flow to hire experienced professional staff and attract highly motivated and qualified PhD students. Scholars and professionals developed a critical mass of institutional theory that developed new research programmes and generated an innovative theoretical and conceptual platform from which a dynamic micro-analytical executive education framework was to emerge (Cook, 1995). Concepts developed by Oliver Williamson, Bengt Holström, Elinor Ostrom, Douglass North, Herbert Simon, Richard Thaler, Oliver Hart, Leonid Hurwicz and James Buchanan, some of them Nobel Prize recipients, challenged the assumptions of neoclassical economics and social science. They introduced the concepts of incentives, self-seeking behaviour with guile, and the inability of transactors to know all attributes of a transaction. Insights from institutional and behavioural economics, psychology, sociology, political science, law and anthropology allowed for a more realistic analysis of the complexity of patron-controlled entities such as co-operatives.

This institutionalized framework created a dynamic learning ambience among staff, students and scholars. At the top of the circle in Figure 5.1 are the GICL outputs: Summer Institute, Board Chair/CEO, workshops, customized programmes, graduate seminars and undergraduate courses. Each programme fosters new networks that in turn generate additional research ideas and stories as well as student opportunities. These research ideas and stories are shared with academic colleagues in social sciences and management studies. They inform conceptual model development, leading to empirical testing and academic outputs that are then translated into practitioner language through teaching, case studies, histories and stories that are immediately embedded into the aforementioned outputs. This circular and dynamic approach has fostered a growing multidisciplinary collaborative enthusiasm for studying and analysing complex interdisciplinary group action.

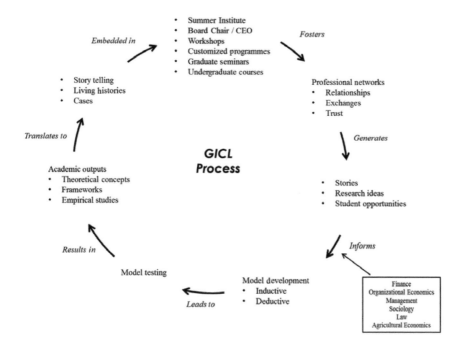

Figure 5.1: The Graduate Institute of Cooperative Leadership process
Source: author

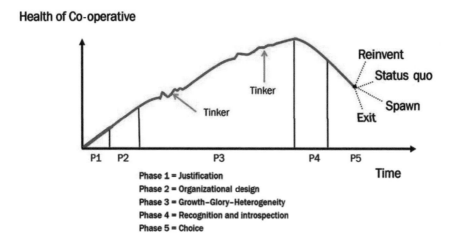

Figure 5.2: The co-operative life cycle
Source: Cook, 2018: 5

The basic platform employed in these varying co-operative education efforts is the 'Co-operative Life Cycle Framework' (Cook, 2018). The life cycle framework is the result of interaction between co-operative management and board of director participants and organizational social science and management scientists. The framework divides the evolution of a co-operative life cycle into five separate and sequenced phases (see Figure 5.2).

Phase 1, economic justification, discusses producer reasoning behind the decision to enter the costly process of determining whether collective action is justified. During phase 2, organizational design, producers determine the legal–business–organizational model that best fits their group's needs and preferences. They also decide the rules of the game: responsibilities, benefits, penalties, adjudication processes, purpose, co-operative health and performance measure(s).

Once the organizing phases are complete, the co-operative enters phase 3, which is designated the 'growth, glory and heterogeneity' phase. In this phase, the decision-makers address the rate of growth or non-growth, the glory and success achieved, and disagreements generated by the heterogeneity of preferences emerging as time passes. Because of the broad and diverse objective functions of members and agents in a patron (user)-owned and -controlled entity embedded in the performance metrics, potential disruptive frictions may result and must be ameliorated if the co-operative is going to continue meeting member needs. Disruptions may also be caused externally by rivals within the industry or by macro phenomena such as trade, economic or political policy shifts and/or intra-firm frictions. We have found that the surviving co-operatives have developed a collective process called 'co-operative genius' associated with the longevity of agricultural co-operatives in North America. However, compromise is not always attainable and subgroup frictions turn into rudiments of factions. At this stage of phase 3, co-operative leaders assess what probabilities exist for co-operative survivability. To assist in making this decision, the co-operative engages in an introspective analytical process charged with determining what factors give rise to the collective decision-making cost frictions and sometimes resultant factions.

During this introspective phase 4, root causes of these friction/faction disturbances are identified. They usually emanate from a set of unique co-operative structural characteristics embedded in capital constraints and control/governance policies and practices. Generic solutions – in the form of realigning user incentives, policies balancing supply and demand, member retention investments and transparency practices – that have the potential to regenerate the level of co-operative health are also evaluated (Cook and Iliopoulos, 2016).

Having identified the causes and potential solutions in phase 4, the membership moves towards deciding the future of the co-operative in phase 5. The members have the following options: (a) exit through liquidation, merger or bankruptcy; (b) maintain the status quo with little or no change; (c) spawn; and/or (d) reinvention or significant overhaul. If the patrons reject the exit, status quo or spawn options, reinvention is chosen. Reinvention occurs because one or a combination of major elements is identified, each of which will vary across business entities: (a) modification to residual claim rights or rules that determine who receives what proportion of the earnings/savings; (b) readjustment to control rights that define how votes and power are distributed; (c) a significant change in the purpose of the co-operative; or (d) a dramatic shift in co-operative culture and/or mindset (Figure 5.3).

Health of Co-operative

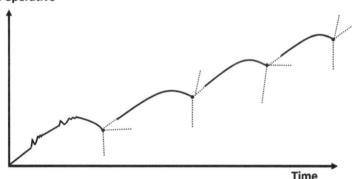

Time

Figure 5.3: Example of multiple co-operative life cycles
Source: Cook, 2018: 13

The participants engage in studying, discussing and interacting at each phase. This exercise takes approximately 30 hours at the Summer Institute session. Participants are placed into two teams: one is a 'similar function team' and the other is a 'similar or related co-operative team'. The assignment at the end of the week is for the participants to write a rough draft of their co-operative's most recent life cycle.

Observations
Analysing detailed participant evaluations and shared experiences provides important insights into this process. Co-operative educators have learnt about the experiential learning process and participants have gained a better understanding of how their co-operatives move through their current

and past life cycles. The participant behaviours described below come from co-operative management employees, the vast majority of whom have a minimum of five years' management experience either with an agricultural-oriented co-operative or with a non-co-operative agribusiness entity. GICL has programmes for directors, mixed functions and academics, but these observations are from approximately 3,000 co-operative management participants.

Co-operative employee participants prefer to be guided by a conceptual framework when involved in a learning process – they initially attach their personal and co-operative experiences to the framework in an unorganized manner and subsequently rearrange their experiences once exposed to the logic of a chronologically organized architecture. Participants immediately identify with the simplicity of the skeleton framework of the life cycle and co-operative health being a function of time. Over time, as co-operative health increases, frictions begin to emerge and the rate of growth in co-operative health begins to slow and eventually decreases. After recognizing and analysing this change in direction of co-operative health, the membership must decide whether to continue as a co-operative. The subsequent curvatures in succeeding life cycles indicate that co-operatives are quite resilient. Participants identify with this optimism as it suggests that their future is in their hands.

Once confronted with the abstract and simple Figures 5.1 and 5.2, participants begin to think conceptually. Indeed, the selection process conducted by senior co-operative leadership in choosing participants uses 'comfort with abstractness' as a criterion. This supports the supposition that 'managers love theory'. Managers agree with empirical studies where one of the key factors in successfully leading complex organizations, such as co-operatives, demands comfort with flexible abstractness. The waiting list for participating in GICL workshops is quite lengthy for some co-operatives.

Given the interest expressed by the participants through both verbal and written reaction, we conclude that the employment of historical context is underused in co-operative education. There is a need to understand the significant continuities with the past as well as the ways in which such insights can be used to respond to future challenges. Moreover, participants enjoy learning from stories. The original purpose and reasons for forming a co-operative garnered more attention when embedded in 'real world stories' that were formulated and derived from historical documents.

The importance of history highlights the fact that longevity is crucial to co-operatives, which are formed to meet member needs rather than shareholder returns. Discussion of the original purpose of the co-operative's founders leads to another interesting observation. The closer the current purpose is to the original purpose of the founding members, the lower the level of anxiety encountered by current co-operative leaders and employees; anxiety is caused by rapid change emanating from volatile competitive and global environments. One of the refreshing lessons drawn from this exercise is that 'the power of the original purpose' attracts interest in the history of the organization, including decisions that have led to the co-operative's enduring longevity. This interest contributes to a culture of respect for understanding survivability factors.

However, participants also like telling stories. They appear to learn from reacting to other people's stories and then countering with stories of their own. Embedding critical structural and strategic decisions into historical story contexts creates a learning environment that motivates participants to contact veteran employees 'back home' to probe, extract and construct 'even better' stories related to the organizational concepts under discussion in the workshop. Before attending the workshop, a future participant is asked to contact other employees with a historical appreciation of their co-operative's past – these veterans are also forewarned that the participant might contact them, seeking validation of certain concepts and supporting stories.

Increasingly, the participants arrive with more advanced formal education (50 to 75 per cent of the participants in recent years have advanced graduate degrees), thus demanding more rigorous theoretical underpinnings and more sophisticated solutions to co-operative challenges. Yet almost none of the participants have been exposed to formal instruction or experience in confronting uniquely co-operative problems and issues – concepts such as vaguely defined property rights, patron-oriented ownership rights, member responsibility contracts, imbalances between control rights and residual claim rights, co-operative health, reinvention, etc. These concepts, which rarely appear on MBA courses, are addressed in detail in GICL workshops and are supported by evidence-based social science research.

Many of the participants graduated with an academic discipline degree rather than a professional degree. This means their analytical skills are formed by a specific set of theories and a predetermined outline for solutions. GICL uses a more inter/multidisciplinary approach emanating from social sciences and management sciences because of the complexity of the co-operative organization. Understanding a co-operative, its members, organization, governance, management and life cycle demands a broad understanding of conceptual approaches and the ability to use them to inform complex co-operative problems. Participants enjoy knowing the relevance of these differing views when addressing the problems and challenges faced by co-operative decision-makers – particularly when digesting phase 3 of the aforementioned life cycle framework, where exploring the positive, neutral and negative implications of growing forms of heterogeneously created frictions (Cook and Iliopoulos, 2016).

Participants thrive in a learning environment where peers have experienced the same 'co-operative' user–patron–member issues. When engaged in team exercises, where teams have experienced similar functions and common histories, trainees are frequently surprised by the number of solutions that address similar problems. They also celebrate the learning of a new vocabulary. By sharing stories of issues, concerns and behaviours that are difficult to define or describe, they become excited when phenomena such as temporal asset specificity, tinkering, co-operative genius process, influence costs, internal versus external free-rider constraints, and ownership costs are defined and put into a context in a co-operative-laden story. We find them practising this new vocabulary during breaks and mealtimes. We receive feedback once they return to their co-operatives about how their use of certain terms raises the interest of a peer or colleague, thus presenting them with the opportunity to share their newly acquired co-operative knowledge and education. There is indeed some evidence that this method of training is implemented and shared with other employees.

The debate on co-operative health is always a highlight and never a disappointment in a GICL workshop. How does a group define co-operative health, or measure it, or achieve a consensus about its meaning among members, management, employees, and subgroups of each? This is one of the most fundamental elements of co-operative education and co-operative success. When conducting member surveys, we find a multitude of responses or measures. Exercises within GICL workshops have resulted in more than 80 definitions. We have found that truly understanding co-operative health requires an acceptance of the concept as 'self-defined' by each individual co-operative. This is a difficult reality for co-operative researchers to accept but reflects the fact that co-operatives are autonomous enterprises and developing their own criteria for success is crucial to building an engaged democratic team.

The management participants at GICL sessions have primarily been chosen by senior leaders in their co-operatives. The participants are known explicitly or implicitly as the future senior leaders of their organizations. They arrive with a high degree of confidence and elevated standards, yet few of them know anything about co-operatives. Many have the impression that co-operatives are considered an inferior or inefficient form of business governed by an inexperienced body of patrons. This presents the co-operative educator with a unique challenge. GICL confronts this challenge by working through an exercise on the advantages of being a co-operative, which includes 26 advantages organized into five categories: (a) competitive advantage elements; (b) public authorization advantages; (c) positive externalities; (d) defensive gain advantages; and (e) offensive gain advantages. Discussion of these points brings participants' attention to the stories of how each of the long-enduring co-operative entities in US agriculture has employed these advantages to serve their members for more than five times longer than their investor-owned rivals. More than 140 agricultural co-operatives in the USA are over 100 years old, with a large number approaching 100 in the near future. The average investor-owned firm in the USA has a life span of less than 20 years. Thus, the supposed inefficiencies of co-operatives are not borne out by the facts. Combining these facts with stories of success and of near failure with the ability to rebound and continue appears to change attitudes. When stories and readings on whether competitor entities are more efficient, participants are surprised to learn how professionally managed and governed existing co-operatives are and that many are considered to be leaders in their value chains. In discussing the participants' inferiority attitude, the importance of defining and understanding purpose and co-operative health becomes apparent.

Conclusion

In the USA, the consolidation at the farm level and the advances in agribusiness and management education have had considerable impact on the concept of collective action. Farmers are becoming more individualistic and more demanding of their collectively controlled assets. As this phenomenon was fostered by the agricultural depression of the 1980s and rekindled in the early 2000s, co-operatives consolidated very rapidly and farming became driven almost entirely by business and economics. There are a few exceptions to this pattern, but even the organic co-operatives are now reaching a large scale. On observing these trends, we examined new advances in institutional and behavioural research and in social and management science. The insights from these advances informed the theoretical underpinnings of the predecessors to the life cycle framework, particularly the development of concept of vaguely defined property rights (Cook, 1995; Chaddad and Cook, 2004). The assumptions underlying the theoretical concepts were tested with the participants (particularly the assumptions of bounded rationality and opportunism) and were found to be non-heroic. A basic premise of classical social science is that the parties of a transaction both have perfect knowledge of all attributes of the thing being exchanged, such as cost, quality, price, etc. The new institutional and behavioural approach draws on Herbert Simon's findings that humans do not have the capacity to know everything and do not have the time to gather the information because of the complexity involved. A further premise is that parties to a transaction want to know the rules of a game so they can play by those rules. Oliver Williamson describes a behaviour called 'opportunism' that suggests people want to know the rules so they can determine how far they can bend them. Free-riding behaviour is often observed in co-operatives. Relaxing these two assumptions, perfect knowledge and non-opportunistic behaviour, enables co-operative scholars to develop greater understanding of frictions, factions and broken norms and rules with more predictability. Participants identify these behaviours and much time is spent discussing the solutions to the resultant opportunistic behaviours (Cook and Iliopoulos, 2016). Thus, advances in organization economics formed the basis of a new conceptual framework that has served as a lightning rod for co-operatives (Royer, 1987).

Identifying conceptual approaches to explore the complexity of co-operatives is only one of the challenges for co-operative educators working in this narrow yet important agricultural field where co-operatives play very important economic, community and social roles. In the mid-1990s, GICL staff faced a number of serious challenges. They realized that federal and state resources were decreasing; that co-operative employees and farmer members were becoming more educated and sophisticated; that co-operatives themselves were becoming more complex and their design was more of a hybrid form than a traditional co-operative organization; and that scientists were making great strides in fields such as mechanistic design, organizational architecture, contract formulation, governance, property rights enforcement, and individual and group incentive understanding. GICL staff and board members questioned whether co-operative education had a future. This is a story, albeit incomplete, of what they decided. They combined new conceptual fields and designed programmes that would engage with and extract knowledge from participants as to what skills and concepts they really needed in order to lead a sustainable and competitive agricultural co-operative. In doing so, GICL staff built a process that facilitates interactive learning and started a process that they never stop modifying. Participants and educators co-design methods to explore alternatives to finding group solutions, how to ameliorate frictions, how to design co-operative genius processes and develop individual genius, and to determine how to communicate to a leadership that might not understand how rapidly the world is changing.

Many opportunities remain untapped and under-exploited. Several challenges face the North American co-operative educator, in particular the decreasing supply of educators who can raise co-operative education to another level as the constraints facing co-operative leaders accelerate on a daily basis. However, there are a growing number of young, audacious academics and co-operative organization leaders who may soon make this an outdated statement. Farmers in rural North America have seen their opportunity cost increase significantly while the role of governing has become increasingly complex in specialized and large co-operatives. The final challenge exists in the distribution of co-operative knowledge, which has stagnated in an outdated set of delivery institutions and methods. As participants on this bumpy road, we must become even more creative. Collective action in the real world is gaining favour because of its organizational form that promotes community capital, social capital and financial capital. This is probably what Leland Stanford, founder of Stanford University, meant when he spoke before the US Congress in 1887:

> With greater intelligence, and with a better understanding of the principles of co-operation, the adoption of them in practice will, in time I imagine, cause most of the industries of the country to be carried on by these co-operative associations. (Schneider, 2016)

References

Bakken, H.H. and Schaars, M.A. (1937) *The Economics of Cooperative Marketing*. New York: McGraw-Hill.

Chaddad, F.R. and Cook, M.L. (2004) 'Understanding new cooperative models: An ownership-control rights typology'. *Review of Agricultural Economics*, 26 (3), 348–60.

Cook, M.L. (1995) 'The future of US agricultural cooperatives: A neo-institutional approach'. *American Journal of Agricultural Economics*, 77 (5), 1153–9.

Cook, M.L. (2018) 'A life cycle explanation of cooperative longevity'. *Sustainability*, 10 (5), Article 1586, 1–20. Online. www.mdpi.com/2071-1050/10/5/1586 (accessed 24 January 2019).

Cook, M.L. and Iliopoulos, C. (2016) 'Generic solutions to coordination and organizational costs: Informing cooperative longevity'. *Journal on Chain and Network Science*, 16 (1), 19–27.

Cramer, C.L. (1994) 'Graduate Institute of Co-operative Leadership: Meeting changing needs of co-operatives'. In Keller, L.L. (ed.) *Co-operative Economic Summit Proceedings*. Washington, DC: National Council of Farmer Co-operatives, 179–82.

Helmberger, P. (1966) 'Future roles for agricultural cooperatives'. *Journal of Farm Economics*, 48 (5), 1427–35.

Knapp, J.G. (1969) *The Rise of American Cooperative Enterprise: 1620–1920*. Danville, IL: Interstate Printers and Publishers.

Knapp, J.G. (1973) *The Advance of American Cooperative Enterprise: 1920–1945*. Danville, IL: Interstate Printers and Publishers.

McDowell, G.R. (2003) 'Engaged universities: Lessons from the land-grant universities and extension'. *Annals of the American Academy of Political and Social Science*, 585 (1), 31–50.

Royer, J.S. (ed.) (1987) *Cooperative Theory: New approaches* (ACS Service Report 18). Washington, DC: Agricultural Cooperative Service.

Schneider, N. (2016) 'Curricular cop-out on co-ops'. *Chronicle of Higher Education*, 9 October, 237–46.

Torgerson, R.E. (1996) 'New public and private sector strategies in co-operative education'. St Louis, MO: National Institute on Co-operative Education, speech, 6 August 1996.

Chapter 6

The nature, purpose and place of co-operative education in new times: Learning to know, do, be and live together[1]

Cilla Ross

It's how you live co-operation that matters. You don't learn how to do that externally on a course but by building up trust with people who inspire you and who you share the same values with. Well, a course can give you the practicalities ... but you learn what's best for you and the co-op being with other co-operators. You make it work by being with each other and learning from each other. (Interview with education co-operative worker)

Co-operative education was historically about co-operation as a common good but more recently, it has been training for managers and governance. Co-operative education is badly under-theorized, it came out of the past and was not ready for the future. (Interview with co-operative researcher and educator)

There is a need to explore the nature, purpose and place of co-operative education in an age of disruption and the responses of a new generation of co-operators. Co-operatives are by nature and instinct deep, transformational, learning spaces (Senge, 1990; Mezirow and Associates, 1990), characterized by participatory, collaborative, creativity (Clapp, 2016). While acknowledging the innate essence and embodied nature (Stolz, 2015) of co-operative skill and identity acquisition, the focus of this chapter is on formal, post-compulsory, co-operative education and training (CET), of the kind advocated by nineteenth-century co-operators and delivered subsequently by the Co-operative College internationally and in the UK. 'New times' refers to the seismic structural and ideological shifts unleashed by technological and other change and precipitated by the 2007–8 global financial crisis. These changes are transforming mainstream educational policy, theory and practice (Illeris, 2018), recasting the co-operative and social economy and provoking various imperatives and discourses around 'austerity', automation, education and the future of work (Conaty *et al.*, 2017; Mayo, 2015).

One consequence of these changes is a renewed interest in the co-operative as an alternative (and resilient) business model as existing economic and social forms fail (Roelants *et al.*, 2012; Webster *et al.*, 2016; CICOPA, 2018). The trend towards non-standard employment also favours co-operative models and, although reliable figures are hard to come by, a recent survey by CICOPA (the International Organisation of Industrial and Service Cooperatives (see www.cicopa.coop) indicates a rise in young people attracted to worker and social co-operatives, particularly in high-income countries. As a result, the UK co-operative model now reaches into previously 'uninhabited' spaces such as social care, energy and the gig economy. While some of this change is a response to privatization and the rolling back of the state, it is also the outcome of cultural, political and social choices (Mayo, 2015). Indeed, at a time of work precarity and immiseration, co-operatives appear to offer a solution to the 'race to the bottom' and to securing decent work (Conaty *et al.*, 2017).

Education and training are fundamental to co-operative development and must be fit for purpose in order to facilitate a fusion with experiential and situated learning as well as proactively build knowledge for successful enterprise and the future co-operative movement. CET may be relevant to new and emerging co-operators, especially those working in 'undisciplined' contexts (Graff, 2015) where the meaning and place of co-operative education are growing in importance. Alternatively, this chapter asks if a new paradigm might be necessary to meet the educational needs of the existing and future co-operative movement.

The broad definition of CET is of relevance to the work of the Co-operative College. This chapter offers a short history of the role that co-operators have ascribed to CET in relation to individual, movement and social progression across changing co-operative and educational landscapes. The analysis of interviews with a small number of young co-operators on the nature and role of co-operative education provides important insights into CET.[2]

While existing co-operative education can play a powerful role in the making of co-operators through associative, interdisciplinary and experiential learning, co-operative educators must also reflect on the relationship between CET and other constituencies within and without the co-operative movement. Although formal CET has numerous strengths and a robust provenance, it is suggested that there is a need for repositioning it in order to appeal to those seeking to construct alternative economic and social systems and to those new to co-operation more generally.

In her excellent mapping Shaw (2012, 2013, 2015) reminds us of the multiple meanings associated with co-operative education, and Woodin (2015) argues that the global reach and long, complex history of co-operation makes a straightforward definition elusive. For example, the scale of the UK co-operative consumer movement throughout the nineteenth century and the first half of the twentieth meant that numerous autonomous societies provided their own educational services in addition to working with the Co-operative Union from the 1880s and the Co-operative College from 1919. This resulted in a 'rich ecology of educational provision' (Shaw, 2015: 162). Shaw proposes a definition that constructs and then draws upon a number of fundamental core principles. If these principles are met, Shaw argues, they result in best CET practice across the global co-operative movement and in all co-operatives, regardless of size or type.

First, CET must be underpinned by values and principles with active teaching, learning and research focused on how values and principles can be realized – particularly in relation to co-operative governance and behaviours. As with any education that draws upon Freirean ideas of understanding cultural contexts, effective CET will first establish needs and then develop programmes around real lived experiences and issues (Freire, 2000). However, as the business failure of co-operatives is so often a failure of governance and culture, this is usually a strong focus of CET. In the Co-operative College's national and international work, the practical application of values and ways of putting principles into practice through active learning is fundamental to board and member training, with co-operative team building and conflict resolution an essential part of the College's work.

Second, CET should offer a distinctively co-operative identity that is 'movement focused' and committed to developing the skills and knowledge needed for successful co-operative growth through the active engagement of members. Co-operative values and principles underpin much CET identity building, and co-operative history and international co-operative examples are drawn upon extensively to exemplify values-based identity. For instance, when working with co-operatives, the College focuses CET on programmes and workshops that foster member engagement and movement building among and between co-operatives.

Third, CET must reflect the unique nature of a co-operative, that is, its associational as well as enterprise aspects. This necessitates a holistic, interdisciplinary approach to meeting the learning needs of the whole co-operative movement – ranging from enterprise to personal and social education, and delivered to all co-operative stakeholders. MacPherson discussed the importance of 'associative intelligence' (MacPherson, 2003), and association, 'labour's own capital' (Yeo, 1988), as a 'special kind of knowing that emerges when people work together effectively ... [making] collective behaviour more economically rewarding, socially beneficial and personally satisfying' (MacPherson, 2007: 372). Associationism is embedded in the peer-to-peer and values-based programmes run by the College as this 'special kind of knowing' emerges from and helps to construct new co-operative knowledge.

Finally, CET should be characterized by solidaristic, non-competitive pedagogies and value both informal and formal learning. Indeed, the College's international development work, for example, uses participatory approaches such as action learning, enabling collective rather than individualized knowledge production (Woodin, 2011).

We have examples then of Shaw's principles being met through the good practice of co-operative educators, although the principles enjoy greater or lesser priority depending on what are considered to be the needs of the co-operative movement in specific social, historical, economic and political contexts. For example, at times, following its founding in 1919, the College favoured hierarchical approaches with changing pedagogical and epistemological considerations inevitably shaping educational praxis. Similarly, in the early days of co-operative development, co-operative education intersected with multiple forms of adult education such as that of the emerging labour movement and shared many pedagogic and ideological approaches. Education happened through solidarity, association and informally, 'by collision' (Dobbs, 1919), and was generally a response to popular discontent and demands for 'really useful knowledge' (Johnson, 1988). However, attitudes change and while Owenites, trade unionists and co-operators were largely the architects of nineteenth-century radical, adult education (Woodin, 2015), the expansive understanding of the transformative possibilities of co-operative education as envisaged in Law First – the rules drawn up by the Rochdale Pioneers in 1844 – was alien to the vast majority of pragmatic co-operators (Robertson, 2010; Harrison, 1961). Despite this, education has always been regarded as fundamental to movement development and has stimulated much inventiveness (Atkinson *et al.*, 2012).

Woodin and others describe, for example, how reading groups, peer-to-peer, collective and group learning, and study circles were used in community-based co-operative education from the mid-nineteenth century onwards (Woodin, 2011). Co-operative education also had widespread visibility in co-operative 'places' such as in reading rooms and libraries above co-operative shops, where it had a significant impact on individual and community aspirations (Woodin, 2011). At the same time co-operative education, while not interdisciplinary in the contemporary sense (Barry and Born, 2013), was wide-ranging with learning across a number of disciplines considered important to the flourishing and 'making' of the whole co-operator. For example, students studying with the Co-operative Union in 1898 were offered courses in industrial history, politics, citizenship, bookkeeping and co-operative accountancy (Twigg, 1924).

Vernon, in turn, describes how co-operative education was an early innovator in technical education and workforce development (Vernon, 2011), offering correspondence, blended and distance learning methods to tens of thousands of co-operative employees in the UK and internationally. Career pathways were forged through a mixture of 'in-house training, itinerant lecturers, specialist residential courses and correspondence' (ibid.: 49). While building the co-operative character was always an aim, this was fundamentally what we might understand today as professional development, offering a distinctively 'movement focused' experience. Finally, Shaw alerts us to the role of the Co-operative College in supporting the growth of co-operative colleges internationally and describes the early years of the UK College when the aspiration was for co-operative higher education and when programmes were offered to large numbers of residential, full-time, international and UK students (Shaw, 2012: 13). The College's use of participatory methods and its experimentation with blended approaches throughout this time, while uneven, were rich with potential and need to be understood and critically evaluated.

So what is the current situation with regard to CET and the existing, 'traditional', co-operative movement? One important development, a result of mergers and through seeking economies of scale, has been that many co-operative societies have taken CET 'in-house', with training on co-operative management and governance at board and member level a priority. Such provision is almost solely for the society's own employees and members, although increasing effort is being put into community as well as member engagement. While independent societies continue to do vital educational work with the College, particularly around values, principles and co-operative identity, the College, in turn, has sought to reconcile its organizational autonomy with its links to the UK co-operative movement through diversification. Thus, the College has developed a portfolio of CET, including UK and international projects, and participates in research and education partnerships with UK higher education as well as with the global co-operative movement. Changes to UK higher education legislation in 2017 also allow the possibility of a new co-operative higher education offer through a federated co-operative university.

Yet the need for funding and a dominant discourse that privileges employability above wider learning imperatives (Garratt and Forrester, 2012) affects CET as it does all educational projects, by constraining some of the more visionary possibilities for co-operative education. For example, community adult education, which characterized so much early CET, has largely disappeared and links with other social movements have fragmented. As a result, CET overall tends to have a limited curriculum and to be relatively inward-looking. Even in higher education, where a limited co-operative offer exists in business schools and education departments, there have been low levels of engagement from the formal co-operative movement. Some would see this as a missed opportunity. A commitment to developing innovative and reflective forms of democratic, co-operative leadership combined with the co-operative ethos, for example, might have challenged the dominant employability paradigm so prevalent in mainstream business education. This almost universally focuses on individual social mobility and misses wider social, co-operative and collective imperatives (Garratt and Forrester, 2012). Finally, the relatively non-academic nature of much UK CET has also had a negative impact on research and, despite the best efforts of many co-operative educators, has resulted in the co-operative project remaining a 'hidden alternative' (Webster *et al.*, 2011). Practice-based research helps to inform CET but it has its limitations and MacPherson's call for greater attention to be paid to developing a key attribute of co-operative scholarship – interdisciplinarity – has been little heeded (Woodin, 2015).

It is clear then that the existing co-operative movement enjoys a limited CET offer and that a number of innovations, where Shaw's principles are met, make a useful contribution to co-operative learning experiences. But what about the relationship between formal CET and the 'new' and emerging co-operative movement? It will be remembered that one of the aims of this chapter was to establish whether the CET available is fit for purpose in terms of meeting the existing and future needs of new co-operators, many of whom, especially from worker co-operative and social solidarity backgrounds, are not aligned to the traditional movement. A second concern was to understand what co-operative education means to young co-operators. To answer these questions authoritatively would necessitate a wide-ranging research project that would seek to establish the nature of existing and likely future needs, while also drilling down into demographics, educational experience and sectoral aspirations. In order to open up these issues, this chapter offers an analysis of semi-structured interviews with ten co-operators, all of whom consider themselves to be innovators, working in technology, food, education or entertainment co-operatives. With the exception of a large food co-operative employing over 40 people, the remainder work in co-operatives of between four and ten members. Six respondents were women and four were men and all were aged below 35. Widening participation or perhaps class location meant that all but one had participated in higher education and three had studied at postgraduate level, a not inconsequential point. Additionally, two adult educators who worked in education co-operatives were interviewed. Interviews took place face to face and lasted for about an hour, with two conducted virtually.

Importantly, all respondents considered values to be a fundamental part of co-operative education, their own practice and who they are as individuals. One described how pre-existing shared values and association through political networks was an important motivation for her becoming a co-operator:

> I decided to start a co-operative with people I already share a set of values with. These were people I met through the anti-globalization movement. I got into co-operatives because of the people I knew, people who had my values and then you decide you want to share with others. Sharing rather doing things for yourself is a value. Getting into a co-operative is part of your individual development as a person. Then you want to co-create something, in my case, something collective.

In the case of this respondent, we can see the interlocking nature of social movements. Through participation and activism, values and individual and collective development find expression and agency. Network building based on shared values was important to a number of those interviewed. From this flowed solidarity, also one of the core international co-operative values. One said:

> I see myself as being in a co-operative network with like-minded people with similar values. The co-operatives are in a network

and the people are networked. The solidarity is powerful; it is a movement of people with the same values.

The solidarity engendered by co-operative and social movement participation was seen as an expression of values and ethics in addition to being a co-operative value in its own right. The respondent went on to say:

> I wanted to be involved in something I considered to be more ethical than a straightforward business. That's why I applied to work at the co-op. I hoped, well knew, it probably shared my values.

While one respondent described how 'the co-operative values of the Rochdale Pioneers are important if you want to know about the history', they also believed that 'history was something you could come to later'. Rather than needing to 'learn the values' of co-operation in order to develop co-operative identity, a focus of much formal CET, it may be that co-operators are drawn to co-operation precisely because of their pre-existing, already acquired, values. Learning how to apply the values practically, however, was acknowledged by most respondents to be an important element of CET and indeed of their own co-operative learning. In this sense young and emerging co-operators view themselves as practical people, a perspective shared by co-operators historically (Woodin, 2011). This interviewee describes both that practicality and their personal commitment to the wider collective:

> You need to work out how to have co-operative relationships with the people you work with. We have done a lot of work on conflict resolution and equality in our co-operative, so yeah, that has been good to do and we did that together.

Another commented that 'putting principles into practice is the most important thing because anyone can say they have the values, it's what you do with them that counts'.

In all cases, respondents described how they valued peer-to-peer learning as well as learning through experience. For one workers' co-operative member:

> I have learnt the soft skills through experiential learning with my mentors. At school your learning is about facts, not how to adapt and experiment. I've learnt about models and structures from other co-operators. You are working for the whole organization so you co-operate to make that work. In my previous jobs I was working for me, as an individual. It is a very different mindset in

the co-op but though you think about it, it just sort of happens. Peer-to-peer helps you to think how to move the co-operative forward by putting the learning into real life practice.

Another described how he 'learnt by doing' rather than through participating in formal co-operative education programmes. In this quote there is also a suggestion of some of the possible tensions of being in a co-operative, for example, reconciling personal and collective notions of fairness and how these might change depending on the size and situation of the co-operative:

> You do have a lot of learning to do once you start at the co-op. There is a sort of culture about trying to be fair and doing the right thing. The thing is, you really want it to be different and you behave differently because you are in it together and you want it to be a better place to work. Just being in a co-op teaches you to behave in a certain way.

A number of interviewees engaged in 'external' learning but, even then, this tended to be unstructured and informal. One said, 'Any learning like that I need to do, I do through a MOOC [Massive Open Online Course], so I can pick and choose.' Another described how:

> If I need to know anything I just go on the internet or talk to other co-operators. I have been on some co-operative courses and learnt about the history. It was good going on a course to talk about solutions to co-operative conflict and stuff like that, how to work together, how to co-operatively resolve disputes. I mean you can talk about it day to day anyway but it's useful to get ideas off other people too.

Respondents also talked extensively about the role of technology in their learning as well as about their individual learning styles. All interviewees had experienced both formal and informal learning through a range of devices and learning 'episodes', using digital assets. Most had experienced peer-assisted approaches and were deeply comfortable with open and non-competitive learning. Until relatively recently, it was only in non-traditional adult and community education, including co-operative education, that understandings of situated and experiential learning could be found. Now, in mainstream education, student-centred, 'authentic' and distributed approaches intersect with the notion of learner as co-producer and understandings of collaborative and co-operative learning are commonplace (Jowers *et al.*, 2017). It is important for co-operative educators to note this and to reflect on what this means for CET and how co-operatives might respond. One respondent described how using co-operative learning approaches was widespread in her own university experience: 'On my recent MA a lot of it was peer-assisted learning and working co-operatively, choosing what you wanted to learn about and, yes, you took modules in lots of different subjects.'

Respondents were also committed to interdisciplinary approaches to learning – which are increasingly facilitated through technology. In the words of one co-operator:

> Why would I want to work my way through someone's idea of what a subject should be? I should be able to jump around until I feel I have enough knowledge about something. I tend to ask people to recommend things I should read or I get into webinars or I talk to people when I'm out. That's how I get involved in learning.

While some commentators might express concern that such an approach risks learning that is fragmented and superficial (Jukes *et al.*, 2010), this respondent, who also possesses a higher degree, is confident and digitally fluent.

Another set of views on the role and place of co-operative education links to a belief among interview respondents that 'new co-operation' transcends traditional, co-operative boundaries and can be found woven through 'non-co-operative' communities of practice. One adult educator explains:

> Well, I haven't been in the traditional co-op movement, I mean we shopped at the co-op but what I found out was that co-operating is a really good way of thinking about education and the economy and when I did my own degree, I realized I didn't like competitive learning. So I got involved in a co-op and I'm out there, working in co-operative ways in my teaching with trade unions. Trade union education uses the same methods as co-ops but I wouldn't say I was a co-operative educator.

While this respondent is not delivering education 'to make co-operators', she is using what she considers to be co-operative pedagogies and approaches, suggesting that co-operative education is part of a wider diaspora than education and training delivered to the co-operative movement. Another respondent, more explicitly working to develop co-operators, describes how she uses co-operation as a frame of reference for all of her educational practice:

> I work at all levels of education but I want to work in communities because I think co-operatives are a really good way to change the world, especially if you are poor. So I work in a co-operative, I use co-operative methods in my teaching and I encourage other people to set up co-operatives by learning about the whole experience of co-operation. I work closely with university outreach people and local projects, councils, so I think we are really getting the co-operative idea out into communities. And it's not only about getting people work ready that I'm interested in. People co-operate all the time in families and communities. So everyone does it about everything!

Finally, one worker from another education co-operative describes how she is beginning to engage in co-operative adult education:

> Yes, well, I am in a co-operative and I use co-operative methods but I work with all people I have things in common with. It's not the old co-operative movement but alternative things like food co-ops and land trusts. I also work in the community with people doing literacy and numeracy courses and citizenship. I have really learnt a huge amount. I think co-operation is a better way of running the world but I think it's different now and more alternative.

So what do the views of this group of young co-operators and educators tell us about whether existing CET is fit for purpose? How can we map these perspectives against the principles outlined by Shaw? First, it is clear that values have a central place in the lives and learning of those interviewed. However, respondents described how they acquired their values before becoming co-operators. Indeed, a number said that it was because of their existing values that they became co-operators. This is at odds with much CET, which remains focused on teaching values to co-operative groups once they have formed. This points perhaps to a failure to understand the strong ethical and values-based friendships and approaches that people can acquire in the early part of their lives, particularly through access to post-compulsory education. Shaw also discusses the need for CET to focus on principles – that is, how values can be practically applied to governance and behaviours. Respondents are in agreement with this view. Co-operative team building was just one example cited of a learnt co-operative behaviour, based on values. It is also clear that interviewees enthusiastically embraced what can be termed 'active learning', a further principle of CET. Respondents described how they learnt best in active relationships, in collective, authentic environments and when they were clear about the purpose of their learning (Knowles *et al.*, 2011).

Second, more research is needed on the importance of learning about co-operatives and co-operative identity for this new generation of co-operators. Superficially at least, historical and international examples – so fruitfully drawn upon by much CET – do not appear to have the same resonance for these respondents, although identity is important. Indeed, a majority came to the historical narrative of traditional co-operation long after they were functioning as co-operators. Likewise, these co-operators see themselves primarily as belonging to peer networks, rather than to a social movement, although there is a tendency for them to use the terms 'network' and 'movement' interchangeably, despite their being conceptually distinct (Diani and McAdam, 2003). However, the second principle includes a commitment for CET to develop the skills needed for successful co-operative growth and that perspective is clearly shared by interviewees. Learning is immersive, in the everyday, and young co-operators appear to learn what they need, when they need to learn it.

The third principle focuses on the value of the associational as well as enterprise aspects of co-operation and how this should be reflected in CET. It is evident from these interviews that respondents have a strong understanding of the role of association in their learning. While external, formal, co-operative learning retains some relevance for innovators, they believe that this becomes ever more valuable when they are learning with others, through association. Indeed, respondents were acutely aware of how they learnt by doing (through experience) and had preferences for informal, peer-to-peer learning with their mentors, rather than through formal programmes with experienced educators. However, it may well be of relevance that those who were interviewed were speaking from a context of positive work situations and already had graduate capabilities that enabled them to feel confident about their learning and working lives.

The fourth CET principle referred to the use of solidaristic, non-competitive pedagogies and these were clearly embraced by respondents. What is more, the solidarity implicit in co-operative learning, and discussed by at least one interviewee, points to the valuing of interdisciplinarity in learning. MacPherson (2015) discussed the virtues that interdisciplinarity can bring to co-operative studies and as co-operators learn to 'do and be'. Co-operative learning tends to be drawn from a range of academic and subject disciplines – from economics to psychology, history to sociology, business studies to communications. This is an important, timely and a fundamental characteristic of co-operative educational practice. We know that 'while disciplines will continue to underpin the foundations of our knowledge, the issue of interdisciplinary learning becomes ... increasingly relevant ... for a changing world' (Lyall *et al.*, 2015: v). Future thinking about effective co-operative educational practices should foreground and theorize interdisciplinarity as one of the defining strengths of co-operative pedagogy and CET (Repko *et al.*, 2013).

This chapter has considered the nature, purpose and place of co-operative education in the new times resulting primarily, but not only, from the 2007–8 global financial crisis. It is clear that many elements of existing CET are fit for purpose – particularly when there is a strong emphasis on learning that prioritizes the practical application of co-operative principles, recognizes that co-operative values and principles have a broad social relevance, and is learning that privileges peer, active, solidaristic and participatory pedagogies. Less relevant for respondents appears to be CET that might over-prioritize formal, narrow learning about co-operative values, the history of the co-operative movement and movement building more generally. However, these respondents are already active co-operators, are acquiring practical co-operative education when it is needed, are using co-operative pedagogies and solidaristic learning, associating and, what is more, in many cases, are learning 'to know, do, be and live together'. Testimonies additionally point to areas that are important to interviewees as they reflect on their existing and future learning preferences and practices. They include not only interdisciplinarity but also education 'beyond the classroom' and relations with wider social networks. We might equally ask then, what can traditional CET learn from the educational practice of young and emerging co-operators?

It will be remembered that interviewees came to co-operation from a range of values-based social movements so future CET should consider rebuilding relational links with old and new social movement allies. CET should also acknowledge where collaborative and networking learning practices are in play beyond the classroom in higher, adult and community education settings so as to work more closely with new and potential co-operators of the type contributing to this chapter. Finally, CET needs to revisit its roots and original aspirations by advocating for education for the whole co-operative person and not just for employability or a narrow conception of 'movement'. This would encourage democratic co-operative solutions that privilege learning ecologies, placemaking, and individual and collective livelihood building (Jackson, 2016; Conaty and Large, 2013).

In conclusion, economic, social and educational change suggests that co-operatives will increasingly be seen as whole social organizations that can deliver a better world. Co-operative education – interdisciplinary, eclectic, values-based and inclusive – could be the defining and transformational educational paradigm of the coming age, not one whose time has gone. However, while the holistic nature of co-operative education means that deep learning continues to take place experientially, these young co-operators remind us that if we wish to purposefully make a movement for all co-operators, actual and potential, synergies must be built between typologies and understandings of co-operative education, and between ever-changing co-operative and associated constituencies.

Notes

[1] The subtitle references the four pillars of education outlined by UNESCO in 1996 (Delors, 1996) as imperative for democratic and fulfilled citizenship. The UNESCO understanding of education was holistic, similar to the conceptualization of co-operative education at its most powerful.

[2] Research first reported upon in *STIR* magazine, 2017.

References

Atkinson, S., Fuller, S. and Painter, J. (eds) (2012) *Wellbeing and Place*. Farnham: Ashgate Publishing.

Barry, A. and Born, G. (eds) (2013) *Interdisciplinarity: Reconfigurations of the social and natural sciences*. London: Routledge.

CICOPA (2018) *Global Study on Youth Co-operative Entrepreneurship*. Geneva: ICA.

Clapp, E.P. (2016) *Participatory Creativity: Introducing access and equity to the creative classroom*. London: Routledge.

Conaty, P., Bird, A. and Ross, C. (2017) *Organising Precarious Workers: Trade union and co-operative strategies*. London: Trades Union Congress.

Conaty, P. and Large, M. (eds) (2013) *Commons Sense: Co-operative place making and the capturing of land value for 21st century garden cities*. Manchester: Co-operatives UK.

Delors, J. (1996) *Learning: The treasure within: Report to UNESCO of the International Commission on Education for the Twenty-First Century*. Paris: UNESCO Publishing.

Diani, M. and McAdam, D. (eds) (2003) *Social Movements and Networks: Relational approaches to collective action*. Oxford: Oxford University Press.

Dobbs, A.E. (1919) *Education and Social Movements, 1700–1850*. London: Longmans, Green, and Co.

Freire, P. (2000) *Pedagogy of the Oppressed*. Trans. Ramos, M.B. New York: Continuum.

Garratt, D. and Forrester, G. (2012) *Education Policy Unravelled*. London: Continuum.

Graff, H.J. (2015) *Undisciplining Knowledge: Interdisciplinarity in the twentieth century*. Baltimore: Johns Hopkins University Press.

Harrison, J.F.C. (1961) *Learning and Living, 1790–1960: A study in the history of the English adult education movement*. London: Routledge and Kegan Paul.

Illeris, K. (ed.) (2018) *Contemporary Theories of Learning: Learning theorists ... in their own words*. 2nd ed. London: Routledge.

Jackson, N.J. (2016) *Exploring Learning Ecologies*. Chalk Mountain. Online. www.normanjackson.co.uk/uploads/1/0/8/4/10842717/lulu_print_file.pdf (accessed 12 February 2019).

Johnson, R. (1988) '"Really useful knowledge" 1790–1850: Memories for education in the 1980s'. In Lovett, T. (ed.) *Radical Approaches to Adult Education: A reader*. London: Routledge, 3–34.

Jowers, I., Gaved, M., Dallison, D., Elliott-Cirigottis, G., Rochead, A. and Craig, M. (2017) 'A case study in online formal/informal learning: Was it collaborative or cooperative learning?'. *Design and Technology Education: An International Journal*, 22 (1), 1–24. Online. https://ojs.lboro.ac.uk/DATE/article/view/2213 (accessed 24 January 2019).

Jukes, I., McCain, T. and Crockett, L. (2010) *Understanding the Digital Generation: Teaching and learning in the new digital landscape*. Thousand Oaks, CA: Corwin.

Knowles, M.S., Holton, E.F. and Swanson, R.A. (2011) *The Adult Learner: The definitive classic in adult education and human resource development*. 7th ed. Oxford: Butterworth-Heinemann.

Lyall, C., Meagher, L., Bandola, J. and Kettle, A. (2015) *Interdisciplinary Provision in Higher Education: Current and future challenges*. York: Higher Education Academy.

MacPherson, I. (2003) *Encouraging Associative Intelligence: Co-operative learning and responsible citizenship in the 21st Century* (Working Paper 1). Manchester: Co-operative College.

MacPherson, I. (2007) *One Path to Co-operative Studies: A selection of papers and presentations*. Victoria, BC: New Rochdale Press.

MacPherson, I. (2015) 'Mainstreaming some lacunae: Developing co-operative studies as an interdisciplinary, international field of enquiry'. In Woodin, T. (ed.) *Co-operation, Learning and Co-operative Values: Contemporary issues in education*. London: Routledge, 177–94.

Mayo, E. (ed.) (2015) *The Co-operative Advantage: Innovation, co-operation and why sharing business ownership is good for Britain*. Manchester: Co-operatives UK.

Mezirow, J. and Associates (1990) *Fostering Critical Reflection in Adulthood: A guide to transformative and emancipatory learning*. San Francisco: Jossey-Bass.

Repko, A.F., Szostak, R. and Buchberger, M.P. (2013) *Introduction to Interdisciplinary Studies*. Thousand Oaks, CA: SAGE Publications.

Robertson, N. (2010) *The Co-operative Movement and Communities in Britain, 1914–1960: Minding their own business*. Farnham: Ashgate Publishing.

Roelants, B., Dovgan, D., Eum, H. and Terrasi, E. (2012) *The Resilience of the Cooperative Model: How worker cooperatives, social cooperatives and other worker-owned enterprises respond to the crisis and its consequences.* Brussels: CECOP-CICOPA Europe.

Senge, P.M. (1990) *The Fifth Discipline: The art and practice of the learning organization.* New York: Doubleday.

Shaw, L. (2012) *Co-operative Education Review 2011.* Manchester: Co-operative College.

Shaw, L. (2013) *What is Co-operative Education?* Unpublished paper. Manchester: Co-operative College.

Shaw, L. (2015) 'A turning point? Mapping co-operative education in the UK'. In Woodin, T. (ed.) *Co-operation, Learning and Co-operative Values: Contemporary issues in education.* London: Routledge, 161–76.

Stolz, S.A. (2015) 'Embodied learning'. *Educational Philosophy and Theory*, 47 (5), 474–87.

Terrasi, E. (2018) *Global Study on Youth Cooperative Entrepreneurship.* Geneva: CICOPA.

Twigg, H.J. (1924) *An Outline History of Co-operative Education.* Manchester: Co-operative Union.

Vernon, K. (2011) 'Values and vocation: Educating the co-operative workforce, 1918–39'. In Webster, A., Brown, A., Stewart, D., Walton, J.K. and Shaw, L. (eds) *The Hidden Alternative: Co-operative values, past, present and future.* Manchester: Manchester University Press, 37–58.

Webster, A., Brown, A., Stewart, D., Walton, J.K. and Shaw, L. (eds) (2011) *The Hidden Alternative: Co-operative values, past, present and future.* Manchester: Manchester University Press.

Webster, A., Shaw, L. and Vorberg-Rugh, R. (eds) (2016) *Mainstreaming Co-operation: An alternative for the twenty-first century?* Manchester: Manchester University Press.

Woodin, T. (2011) 'Co-operative education in Britain during the nineteenth and early twentieth centuries: Context, identity and learning'. In Webster, A., Brown, A., Stewart, D., Walton, J.K. and Shaw, L. (eds) *The Hidden Alternative: Co-operative values, past, present and future.* Manchester: Manchester University Press, 78–95.

Woodin, T. (ed.) (2015) *Co-operation, Learning and Co-operative Values: Contemporary issues in education.* London: Routledge.

Yeo, S. (ed.) (1988) *New Views of Co-operation.* London: Routledge.

Chapter 7

Building sustainable co-operatives: Education and international development practice

Linda Shaw

Building successful and sustainable co-operatives represents a considerable challenge wherever it is undertaken and there can be no simple blueprint for success, with much depending on context. As this volume attests, education has long been viewed as an essential ingredient for ensuring the growth and sustainability of co-operatives. This has been as much the case for co-operatives in the developing as in the developed world.

In reviewing the history of co-operative development, it becomes clear that education and training have long played a key role. This recognition was not just limited to the movement. In 1977, for example, a conference on co-operatives and the poor held at the UK's Co-operative College brought together experts from the United Nations and the World Bank as well as from the co-operative movement. They concluded that education was the most important ingredient in co-operative development. They also noted that co-operative education was also primarily adult education (Münkner, 2012: 99).

At the time of the conference, co-operatives still played a significant role in international development discourse and practice but over the following fifty years perceptions and practices have altered greatly. Support for co-operatives has waxed and waned. Co-operatives were 'off the radar', for example, during the 1990s and into the 2000s when they were often dismissed as a 'failed' model of economic and social development (Johnson and Shaw, 2014). During the past decade or so this narrative has begun to change and there is a renewed interest in co-operatives, especially in the context of the need for inclusive development in the agricultural and financial sectors (Saner *et al.*, 2012). Today co-operative development is central to the economic strategies of many developing countries such as Ethiopia (Tesfarmariam, 2015). Large development actors and donors such as the European Union (EU) have recognized co-operatives as important development actors in their own right (Cooperatives Europe, 2015).

With this growing recognition of the role that co-operatives can play in international development, questions around the practice of how to build successful and sustainable co-operatives have become much more pertinent. It is also therefore timely to review current approaches to education and learning, especially for adults within the wider international context for co-operative development.

A starting point for all co-operative development has to be to ensure that the overall legal and policy framework – the enabling environment – is supportive of co-operatives. In 2002, the International Labour Organization (ILO) – the United Nations agency working with all types of co-operatives – published guidelines on the legal and policy framework for co-operatives. The guidance embodied in ILO Recommendation 193 (Smith, 2014) states that the promotion of co-operatives should be considered as one of the pillars of national and international economic and social development. Governments need to provide a supportive policy and legal framework consistent with the nature and function of co-operatives and guided by the co-operative values and principles.

The Recommendation also urges governments to develop the technical, vocational and managerial skills of members, workers and managers to improve levels of productivity and competitiveness. The emphasis on skills development reflects a wider discourse within international development, which has adopted a utilitarian vision of education framed within the human capital approach that foregrounds the economic benefits of education and prioritizes skills acquisition (UNESCO, 2015: 37).

Alternative visions for education have been rooted in community-based approaches often linked to social movements, perhaps best articulated in the work of Freire (2000). More recently the work of Amartya Sen (1999) has been hugely influential. Sen has argued for the expansion of human capabilities rather than simply economic development as the overarching aim of development. The expansion of human capabilities includes not just personal and economic development but also the capability to interact socially and participate politically. It is a vision of development that emphasizes the role of education in helping people to develop their capabilities to lead meaningful and dignified lives. Although learning and education specifically for adults clearly has a pivotal role to play here, it has remained low down in developmental and educational priorities nationally and internationally. UNESCO has also defined three main types of adult learning that will be used to frame the following discussion: formal learning, which consists of accredited courses delivered by educational institutions; non-formal learning, which consists of education delivered by outside institutions for specific groups such as agricultural extension courses for co-operative members; and informal learning resulting from everyday activities (UNESCO, 2009: 27).

The capabilities approach has been widely adopted by many agencies and a consensus has emerged around the importance of capacity building within development practice. However, there has been much less agreement as to what capacity building actually means in practice, together with a lack of clarity about the concept, its effectiveness and appropriate methodologies (Bergström, 2002; Eger *et al.*, 2018). Nonetheless, education and training have become core to capacity-building programmes but there has been little discussion, for example, over methodologies and pedagogies. However, in terms of broader discussions over adult education, UNESCO has argued that a prime marker of quality is a pedagogy based on the learners' own knowledge and needs, which leads to active participation (UNESCO, 2009: 19). While arguing for the central role of good pedagogy for achieving the education targets as part of the Sustainable Development Goals for 2030, UNESCO cautions against a 'one size fits all' approach (Livingston *et al.*, 2017).

Reviewing the co-operative context, it becomes apparent that these two differing and sometimes competing views of education and learning are both currently informing policy and practices. Some co-operative development projects have focused primarily on the acquisition of business and managerial skills. Indeed, much of the literature on co-operatives has focused on the lack of managerial capacity and business skills and on the problems faced by co-operatives, especially smallholder ones, in accessing markets. To this can be added the lack of requisite knowledge and resilience needed by farmers to mitigate the impact of climate change (IFC, 2013: 1–4). Many programmes have specifically set out to address this skills gap in order to improve the competitiveness of co-operatives in the marketplace.

The Co-operative Life Cycle Framework developed by Michael Cook and colleagues focuses on the economic aspects of co-operative development and is also designed to help frame training interventions. The model involves a five-stage process charting the foundation, increasing membership and initial economic growth of co-operatives. Cook's model, however, also posits a further stage for successful co-operatives stemming from growing a heterogeneous membership with diverging interests leading to agency issues and problems such as side-selling, when members do not sell their produce via the co-operative but instead use itinerant middlemen.

At this point, co-operatives then enter a period of introspection looking at ways to tackle their problems. Many do not find solutions, struggle with the status quo and eventually enter a state of dormancy. Yet, others do manage to reinvent and reorient themselves (Cook, 2018). Francesconi has contended for the applicability and validity of this approach in the African context, arguing for programmes to assist co-operatives to have well-defined membership rules and decision rights. In addition to relevant changes in the policy environment, Francesconi also argues that training and coaching sessions for co-operative leaders to strengthen their leadership capacity are needed if co-operatives are to reinvent themselves. In this approach, training interventions are there to help support economic and business viability but leadership issues are also not ignored (Francesconi *et al.*, 2015; Francesconi, 2015).

An approach to education and learning based on the capacity-building approach has been commonly adopted by European co-operative development agencies according to a recent study, *Good Practices in Co-operative International Development* (Cooperatives Europe, 2017). The research found that capacity building, particularly in the form of education and training, was the main approach used. The study investigated the methodologies used by nine co-operative agencies working in the field of international development, which are currently active in 74 countries across several sectors including agriculture, housing, finance and education. The most common activities carried out under the rubric of co-operative development were institution building and training/capacity building. For the latter, participatory methods were commonly used, with programmes developed after consultation with local partners. Training was delivered at different levels – sometimes for leaders but also for members, especially women members. Most agencies aimed to strengthen organizations, their members and local communities via a bottom-up approach to build skills and improve capacity. The methodology used for institution building also relied heavily on training for improving governance and related knowledge transfer. All sought to keep their work informed and in line with the co-operative values and principles. Many reported that they also drew on the expertise gained in co-operative development projects in their home countries in Europe and worked closely with local co-operative partners. These co-operative development agencies shared an approach that was based on capacity building, using a multi-level approach to work closely with local co-operative partners, which involved skills and wider movement-building strategies as well as support for organizational development.

This broad-based approach to capacity building is congruent with the findings of a recent literature review that discusses the factors that contribute to the organizational resilience of co-operatives. It emphasizes the importance of collective capabilities. This concept of collective capabilities has evolved as a way of extending the analysis of capabilities from the individual to the collective. It recognizes the importance of social institutions for the expansion of human capabilities (Stewart, 2005), although there is debate over whether collective capabilities are more than the sum of individual capabilities or represent new collective ones (Rauschmayer *et al.*, 2018). To date, there has been only limited discussion of it in relation to co-operatives. The review argued that, in the case of co-operatives, collective capability lies in large part in their multidimensional nature. Resilience is linked to the multidimensionality of co-operatives and their need to develop collective capabilities in five mutually reinforcing areas of activity. These are: membership, networks, collective skills in governance, innovation, and engagement with governments. Together, they strengthen co-operatives' resilience but, where lacking, they undermine it (Borda-Rodriguez and Vicari, 2015; Borda-Rodriguez *et al.*, 2016). Importantly, the review contends that the development of collective capabilities is rooted in both formal and informal learning.

Based on five in-depth studies of youth co-operatives in Lesotho and Uganda, Hartley emphasizes the central role of informal and non-formal learning in co-operatives. Drawing on the literature on situated learning, which conceptualizes learning as a social process embedded in specific activity, context and culture, Hartley envisions co-operatives as a learning space that facilitates groups of members to learn together and generate collective knowledge (Hartley, 2014). In her analysis, four broad areas of collective knowledge emerged: business, co-operative philosophy, structure and operations, and co-operator identity. Both non-formal and informal learning occurred through external course provision, sharing experiences and through participation in the democratic and deliberative processes of co-operative governance, which in turn has facilitated the development of values-based co-operatives. Hartley argues that this understanding of learning needs to shape a more supportive policy environment for the development and revival of co-operatives.

In her case studies of Kenyan dairy co-operatives, Hannan has deepened our understanding of learning processes within co-operatives and the ways in which informal and non-formal learning can play an important role in co-operative development. In particular, she highlights how the co-operatives have provided a vehicle for training from external agencies such as agricultural extension departments. Through the co-operative, members were able to access a range of training sessions (Hannan, 2014) that had a demonstrable and favourable impact on their standards of living. Hannan also posited a connection between governance and training. Good internal co-operative governance, she argued, facilitated the process of identifying training needs, networking, and negotiating with external training providers (Hannan, 2016). Informal learning also played an important role for members. In this case, staff at the seed and farm inputs shop run by the co-operative also provided advice and information on agricultural issues for both members and non-members. This was also valued within the wider community.

Other studies also cite the role of co-operatives in enabling non-formal education for members. In Guatemala, coffee co-operatives also acted as a conduit for training and other extension services. These services were of great benefit to women who had less knowledge of agronomic production and less access to technical assistance. Members from all four co-operatives requested on-farm training as a complement to centralized training – ideally in local languages. Local delivery was also of great value for women members, who were less able to leave their communities (Root Capital and Multilateral Investment Fund, 2014). In East Africa, in a study of youth and co-operatives in Rwanda, Uganda and Tanzania, the participants from all three countries stated that a key reason to join was to access training and to share experiences among members (Flink and Vast, 2018).

Co-operatives, therefore, can provide important spaces and opportunities for all kinds of learning. But, as with the case of adult education globally, the availability of formal and non-formal provision for co-operatives is limited. The experience of the UK Co-operative College in its international development programmes is that there is an extensive and unmet demand for education on co-operatives and co-operation from primary- or village-level societies in Africa and South Asia. The following section therefore draws on the largely unpublished findings from projects in Ethiopia, Rwanda, Sri Lanka and Malawi. It relies most heavily on the work done in Malawi and Sri Lanka as this has been the most recent, being based on research carried out from 2016 to 2018.

Unsurprisingly, what is most evident from this research is that formal learning opportunities for co-operatives remain limited. In a review of education for co-operatives globally in 2011, I proposed a fourfold typology of major providers of education and training: universities, government co-operative departments, co-operatives themselves, and non-governmental organizations (NGOs) and co-operative colleges (Shaw, 2011). Currently, in the African context, the co-operative colleges continue to provide formal accredited learning programmes (see Chapter 3 in this volume). Government co-operative departments are still responsible for the delivery of non-formal programmes as well as auditing, but resources and capacity are insufficient to meet demand. In many cases, the civil servants delivering the programmes are not trained as educators and are unfamiliar with learner-centred pedagogies. NGOs can provide access to programmes delivered by more skilled trainers using participatory methods and on a wider range of topics. However, the training provided by NGOs is typically project-funded and limited to the lifetime of a project. Typically, this has resulted in provision that has been fragmented and uneven in quality. A co-operative member from Malawi summed up the situation:

> We need education as we have not been educated as to what a co-op really is – sometimes government officers come for a few hours but that's all. NGOs come to help but they don't touch on the roles we have to play.

This was a common story. Much of the provision was related to skills development for better farming, business development and market access. This is valued by the members and clearly much needed, but quality and consistency varied widely. Some training adopted a generic business approach, which did not always have a good fit with the specificities of the co-operative business model. Overall, agricultural technical assistance and training formed the major part of the training portfolio in Malawi and other countries.

Some of the large co-operatives had the resources so were able to fund and deliver their own training programmes. This they had been forced to do because they had problems attracting staff with the requisite co-operative expertise. The members interviewed in Malawi pointed out that there was a great need for ongoing training, refresher programmes after a year or so, and training for new and prospective board members. In addition, board members could change and refresher training was needed to help keep the co-operative on track. Training on governance and organizational development were often put on the back burner until the later stages of a project. There was little provision of training that reflected the multidimensionality of co-operatives.

The variety of providers and projects meant there was little information sharing or opportunities to build communities of practice around co-operative learning. There was little or no discussion about aims, approaches or pedagogies. This was evident in several countries. NGO providers commented on the scarcity of good trainers who were well versed in co-operatives. As a result, bringing in external experts and co-operative leaders to national or regional workshops was a common pattern. These could be external to the movement or external to the country. While certainly valuable, there was often no follow-up or monitoring of how or whether the leaders used their training for the benefit of the co-operative. Many external consultants and trainers used generic business models that could be at odds with the co-operative values. Some providers did not use the definition of a co-operative agreed by the International Co-operative Alliance and the International Labour Organization or recognize the difference between co-operatives and other organizations. This could confuse members and also could be at odds with the legal and policy framework within a country.

Online and distance learning programmes such as the ILO's 'My Coop' and the International Finance Corporation's agribusiness leadership programme also make a valuable contribution to co-operative education. Both represent an important step away from short-lived programmes that are disconnected from the real-world problems facing co-operatives (ILO, n.d.; IFC, 2018).

Business and marketing skills-based programmes were needed but did not address all of the challenges facing co-operatives. In Malawi, college project staff spoke of an underlying need to promote attitudes of self-help as well as provide information on better farming or business techniques. This was typical where co-operatives had been viewed as part of the government infrastructure with little incentive for them to develop as autonomous and self-directed enterprises. A culture of waiting for government assistance to solve problems had developed. To tackle this in Malawi, the trainers used storytelling, role plays and drama as part of the learning process. Spaces where different co-operatives can meet and exchange views provided opportunities for these views to be challenged not only by project staff but also by fellow co-operators. Drama and storytelling were used to tackle underlying issues such as commonly held attitudes to women that limit their participation in co-operatives.

In all these projects, centring the learning around co-operative values and principles has proven to be vital. In Kenya, a co-operative start-up training programme run by the Kenyan college tackled technical tea production issues and also focused on co-operative identity and values. Co-operative values, including self-help, were introduced from the beginning. Local co-operative trainers and partners were used to deliver the programmes. Since their establishment in 2012, the five primary co-operatives have grown successfully to over 10,000 members and have also come together to form their own secondary-level union. To date, in 2018, they are still operating successfully (Fairtrade Foundation, 2019).

Working on a project in Sri Lanka, funded by the UK co-operative movement, the UK's Co-operative College developed a programme that sought to move beyond the limitations of project-funded training and trainers. This was done by working with a local co-operative organization, the Northern Federation of Thrift and Credit Societies. The aim was to improve their capacity to deliver effective learning and, in particular, to use participatory methods. Staff benefited from an intensive Train the Trainers (ToT) programme that focused on a cluster of courses around co-operative identity, leadership and better governance. In addition, a similar ToT programme was offered to some of the local co-operative department staff – the co-operative development officers (CDOs). Neither group had received formal training as trainers although both had to deliver training and information sessions to village-level co-operatives Ongoing support, manuals and sample workshops were provided. In addition, staff from both organizations were encouraged to work more closely together. Federation and department staff now do work together more often and sometimes run joint workshops in the villages.

The strategy of building the training capacity of local partners appears to have been an effective one. The local staff were enabled to adapt and devise new courses or sessions, where needed, to meet the needs of individual societies. Course delivery is in local languages and does not need much in the way of external resources. This reflected the reality of life in many villages where access to electricity, for example, is very limited. One federation staffer reported that they:

> can offer training to societies without fear and without waiting for CDOs. We can speak to a crowd without fear. We are sometimes worried that the villagers will not appreciate new methods but at end of day they all like it and even the educated ones learn new things. (Respondent from Mannar District, Sri Lanka)

Until the programme, staff were not familiar with participatory methods or the process of encouraging an active approach to learning. Many would typically lecture villagers at length without checking what was being understood. The project experience underlined the fact that pedagogy is important. A lecture-based approach is simply not a very effective model of learning by comparison with participatory methods (Johnson *et al.*, 2014). The more engaged the learner, the more they learn (Trowler, 2010).

For co-operatives, a participatory approach that encourages active learning builds on the reality that the learners are adults who often have considerable experience of life and work. Participants learn through activities that enhance co-operation. The activities are designed so that participants can share experiences and learn from each other. They are often problem-centred and participants work together to solve common problems from their co-operative. This approach also begins to recognize the ways in which co-operatives can provide learning spaces where members share knowledge and learn from each other.

It was also evident that governance needs to remain a key element in all programmes and not be just dealt with as a one-off issue. It is often the case that governance challenges grow as the co-operative itself expands and becomes commercially successful. Courses at the village level can also include members and help to make them aware of their rights and responsibilities – all essential for good governance. Local delivery enables many more members to be reached, especially women and youth who are less likely to travel outside their community.

The question of how best to promote more women leaders in co-operatives is another pressing challenge in terms of education and training. An ILO survey of women in African co-operatives, Promising Practices, outlined some valuable initiatives to challenge the under-representation of women. One example cited was the Uganda Co-operative Alliance, which has been working hard to promote women's participation, including instituting a requirement that a third of all members attending training should be women (Majurin, 2010). All the evidence underlines the importance of education and training as a tool to increase women's participation in co-operatives. In rural communities, women trainers or board members can be a powerful trigger to encourage other women to participate. Mentoring schemes for women leaders can also help. Workshops in Kenya bringing women together from different co-operatives provided valuable insights into the barriers for women's participation and some proposals for tackling them. This is one area where much more research is urgently needed.

Both the literature on co-operatives and the international development programmes of the UK College underline the importance of education and learning for sustainable co-operatives. Undoubtedly, far more research is needed as even basic data on co-operative education is lacking, especially in the developing world. There is also a need for internal debates and dialogue in the movement on the nature or purpose of co-operative education and learning.

In addition, as this chapter has shown, these debates can gain much from being informed by the wider discussions taking place about adult education within the context of global development. Indeed, current co-operative practices already reflect some of the wider conceptions of education and encompass both a narrower skills-based agenda and a broader conception that draws on the capabilities approach. The latter approach, for example, is evident in the capacity-building programmes widely adopted throughout the work of the European co-operative development agencies with their strong focus on education and training as key development tools.

The approach used by the UK College has drawn on the theories and expertise from global adult education perspectives. This has been reflected in the emphasis on developing effective learner-centred pedagogies and the need for training local co-operative development workers to use them. Building local capacity in this manner has helped embed good practice with long-term benefits. It has also addressed the common problem of the shortage of effective co-operative trainers.

Studies of village-level, grass-roots co-operatives reveal how important they can be in providing opportunities for non-formal and informal learning. They remind us that co-operatives offer learning opportunities in a number of ways and should not be viewed simply as empty vessels waiting to be filled with external knowledge and expertise. Hartley's (2014) conceptualization of co-operatives as a site for situated and social learning interacting with training provided by external agencies, such as agricultural extension agencies, is a valuable one. Other studies have also underlined the importance of the access co-operatives can bring to this type of non-formal learning, which is a feature much appreciated by the membership. Such access has the potential to bring about significant improvements in living standards not only for members but also for the communities in which they live. When planning for sustainability, it is crucial that co-operative developers and policymakers take into account the existence and value of these informal and non-formal learning opportunities provided by co-operatives.

However, many challenges remain and one of the most pressing is the huge and unmet demand for education, especially from primary-level co-operatives. This chronic under-resourcing, of course, is not just confined to co-operatives but is common to most forms of educational provision for adults globally. Addressing gender inequity in co-operative education is another major challenge in co-operatives as in other sectors.

Looking to the future, despite these issues, one of the major strengths of co-operative education continues to reside in its connection to the wider co-operative movement and its values. Ensuring that education and learning, especially for adults, is fit for the twenty-first century means developing provision that is strongly rooted in some core values. In its report *Rethinking Education*, UNESCO stated that humanistic values should be the foundations and purpose of education (UNESCO, 2015). Among others, these values include solidarity, shared responsibility, equal rights and social justice. It should scarcely need saying that there is a considerable overlap here with the co-operative values.

The multifaceted and complex nature of co-operatives undoubtedly poses enormous challenges for development programmes and agencies. However, if we are to see real change and improvement in the long term, then investing in effective strategies that recognize and build on the many dimensions of co-operative learning has the potential to make an enormous contribution to building sustainable co-operatives. But, just as importantly, we also need to ensure that our co-operative values sit at the centre of co-operative education if we want it to meet the learning needs of co-operatives in the twenty-first century.

References

Bergström, L. (2002) *Methods for Capacity Development: A report for Sida's project group "Capacity development as a strategic question"* (Sida Working Paper 10). Stockholm: Sida. Online. https://tinyurl.com/y7dbua6k (accessed 1 February 2019).

Borda-Rodriguez, A., Johnson, H., Shaw, L. and Vicari, S. (2016) 'What makes rural co-operatives resilient in developing countries?'. *Journal of International Development*, 28 (1), 89–111.

Borda-Rodriguez, A. and Vicari, S. (2015) 'Coffee co-operatives in Malawi: Building resilience through innovation'. *Annals of Public and Cooperative Economics*, 86 (2), 317–38.

Cook, M.L. (2018) 'A life cycle explanation of cooperative longevity'. *Sustainability*, 10 (5), Article 1586, 1–20. Online. www.mdpi.com/2071-1050/10/5/1586 (accessed 24 January 2019).

Cooperatives Europe (2015) *Building Strong Development Cooperation: Partnership opportunities between cooperatives and the EU*. Brussels: Cooperatives Europe.

Cooperatives Europe (2017) *Good Practices in Cooperative International Development*. Brussels: Cooperatives Europe.

Eger, C., Miller, G. and Scarles, C. (2018) 'Gender and capacity builing: A multi-layered study of empowerment'. *World Development*, 106, 207–19.

Fairtrade Foundation (2019) 'Fintea Growers Co-operative Union Ltd, Kenya'. Online. https://tinyurl.com/ya2ns93m (accessed 1 February 2019).

Flink, I. and Vaast, C. (2018) 'Youth in agricultural cooperatives'. Online. www.kit.nl/sed/project/youth-in-agricultural-cooperatives (accessed 18 September 2018).

Francesconi, N. (2015) 'Is the "Cooperative Life Cycle" Framework relevant for rural Africa?'. Presentation. IFPRI/IITA office, Naguru Hill CIAT office, Kawanda. Online. https://cgspace.cgiar.org/handle/10568/56974 (accessed 30 October 2018).

Francesconi, N., Cook, M. and Livingston, K. (2015) *A Policy Note on Agricultural Cooperatives in Africa* (CIAT Policy Brief 26). Cali: Centro Internacional de Agricultura Tropical. Online. https://tinyurl.com/y776k5yj (accessed 1 February 2019).

Freire, P. (2000) *Pedagogy of the Oppressed*. Trans. Ramos, M.B. New York: Continuum.

Hannan, R. (2014) 'Good co-operative governance: The elephant in the room with rural poverty reduction'. *Journal of International Development*, 26 (5), 701–12.

Hannan, R. (2016) 'The co-operative identity: Good for poverty reduction?'. In Webster, A., Shaw, L. and Vorberg-Rugh, R. (eds) *Mainstreaming Co-operation: An alternative for the twenty-first century?* Manchester: Manchester University Press, 221–38.

Hartley, S. (2014) 'Collective learning in youth-focused co-operatives in Lesotho and Uganda'. *Journal of International Development*, 26 (5), 713–30.

IFC (International Finance Corporation) (2013) *Working with Smallholders: A handbook for firms building sustainable supply chains*. Washington, DC: International Finance Corporation.

IFC (International Finance Corporation) (2018) *Agribusiness Leadership Program Course Catalogue*. Washington, DC: International Finance Corporation. Online. https://tinyurl.com/y8vz8ggx (accessed 30 January 2019).

ILO (International Labour Organization) (n.d.) 'My Coop'. Online. http://moodle.itcilo.org/mycoop (accessed 26 April 2018).

Johnson, D.W., Johnson, R.T. and Smith, K.A. (2014) 'Cooperative learning: Improving university instruction by basing practice on validated theory'. *Journal on Excellence in College Teaching*, 25 (3–4), 85–118.

Johnson, H. and Shaw, L. (2014) 'Rethinking rural co-operatives in development: Introduction to the policy arena'. *Journal of International Development*, 26 (5), 668–82.

Livingston, K., Schweisfurth, M., Brace, G. and Nash, M. (2017) *Why Pedagogy Matters: The role of pedagogy in education 2030: A policy advice paper*. London: United Kingdom National Commission for UNESCO. Online. https://tinyurl.com/ycs3srvw (accessed 1 February 2019).

Majurin, E. (2010) *Promising Practices: How cooperatives work for working women in Africa*. Dar es Salaam: International Labour Organization.

Münkner, H.H. (2012) 'Co-operation as a remedy in times of crisis: Agricultural co-operatives in the world: Their roles for rural development and poverty reduction'. *Marburg Studies on Co-operation and Co-operatives Nr. 58*. Marburg.

Rauschmayer, F., Polzin, C., Mock, M. and Omann, I. (2018) 'Examining collective action through the capability approach: The example of community currencies'. *Journal of Human Development and Capabilities*, 19 (3), 345–64.

Root Capital and Multilateral Investment Fund (2014) *Improving Rural Livelihoods: A study of four Guatemalan coffee cooperatives*. Cambridge, MA: Root Capital.

Saner, R., Yiu, L. and Filadoro, M. (2012) *Cooperatives for Inclusive Growth*. CSEND Policy Brief No. 10. Geneva: CSEND. Online. www.wto.org/english/forums_e/ngo_e/csend_cooperatives_inclusive_growth.pdf (accessed 12 February 2019).

Sen, A. (1999) *Development as Freedom*. Oxford: Oxford University Press.

Shaw, L. (2011) *'International perspectives on co-operative education'* . In Webster, A., Brown, A., Stewart, D., Walton, J.K. and Shaw, L. (eds) *The Hidden Alternative: Co-operative values, past, present and future*. Manchester: Manchester University Press, 59–77.

Smith, S. (2014) *Promoting Cooperatives: An information guide to ILO Recommendation No. 193*. Geneva: International Labour Organization.

Stewart, F. (2005) 'Groups and capabilities'. *Journal of Human Development*, 6 (2), 185–204.

Tesfamariam, K. (2015) 'Cooperative movement in Ethiopia: Development, challenges and proposed intervention'. *Journal of Economics and Sustainable Development*, 6 (5), 38–45.

Trowler, V. (2010) *Student Engagement Literature Review*. York: Higher Education Academy.

UNESCO (United Nations Educational, Scientific and Cultural Organization) (2009) *Global Report on Adult Learning and Education*. Hamburg: UNESCO Institute for Lifelong Learning.

UNESCO (United Nations Educational, Scientific and Cultural Organization) (2015) *Rethinking Education: Towards a global common good?* Paris: UNESCO Publishing.

Part Three

Learning from new practices

Chapter 8

On platforms for co-operative knowledge production

Richard Hall

Introduction: The struggle for knowledge

Globally, we witness increasing struggles over the production, circulation and consumption of socially useful knowledge, which tend to pivot around societal responses to crises (De Sousa Santos, 2007; Hall, 2015a). Socio-economic and socio-environmental crises have infected social relations on a transnational level, and have amplified a deeper questioning of the structural realities of capitalism, including its apparent transhistorical nature. In the current instantiation of capitalism, often referred to as neoliberalism, the naturalization of mediations rooted in the market, private property, the division of labour and commodity exchange have made it difficult to generate and sustain alternative conceptions of the world (Mészáros, 2005). Such conceptions rest on alternative narratives and readings, which themselves emerge from alternative governing principles for social reproduction and from developments in the global South, including indigenous knowledges (Breidlid, 2013; Ciccariello-Maher, 2017). The idea of mediations and the possibility for alternative narratives are important because they reveal the abstract way in which life is organized under capitalism, and as a result they force us to engage with ideas of self-mediation as a humanist, co-operative project.

Thus, struggle is immanent to a range of intersecting narratives, giving access to a profusion of reimaginings. These struggles have a long historical lineage, and emerge from the contradictions of the capitalist social relations that catalyse a range of social movements focused on defining alternative forms of social reproduction (Haiven, 2014). Such social movements operate at the intersection of geography, identity and work, and include: the Zapatistas in Chiapas, Mexico, and the Movimento dos Trabalhadores Rurais Sem Terra (MST) in Brazil (Canaan, 2017); the transnational, Black Lives Matters movement, with connected educational struggles like Rhodes Must Fall; transnational commons and peer-to-peer networks (see, for example, the work of the P2P Foundation); Ecuador's Free-Libre, Open

Knowledge Society project (Commons Transition, n.d.); and precarious workers in the digital platform economy fighting for recognition and labour rights (Lorey, 2017). While these movements are not formal co-operatives, they describe forms of co-operative practice and values at the intersection of civil society and the state.

This sense of social movements engaging with what may be termed as co-operativism has historically been reinforced in two critical terrains: first, in the production and sharing of knowledge as a way of challenging hegemonic power over the world; and second, in the use of technology to generate moments of co-operation and solidarity, and as platforms for dissemination. However, at the intersection of those terrains, the possibilities for co-operative practices force us to reconsider how we conceive of knowledge production. This is important because capitalist activity is driven by the desire to make knowledge productive of value (Roggero, 2011; Vercellone, 2007). This has tended towards narratives of immaterial labour and cognitive capital, through which socially useful knowledge has been commodified so that it can become private property and exchanged as a private good. Moreover, knowledge, alongside data about an individual's use of that knowledge that demonstrates behavioural or predictive patterns, has then been weaponized for capital through processes of financialization.

The commodification of knowledge, as a productive moment of capitalist expansion, has led to a re-engineering of education in the name of entrepreneurialism and human capital (McGettigan, 2015; McMillan Cottom, 2017). In terms of responses to this re-engineering, questions have been raised about the possibility of converting existing institutional forms through co-operative practices and governance (Neary and Winn, 2017). The idea here is to refuse the claim that the market should be the sole arbiter of responses to crises that are rooted in ideas of scarcity, and instead to consider ways in which the direct producers of knowledge can co-operate through associations that widen their autonomy. One possibility is for a refusal of marketized knowledge production, and instead to argue for socially useful knowledge developed in institutions or platforms that reflect the open, participative and democratic values of the International Co-operative Alliance (ICA). Here, the use of digital technologies to develop co-operativism-as-a-platform forms a potential moment of amplification for those values.

This potential for reimagining the production of socially useful knowledge challenges the hegemonic idea of transhistorical, educational institutions with a particular focus on knowledge production and its uses. However, this reimagining takes a variety of forms, including inside co-operatives, in peer-to-peer networks, in autonomous centres, in institutional co-creation projects, and in global commons. In this chapter, I am working through a model that investigates co-operative practices that are against the second-order mediations of life, in order to move beyond the market, private property and commodity production. Instead, I point towards forms of direct production as a process of association between individuals, which reflects relationships where there is no state, social class, authority, or private ownership of means of production. There are transitional moments in this process, for instance in questioning how state-supported, producer co-operatives might enable a movement towards such direct production. This responds to the idea of co-operatives as autonomous enterprises in the ICA (n.d.) statement on co-operative identity, but it is also situated against a longer history of co-operative, educational production.

Therefore, in understanding the co-operative potential for knowledge production, meaningful analysis demands a critique of the relationship between the social reproduction of communities and their technologies. One heuristic for so doing might be the development of digital platforms (Kornberger *et al.*, 2017; Srnicek, 2017), in order to discuss whether they enable communities to reconstitute their own lived experiences, or whether capital's cybernetic control mechanisms simply reterritorialize these experiences for value. At issue is how a variety of institutional forms, from actually existing co-operatives to autonomous social centres, can use platforms to dissolve co-operative practices and knowledge production into the fabric of society for more humane ends. A starting point for this is a discussion of the dominance over knowledge production exerted by capitalist organizations in the search for value.

The value of co-operative knowledge

Value is fundamental in understanding the production, circulation and consumption of knowledge. Through capitalist social relations, the production of knowledge is rooted in oppressive social relations, governed by the need to extract surplus value in the production process, through an attrition on labour rights or the proletarianization of that labour. Through a drive for productivity, proletarianization involves the sequestration of human capabilities, skills and knowledge, and their instantiation inside technology (Marx, 2004). As a result, social relations are not free associations between those who directly produce goods or services. Rather, the total social product is a collection of commodities produced for their exchange value, and mediated through the division of labour, private property and the market. This means that social wealth is a function of commodity production, and the regulation of social life is mediated by that production process (Hall, 2018).

Commodities are shaped by and infused with knowledge, in how they are produced, how they are identified or indexed as having social use, and in what they actually contain that is socially useful. However, capitalist production rests on alienated labour such that commodities, including the labour power of individuals, have a fetishized, privatized appearance (Clarke, 1991), and appear to lack any social or collective good beyond their exchange relationship in the market. As a result, the marketization of knowledge is imminent to its exchange value and its ability to generate surplus value. This generates waves of exploitation and tends to deny that another world is possible, precisely because activity has to be productive of value in order to be justifiable inside capitalism. Inside educational institutions in the global North, a focus on efficacy, future earnings and value for money has a tendency to valorize specific subjects and kinds of knowledge. Moreover, across educational sectors the risk of failure to achieve is increasingly borne by individuals and individual institutions, with a reduced focus on collective or social insurance.

There is potential for co-operative reimagination in work that centres on values of democracy, openness, participation and autonomy, and which works to interconnect spaces that embody those values as a network. Such spaces offer alternative conceptions by focusing on spaces for associational, direct production (Cleaver, 2017; Marx, 1991). Here, the work of transformation seeks to address crises by mediating life through humane values rather than value, and by reconnecting with Marx's (1974) conception of species being, as 'humanity's capacity to co-operatively change the conditions of its collective existence' (Dyer-Witheford, 2004: 3). Developing such co-operative capacity is the liberation of those practices that have been commodified for value, such that self-mediated human flourishing might emerge, and it connects a range of struggles for justice that are, for instance, anti-capitalist, ecological or intersectional. This is why informal, solidarity networks inside institutions like the undercommons, extra-institutional spaces for educational protest like Edufactory or Rhodes Must Fall, the educational wings of trade unions, or co-operative alternatives like the Social Science Centre in the UK and Mondragon University in Spain, are important. They each make possible the release of the full potential of human, mass intellectuality for collective use rooted in self-mediation (Hall and Winn, 2017; Vercellone, 2007). They point towards direct, social, knowledge production that is co-operative in practice and values, if not in governance and regulation.

Thus, the analysis of alternatives might usefully be grounded in relation to co-operative principles, regardless of whether those organizations are themselves formal co-operatives. Thus, the value of self-mediation as a humanist project connects to the ICA (n.d.) principles of mutual self-help and self-responsibility (rather than outsourcing solutions to technology or the market), organized democratically and with equal rights, grounded in social justice and social solidarity, and framed by an ethics of care. Thus, throughout this chapter, the focus is on how platforms might be used, in order to identify authentic, interdisciplinary knowledge production, which appropriately reflects the lived experiences and needs of different people and communities. This is being enabled *both* autonomously at the level of society through co-operative practices *and* in formal co-operative institutions.

While Marx (1866, 2008) saw that co-operative societies were pivotal to the transition to communism as self-mediation, he did not fetishize them as utopian, and instead celebrated them as moments in a movement of opposition to the anarchy and fatality of capitalism. In supporting the everyday needs of people inside and beyond the factory, Marx enables us to analyse the movement towards 'self-government for the producers' through specific educational co-operatives, such as Leicester Vaughan College or the Social Science Centre, and in autonomous movements like Edufactory, which point towards forms of education beyond 'the fetters placed upon it by class and government' (Marx, 2008: 47). These forms of education are based on common actions and common claims rooted in co-operation against competition and hierarchies.

In this argument, co-operative education *both* in institutions *and* at the level of society has a critical role in liberating knowledge, skills and capabilities, and in catalysing the collective ability to reimagine the organizing principles for society. This demands a focus on direct, social production achieved by individuals working in association to establish self-mediation, which will eventually subsume co-operative or critical education, at the level of society (ibid.; Mészáros, 2005). In part, this underpins radical or democratic pedagogic practice, which focuses on the integration of values and organizing principles so that the production of education moves beyond its commodification in the curriculum to become an act of co-operative production (Amsler, 2015; Dinerstein, 2015). It is possible to read this into bell hooks' (1994) work on self-actualization and Neary's (2010) work on student-as-producer, and such communal practices matter because they undermine capital's transhistorical rationale.

In this process of developing alternatives through co-operative education, the idea of the commons, in particular as it is facilitated technologically, enables a critique of such communal and co-operative practices at the level of society. Following Marx's engagement with machines and technology (1991), it is important to think cybernetically about how to use digital technology and the forms of organization it enables to reduce necessary social labour or the sphere of heteronomy, which organizes the production of necessities, and to increase the time for free activity or the sphere of autonomy. Effectively, how do we annihilate exploitative labour through the deployment of digital tools that are governed and regulated co-operatively at the level of society? At issue is whether the commons can be situated as a non-commodified space open to specific, co-operative associations of producers (Midnight Collective, 2008; Roggero, 2011). This demands that the use values of the commons (as particular skills, capabilities or knowledge) are governed and regulated reflexively by the community, so that commodification or exchange can be avoided. This moves a discussion around socially useful knowledge beyond ideas of the public good and away from ideas of command management and scarcity (Dyer-Witheford, 2004). The true power of such communal reflexivity lies in its integration of co-operative theory and practice, as a moment of praxis that widens the association of commons or co-operatives for direct, social production (De Peuter and Dyer-Witheford, 2010). However, a crucial issue is the ability of certain bodies, in particular those marginalized by class, race, gender, (dis)ability and sexuality, to contribute to communal reflexivity, or to have equal access to the commons (Ahmed, 2017; Ciccariello-Maher, 2017).

The system of capital is in continuous motion searching out new spaces and temporalities for value production and accumulation. This makes the work of communing, rooted in co-operative values and practices, constantly precarious because it is in tension with hegemonic forces and relations of production. Thus, potential innovations such as the Ecuadorian National Plan for Good Living (National Secretariat of Planning and Development (NSPD, 2013), aimed at generating an ethical and sustainable economy as a co-operative commonwealth, are always at risk of being ruptured by the global circuits and cycles of capital as it revolutionizes production in search of value. One recent mechanism through which capital seeks to reinvent its use of technology for increased productivity and profitability is the platform. At issue is the relationship between this technological assemblage and the generation of co-operative institutions or practices.

The platform against knowledge production

Technology is central in enabling humans to reimagine the world. Technology reveals the active relationship of man to nature, the direct process of the production of his life, and thereby it also lays bare the process of the production of the social relations of his life, and of the mental conceptions that flow from those relations (Marx, 2004: 493).

Here, humanism is framed by production and productive capability. Moreover, Marx (ibid.: 531) was clear that machinery enables humans to redefine the values that frame our activity, precisely because it enables control over the deployment of labour, the length of the working day and the subsumption of the natural world under the law of value. Thus, while it enables labour time to be reduced in principle, in practice technology 'becomes the most unfailing means for turning the whole lifetime of a worker and [her] family into labour-time'; enforces the metronomic control of the 'motion of the whole factory'; separates 'the intellectual faculties of the production process from manual labour'; and is 'continually transforming not only the technical basis of production but also the functions of the worker and the social combinations of the labour process' (ibid.: 531–2, 546, 548, 617).

For Marx (ibid.: 618), under capitalist social relations, technology proletarianizes and immiserates the worker, such that they become partially developed unless they have commodity skills that can be valorized (Newfield, 2010). Inside capitalism, technologically enabled co-operative practices shape the subordination of the individual to the production of 'objective wealth, in the form of capital, an alien power that dominates and exploits' (Marx, 2004: 716), and which is continually separating the labourer from their labour power and the conditions of their labour, in order to reproduce exploitation. Increasingly, the reproduction of exploitation in order to generate value depends on a global production machine assembled from flows of labour, finance and technology, and that deterritorializes existing practices, cultures and relations so that it can reterritorialize these for profit (Deleuze and Guattari, 1983). In this mode, Wendling (2009: 100) argues that human–machine interaction cannot be symbiotic; rather, it must enable capital to parasitize labour.

Exploitation is expanded as technologies are reconceptualized as platforms, through which their users or audiences can be exploited, either in the supply of services that can be commodified through the imposition of competition, or in controlling access to those services as moments of exchange (Deleuze and Guattari, 1987). For Feenberg (1999), this process is legitimated because it is normalized through determinist narratives of technological progress that elide with liberal ideas of freedom and equality. This tends to amplify intersectional and intergenerational injustice, primarily because those determinist narratives tend to be white, male, ableist and heterosexual, and also to predicate salvation upon specific aggregations of human capital, which reinforce the reification of, for instance, entrepreneurialism. Thus, they tend to ignore intersections of class, race, gender, (dis)ability and sexuality across the global labour force, through which proletarianized jobs that are low status, menial, precarious and at risk of outsourcing fall to individuals and communities made marginal (boyd, 2017). They also ignore the ways in which certain bodies are not able to access specific activities or resources, including those on the commons.

This (in)ability to move through the world is reinforced because technology optimizes certain governable spaces, through which individuals can be compared against imposed norms that are disciplinary (Foucault, 1991). Here, *both* the technologies that optimize, in terms of the performance management of certain behaviours, *and* the governance of those technologies, in terms of the data that predict behaviours, serve as fetishes that reinforce the power of the commodity and the interests of a minority over society. Thus, technology serves as an important vector of struggle for social movements wishing to refuse the subjectivity of capital.

Yet, new technological compositions, rooted in the idea of the platform, have been fetishized as emancipating labour from the mediations of capitalists, and enabling them to commission work directly from consumers (Pasquale, 2016). The idea of the platform is one of a controlling, distribution infrastructure acting as an intermediary between contracting parties. However, a critical gain for the platform host is the ability to extract data from the activities surrounding those contracts. In this way, the value of the platform grows as its suppliers or consumers increase in number, because of the potential monopolization of data about actual or predictive behaviours. Moreover, this enables cybernetic control through the ability of the monopoly to smooth barriers to specific forms of valuable knowledge production, circulation and accumulation through the application of dominant protocols and algorithms (Lazzarato, 2014). For Srnicek (2017), this increases the epistemic privilege underpinning the platform, and this reveals a tension among those supporters of open markets in knowledge production, between those who support centralization and those who favour decentralized, distributed networks (Pasquale, 2018). As a result, the platform collapses the digital economy onto a technological infrastructure that is rooted in a specific political economic model for society in which users are always on task and always available (Huws, 2014).

A problem for direct knowledge producers, seeking association or co-operation in order to generate new governing principles, practices, forms of public intellectual activity, and so on, is that platforms tend to operate by collapsing goods into services and extracting rents from them. As Hall (2016) points out, in higher education this tends towards the 'Uberification' of the university, such that knowledge becomes a commodity that is privatized rather than being a social good. Thus, the space inside which existing co-operatives, such as Mondragon University in Spain or co-operative trusts and academies in the UK, have to operate is shaped by policies and practices that commodify education, and then enable access to those commodities through subscription services that amplify financialization and marketization (Hall, 2015b). Technologies like platforms risk amplifying this conditioning where they catalyse dominant, data-driven narratives of behaviour that stand in opposition to the institutional desire to use co-operative values for curriculum design, delivery and assessment.

Equally, where the platform meets discourses of human capital, it imposes constant entrepreneurial and competitive activity upon individuals, who are responsible for repeatedly selling themselves in an increasingly precarious market. This sale of the self is not simply of an individual's knowledge, skills, products or services, but also their attitude and affective position (Southwood, 2017). Thus, engagement on the platform is disciplinary and acts as a form of domination. It enables services to be commodified that: first, mediate those activities against aggregated norms with a focus on generating performative human capital that reduces the risk of failure; second, generate new services to be developed that recalibrate understandings of the world and how they are internalized by individuals; and third, reinforce *both* specific practices as hegemonic knowledge of the world, *and* hegemonic practices for producing the world, as an internalized protocol across the network.

Thus, constant audit and evaluation of knowledge, products, services and experiences by users serve as an evaluative infrastructure, internalized at the level of the individual and aggregated at the level of the platform (Kornberger *et al.*, 2017). Platform data collection as a mechanism for the control of knowledge production is one specific response to capitalist crisis and its negative impact on profitability, and it serves as a material, generative, governmental infrastructure. However, over time the competition between isomorphic platforms exacerbates the tendency of the rate of profit to fall as less surplus value can be extracted from technologically enriched ecosystems. At issue is whether formal co-operatives or autonomous centres and networks that are governed by co-operative principles and values can repurpose the platform.

The knowledge potential of platform co-operativism

The political economy of the platform is a governance risk for societies where those platforms dominate the economic mediation of society by monopolizing its hardware and software. As one response to this, certain city councils have pointed towards platform co-operativism, for instance in the Municipal Action Plan of the Barcelona City Council (Procomuns, 2016), in order to prioritize policies that support infrastructures for social solidarity. In the case of Barcelona, this specifically frames the development of an ecosystem of protocols, websites or applications that enables producers and consumers to interact directly, with co-operative principles and values shaping the governance, regulation and funding of the platform, such that knowledge infrastructures are produced as collective rather than private goods. In extending the possibilities of such collective production for democratic control, participation and autonomous governance, proponents of platform or open co-operatives argue for the use of open licensing to ensure that knowledge, skills and capabilities as goods and services can be shared where possible (Bauwens, 2014). Thus, there is a possibility for connecting concrete co-operative and technological municipal action plans to a history of co-operative social and economic development, for instance as proposed in Chile under Allende or in Ecuador by the FLOK Society, and to the lived reality of co-operatives connected to those plans.

However, such open practices are often rooted in self-mediation of access to the commons, and this risks ignoring the implications of structural forms of privilege and power, alongside differential knowledge and literacy among certain groups. It also risks ignoring how the structure of the commons might act as a barrier to certain groups. As a result, while the Barcelona City Council action plan predicates such economies on open knowledge 'that seeks to promote access and reclaim the resources generated through public or collective ownership', this can equally tend towards a monopoly position on the nature and appropriateness of those resources. Which resources are to be validated and why? This also maps across to statements about open knowledge being enabled by technology that privileges 'the transparency, participation and freedom of citizens, taxpayers and users' (Procomuns, 2016). This challenges and reinforces power because there are issues of privilege and agency in defining who is a citizen, who is able to participate in decision-making, and who is able to describe the technological ecosystem.

These kinds of plans connect to other networked forms of open knowledge production, for instance, through the work of the Platform Cooperativism Consortium and the Internet of Ownership project. These networks argue for principles of collectivism, democracy and a focus on the global commons as a commitment to association for social justice and sustainability. Their approaches stress the idea of technological sovereignty for citizens, such that they have control over their digital lives and the ways in which digital infrastructures might be shaped by the multiplicity of those lives, rather than having those infrastructures deform labour practices and rights, and access to knowledge and services (Scholz, 2016).

This idea of technological sovereignty is not historically specific and is mirrored in Chile's Project Cybersyn during the presidency of Allende, which sought to reimagine society through social networks that connected 'technologies to the function of the state and its management' (Miller Medina, 2005: 22). The critical point here is the ways in which such projects seek to reimagine the world beyond the structuring realities of the law of value: first, by the constant questioning of the governing principles of specific communities, in order to refuse marginalization, privilege and power; second, by sharing narratives about the lived experience of co-operation as a continual form of praxis, constantly questioning assumptions about open knowledge and technologies; third, by sharing access to data such that their use can be defined collectively for the provision of services beyond value; and fourth, by the open sharing of the full range of knowledge, skills and capabilities. The aim is to challenge hegemonic forms of knowledge production, circulation and accumulation, which do not enable societies to engage with crises of social reproduction. While such approaches do not break the law of value, they enable platforms to be reimagined for co-operative ends that point beyond alienating wage labour, and towards full social and economic participation, democratic production and consumption, and open and equitable engagement that supports autonomy.

Another world is possible

The incorporation of platform-based learning tools at the level of society that are governed by specific algorithms and the extraction of data for commercial ends, and that are *both* funded by finance capital *and* regulated by corporate forms, has implications for the governance of educational institutions (Van Dijck and Poell, 2018). Effectively, by predicating education at the level of society upon institutions that can be disrupted and dismantled by platforms offering commodified information, content, data and services, the production of socially useful knowledge comes under threat. The issue then becomes whether platform or open co-operatives, working together as a co-operative of co-operatives, are able to reimagine knowledge production against and beyond the law of value.

However, the ability to imagine that another world is possible situates platform or open co-operatives inside the struggle against capital social relations. Capital drives innovation by increasing the technical composition of labour as an attrition on costs and to build markets. One issue is whether counter-projects can liberate both knowledge and the technological platforms upon which that knowledge is created and shared in the name of an alternative conception of life. At heart, this reflects the idea that capital derives its autonomy and its existence from labour, but that the individual who labours does not need capital in order to live, and is, therefore, potentially autonomous inside new forms of co-operative organization (Tronti, 2012). Here, we are reminded of Chile's integration of technology into social reproduction as a moment of 'struggle for economic and political independence' (Miller Medina, 2005: 31).

A radical form of platform co-operative picks up on Marcuse's (1998) argument (following Marx, 2004) that technics and modern technology have the ability to shatter and then recompose the specific historical form in which they are deployed, in the name of liberation. There are already failed examples from which platform or open co-operatives can learn. For instance, the Ecuadorian National Plan for Good Living (NSPD, 2013) was attempting to blueprint the ways in which education might be transformed through participative practice, in order to generate socially useful forms of knowledge in science, technology and innovation that would reinforce and diversify both individual and social capabilities. This echoes previous reimaginings of the role of really useful knowledge produced communally, collectively and co-operatively, which emphasized the work of radical, working-class organizations such as the Plebs' League and Oxford's Central Labour College, and labour movement plans like the Lucas Plan for socially useful production. Such moments of production, rooted in knowledge at the level of society, begin from a democratic analysis of the conditions of social production, and a focus on militant research undertaken in public. Socially useful production stands against the inhumanity of value, and is grounded in the general, productive knowledge, skills and capacities of society, or its mass intellectuality.

One way of framing the relationship between knowledge production, platforms and co-operative practices is by returning to society's ability to widen the realm of autonomy (Gorz, 1982). This demands spaces for self-mediation inside which human relations and the things that are produced in the activities of humans are not fetishized or commodified, and then privatized, in order to stand over those individuals and their communities (Marx and Engels, 1998). This also demands that humans are allowed true freedom in the creation of knowledge, rather than being fixed inside a division of labour predicated upon isolated, privatized knowledge (ibid.; Marx, 1970). While Marx and Engels emphasize the importance of the productive forces as the precondition for a new mode of social reproduction, in generating the surplus wealth that communist life requires (Clarke, 1991), the governance of those technologies and organizational forms is critical in challenging established hierarchy, privilege and power.

This is important if the co-operative and open development of knowledge through platforms is to challenge intersectional injustice, rather than simply to replicate it. In this way, the development of the realm of autonomy requires that open and platform co-operatives prefigure the world they wish to see (Amsler, 2015; Dinerstein, 2015), which implies a struggle against the limits imposed by the market. In this moment of prefiguration, a co-operative of such co-operatives offers the potential to reimagine the species being of humanity, and to refuse the competitive, entrepreneurial, atomized reproduction of society based on hegemonic knowledge production, circulation and accumulation. It is in this reimagining that the intersection of knowledge production and co-operative governance and values might be enabled through a critical approach to platform technology. This is a knowledgeable moment of struggle against and beyond the law of value.

References

Ahmed, S. (2017) *Living a Feminist Life*. Durham, NC: Duke University Press.

Amsler, S.S. (2015) *The Education of Radical Democracy*. London: Routledge.

Bauwens, M. (2014) 'Open cooperativism for the P2P age'. P2P Foundation blog, 16 June. Online. https://tinyurl.com/y96u7b4u (accessed 29 January 2019).

boyd, d. (2017) 'The radicalization of utopian dreams'. *Data and Society: Points*, 20 November. Online. https://tinyurl.com/ya6cecfs (accessed 29 January 2019).

Breidlid, A. (2013) *Education, Indigenous Knowledges, and Development in the Global South: Contesting knowledges for a sustainable future*. New York: Routledge.

Canaan, J.E. (2017) 'The (im)possibility of mass intellectuality: Viewing mass intellectuality through the lens of the Brazilian Landless Movement'. In Hall, R. and Winn, J. (eds) *Mass Intellectuality and Democratic Leadership in Higher Education*. London: Bloomsbury Academic, 69–80.

Ciccariello-Maher, G. (2017) *Decolonizing Dialectics*. Durham, NC: Duke University Press.

Clarke, S. (1991) *Marx, Marginalism and Modern Sociology: From Adam Smith to Max Weber*. 2nd ed. Basingstoke: Macmillan.

Cleaver, H. (2017) *Rupturing the Dialectic: The struggle against work, money, and financialization*. Chico, CA: AK Press.

Commons Transition (n.d.) 'FLOK Society'. Online. http://commonstransition.org/flok-society (accessed 31 August 2018).

Deleuze, G. and Guattari, F. (1983) *Anti-Oedipus: Capitalism and schizophrenia*. Trans. Hurley, R., Seem, M. and Lane, H.R. Minneapolis: University of Minnesota Press.

Deleuze, G. and Guattari, F. (1987) *A Thousand Plateaus: Capitalism and schizophrenia*. Trans. Massumi, B. Minneapolis: University of Minnesota Press.

de Peuter, G. and Dyer-Witheford, N. (2010) 'Commons and cooperatives'. *Affinities: A Journal of Radical Theory, Culture, and Action*, 4 (1), 30–56.

de Sousa Santos, B. (ed.) (2007) *Cognitive Justice in a Global World: Prudent knowledges for a decent life*. Lanham, MD: Lexington Books.

Dinerstein, A.C. (2015) *The Politics of Autonomy in Latin America: The art of organising hope*. Basingstoke: Palgrave Macmillan.

Dyer-Witheford, N. (2004) '1844/2004/2044: The return of species-being'. *Historical Materialism*, 12 (4), 3–25.

Feenberg, A. (1999) *Questioning Technology*. London: Routledge.

Foucault, M. (1991) *Discipline and Punish: The birth of the prison*. London: Penguin.

Gorz, A. (1982) *Farewell to the Working Class: An essay on post-industrial socialism*. Trans. Sonenscher, M. London: Pluto Press.

Haiven, M. (2014) *Crises of Imagination, Crises of Power: Capitalism, creativity and the commons*. London: Zed Books.

Hall, G. (2016) *The Uberfication of the University*. Minneapolis: University of Minnesota Press.

Hall, R. (2015a) 'The university and the secular crisis'. *Open Library of Humanities*, 1 (1), Article e6, 1–34. Online. https://olh.openlibhums.org/articles/10.16995/olh.15/ (accessed 24 January 2019).

Hall, R. (2015b) 'For a political economy of massive open online courses'. *Learning, Media and Technology*, 40 (3), 265–86.

Hall, R. (2018) *The Alienated Academic: The struggle for autonomy inside the university*. Basingstoke: Palgrave Macmillan.

Hall, R. and Winn, J. (eds) (2017) *Mass Intellectuality and Democratic Leadership in Higher Education*. London: Bloomsbury Academic.

hooks, b. (1994) *Teaching to Transgress: Education as the practice of freedom*. New York: Routledge.

Huws, U. (2014) *Labor in the Global Digital Economy: The cybertariat comes of age*. New York: Monthly Review Press.

ICA (International Co-operative Alliance) (n.d.) Cooperative identity, values & principles. Online. https://ica.coop/en/cooperatives/cooperative-identity (accessed 31 August 2018).

Kornberger, M., Pflueger, D. and Mouritsen, J. (2017) 'Evaluative infrastructures: Accounting for platform organization'. *Accounting, Organizations and Society*, 60, 79–95.

Lazzarato, M. (2014) *Signs and Machines: Capitalism and the production of subjectivity*. Los Angeles: Semiotext(e).

Lorey, I. (2017) 'Labour, (in-)dependence, care: Conceptualizing the precarious'. In Armano, E., Bove, A. and Murgia, A. (eds) *Mapping Precariousness, Labour Insecurity and Uncertain Livelihoods: Subjectivities and resistance*. London: Routledge, 199–209.

Marcuse, H. (1998) *Collected Papers of Herbert Marcuse: Volume 1: Technology, war and fascism*. Ed. Kellner, D. London: Routledge.

Marx, K. (1866) *Instructions for the Delegates of the Provisional General Council: The different questions*. Online. www.marxists.org/archive/marx/works/1866/08/instructions.htm (accessed 31 August 2018).

Marx, K. (1970) 'Critique of the Gotha Programme'. In *Marx and Engels: Selected works* (Vol. 3). Moscow: Progress Publishers, 13–30.

Marx, K. (1974) *Economic and Philosophic Manuscripts of 1844*. Moscow: Progress Publishers.

Marx, K. (1991) *Capital: A critique of political economy* (Vol. 3). Trans. Fernbach, D. London: Penguin.

Marx, K. (2004) *Capital: A critique of political economy* (Vol. 1). London: Penguin.

Marx, K. (2008) *Wage-Labour and Capital*. Cabin John, MD: Wildside Press.

Marx, K. and Engels, F. (1998) *The German Ideology; including Theses on Feuerbach and Introduction to the Critique of Political Economy*. Amherst, NY: Prometheus Books.

McGettigan, A. (2015) *The Treasury View of HE: Variable human capital investment* (PERC Paper 6). London: Political Economy Research Centre. Online. https://tinyurl.com/jlxmozf (accessed 2 February 2019).

McMillan Cottom, T. (2017) *Lower Ed: The troubling rise of for-profit colleges in the new economy*. New York: New Press.

Mészáros, I. (2005) *Marx's Theory of Alienation*. 5th ed. London: Merlin Press.

Midnight Collective (2008) 'The new enclosures'. In Bonefeld, W. (ed.) *Subverting the Present, Imagining the Future: Insurrection, movement, commons*. New York: Autonomedia, 13–26.

Miller Medina, J.E. (2005) 'The State Machine: Politics, ideology, and computation in Chile, 1964–1973'. Unpublished PhD thesis, Massachusetts Institute of Technology.

NSPD (National Secretariat of Planning and Development) (2013) *National Plan for Good Living, 2013–2017: Summarized version*. Quito: National Secretariat of Planning and Development. Online. https://tinyurl.com/ydbx2ww7 (accessed 2 February 2019).

Neary, M. (2010) 'Student as producer: A pedagogy for the avant-garde; or, how do revolutionary teachers teach?'. *Learning Exchange*, 1 (1), 1–12. Online. http://eprints.lincoln.ac.uk/4186 (accessed 31 August 2018).

Neary, M. and Winn, J. (2017) 'There is an alternative: A report on an action research project to develop a framework for co-operative higher education'. *Learning and Teaching: The International Journal of Higher Education in the Social Sciences*, 10 (1), 87–105.

Newfield, C. (2010) 'The structure and silence of cognitariat'. *EduFactory webjournal*, 0, 10–26. Online. www.eurozine.com/the-structure-and-silence-of-the-cognitariat (accessed 31 August 2018).

Pasquale, F. (2016) 'Two narratives of platform capitalism'. *Yale Law and Policy Review*, 35 (1), 309–19. Online. https://tinyurl.com/ybu27opu (accessed 24 January 2019).

Pasquale, F. (2018) 'Tech platforms and the knowledge problem'. *American Affairs*, 2 (2), 3–16. Online. https://tinyurl.com/y9sh7zpr (accessed 24 January 2019).

Procomuns (2016) *Summary: Procomuns statement and policies for Commons Collaborative Economies at European level*. Online. https://tinyurl.com/y76sb9y3 (accessed 2 February 2019).

Roggero, G. (2011) *The Production of Living Knowledge: The crisis of the university and the transformation of labor in Europe and North America*. Trans. Brophy, E. Philadelphia: Temple University Press.

Scholz, T. (2016) *Platform Cooperativism: Challenging the corporate sharing economy*. New York: Rosa Luxemburg Stiftung.

Southwood, I. (2017) 'Against precarity, against employability'. In Armano, E., Bove, A. and Murgia, A. (eds) *Mapping Precariousness, Labour Insecurity and Uncertain Livelihoods: Subjectivities and resistance*. London: Routledge, 70–81.

Srnicek, N. (2017) *Platform Capitalism*. Cambridge: Polity Press.

Tronti, M. (2012) 'Our operaismo'. *New Left Review*, 73, 119–39.

van Dijck, J. and Poell, T. (2018) 'Social media platforms and education'. In Burgess, J., Marwick, A. and Poell, T. (eds) *The SAGE Handbook of Social Media*. London: SAGE Publications, 579–91.

Vercellone, C. (2007) 'From formal subsumption to general intellect: Elements for a Marxist reading of the thesis of cognitive capitalism'. *Historical Materialism*, 15 (1), 13–36.

Wendling, A.E. (2009) *Karl Marx on Technology and Alienation*. Basingstoke: Palgrave Macmillan.

Chapter 9

Co-operative social entrepreneurship: Reflections on a decade embedding co-operative studies in social enterprise courses

Rory Ridley-Duff

Introduction

As I write this, an article in *Stanford Social Innovation Review* (Ganz *et al.*, 2018) is provoking debate within my academic networks. The charge the authors make is that 'solving systemic social problems takes people, politics and power – not more social entrepreneurship' (p. 59). They argue that civil society and the state should act together *against* social entrepreneurship (SE) because the latter is a creature of, and vehicle for, the advance of neoliberalism. This ahistorical and empirically unsound assessment of SE is something I will challenge in this chapter.

My counterargument is that SE was, and once again is, a by-product of developments within the co-operative movement (see Borzaga and Defourny, 2001; Teasdale, 2012; Ridley-Duff, 2015; Ridley-Duff *et al.*, 2018). Specifically, I will set out how UK SE was initially brought into existence by co-operative educators and practitioners who looked beyond consumer ownership to broaden the reach and relevance of the UK co-operative movement. Initially, education initiatives introduced worker co-operatives to social auditing, a multi-stakeholder approach to governance that integrates co-operatives within their host communities (Spreckley, 1981, 2008). Later, the action learning of a new generation of co-operative entrepreneurs catalysed the creation of solidarity and platform co-operatives suited to sustainable development (Ridley-Duff, 2015; Scholz and Schneider, 2016).

It is an appropriate time to reflect on the state of the art for two reasons. First, it is the 100th anniversary of the Co-operative College.

Its archive has enabled co-operative historians to examine the blurred line between worker and consumer co-operation in the development of early co-operatives (Toms, 2012; Balnave and Patmore, 2012; Molina, 2012; Paranque and Willmott, 2014). Second, it is ten years since Mike Bull and I began work on *Understanding Social Enterprise: Theory and practice* (Ridley-Duff and Bull, 2011, 2016). As we work towards a third edition, we encounter rhetoric such as that published by Ganz *et al.* (2018) that misinforms and misleads students about the connections between co-operators, co-operatives and SE development.

While it is possible to agree with Ganz *et al.* (2018) that 'solving systemic social problems takes people, politics and power' and that this cannot be achieved through the adoption of neoliberal doctrine (Klein, 2007; Scholz and Schneider, 2016), I challenge Ganz *et al.* by asserting that co-operative development and co-operators inspired the formation and development of key institutions for SE development. This catalysed a distinctive type of entrepreneurship – co-operative social entrepreneurship (CSE) – that is more mutual, more favourably disposed towards multi-stakeholder design principles (Ridley-Duff, 2018) and gives wider scope to implement co-operative principles 1, 2, 5, 6 and 7 (open membership, democratic member control, education, inter-co-operation and concern for community).

There are good grounds to counter antipathy to co-operative studies in both SE and mainstream management education (MacPherson, 2015; Audebrand *et al.*, 2017). CSE identifies a subset of social entrepreneurship that draws on and applies co-operative values and principles during venture creation. It is characterized by a collective ability to build enterprise networks that emphasize voluntary co-operative action. Such action develops new communities of practice (Wenger, 1998) that favour direct democracy and group ownership over public administration and private ownership (Ostrom *et al.*, 1999). In contemporary debate, co-operative values (self-help, self-responsibility, democracy, equality, equity and solidarity) are advanced both to prevent a 'self-employed precariat' from developing (Conaty, 2014; Conaty *et al.*, 2016: 3) and to oppose neoliberalism by offering alternative approaches to (enterprise) education (see van de Veen, 2010; Neary and Winn, 2017). CSE, therefore, is a form of entrepreneurship in the social solidarity economy (SSE) that connects co-operation with solidarity action. Since Ostrom (2009) received a Nobel Prize for identifying principles of collective action, it has become easier to argue that CSE is a legitimate lens for studying the field of SE (Utting, 2015).

This chapter is divided into two main sections. In the first, I highlight a strategy for challenging Ganz *et al.*'s (2018) ahistorical account of SE. Building on a previous debate (Voinea, 2016), I explore the origins and history of SE in the UK. This leads into a discussion of the way Ostrom's (1990) work on collective action can inform the development and study of mutuality beyond sharing financial risks to encompass governance, resource management, social reporting and conflict resolution. In the second section, I introduce six examples of collective action from outside the formal co-operative movement to develop a new conversation about the principles of 'new co-operativism'. Vieta (2010) argues that new co-operativism has several characteristics: first, it is a response by working people to recent crises in neoliberalism; second, it is 'uninhibited' by the institutions of previous co-operative movements; third, there are new approaches to allocating surpluses that are more egalitarian and emphasize horizontal labour relations; and, lastly, there is a stronger community orientation with social objects and community development goals. To complete the chapter, I argue for the value of SE scholars studying co-operatives and of co-operative scholars studying SEs. It represents a viable strategy for countering neoliberal doctrine by offering new co-operativism within the SSE as an alternative (Ridley-Duff, 2018). Taken together, the two strategies represent separate strands in a course curriculum on SE. The first curriculum strand focuses on the history of SE while the second challenges students to consider how SE can counter neoliberalism.

Strand 1: Rethinking history

In recent years, Sheffield Hallam University and the Co-operative College have worked together to deliver a course to students from the co-operative university at Mondragon. To start, we study first-hand accounts of the conditions among weavers that led to the formation of a co-operative at Rochdale. The co-operative behind the global movement (the Rochdale Equitable Pioneers Society) was initially run by volunteers. Members gave up two hours each evening to run a shop. This operated without a clear distinction between worker and consumer until the introduction of paid employment (Wilson *et al.*, 2012). The situation they faced, of wage cuts and deteriorating social conditions in Rochdale in 1844, was similar to the contexts that trigger SE development today. By today's standards (see Ridley-Duff and Bull, 2016; Defourny and Nyssens, 2017), the members of the Rochdale Equitable Pioneers Society were social entrepreneurs engaged in social innovation – practitioners of CSE.

While it is tempting, politically, to assert that co-operatives are 'businesses' (see Co-operatives UK, 2018), International Co-operative Alliance (ICA) guidance avoids the word 'business' altogether (ICA, 2015). Instead, a co-operative is presented as a voluntary association of members who form an enterprise to meet their economic, social and cultural needs. Their enterprise is jointly owned and democratically controlled. The absence of the word 'business' in the official statement of co-operative identity cannot be accidental. It reflects ongoing contestation about the core characteristics, social and economic contribution, and legal expressions of SE. While Peattie and Morley's (2008) UK review emphasizes business activity for a social purpose, wider European and Asian debates problematize the relationship between SE and 'business' (Teasdale, 2012; Kerlin, 2013; Ridley-Duff and Wren, 2018). Within the EMES International Research Network, there is an emerging consensus on economic activity within and beyond formally constituted businesses, the primacy of social purpose(s), and inclusive governance and/or trading practices that empower marginalized groups (Defourny *et al.*, 2014; Defourny and Nyssens, 2017).

The co-operative origins of English and Scottish social enterprise

While researching a 'hidden history' of SE development, Mike Bull and I received an email from Cliff Southcombe (former Chair of Greater Manchester Co-operative Development Agency and co-founder of the Social Enterprise Partnership).[1] His account of early SE development provides clues to the movement's early dynamics:

> For me, social enterprise emerged from the community enterprise movement that had rejected capitalist, state and charitable solutions to problems caused by the collapse of traditional industries chiefly in the north of England and Scotland [in the early 1980s]. I probably include a rejection of traditional community development in this – seeing the community economy and the ownership of assets as key ... It came too from a frustration with the co-operative movement not being able to give us the models or tools to work with – and so we had turned to creating Companies Ltd by Guarantee and holding companies to increase the democratic nature of our enterprises. This allowed communities to own the assets but workers and volunteers to own the enterprises. The community could use the power of landlord to impose social goals – hence the start of social auditing. (Email, 5 August 2014, reproduced with permission)

It is the existence of 'frustration with the co-operative movement' and the responses to it that represent the umbilical cord between the (old) co-operative movement, new co-operativism and SE development. According to Parigi *et al.* (2005), social auditing has a mixed history that began in the field of medicine, then evolved in corporate, public and third sector evaluation work to understand the impacts of an organization on wider society. The common thread has been a principle that in a democratic culture 'decision makers should be accountable for the use of their powers and that their powers should be used as far as possible with the consent and understanding of all concerned' (ibid.: 15). Social auditing, therefore, is a good vehicle for (re-)establishing the co-operative principles (CPs) of 'education' (CP 5), 'inter-co-operation' (CP 6) and 'concern for community' (CP 7) that the UK's leading trade body has regarded as 'more of an aspiration' than a fundamental requirement (compare Spreckley, 1981 with Atherton *et al.*, 2011: 10).

It is this socially entrepreneurial attitude among co-operators (placing more emphasis on outcomes for labour, citizens and the environment) that spawned new co-operativism (Vieta, 2010). It offers a critique of the way that the market orientation of consumer co-operatives allowed commercial drivers to weaken investments in associational life and wider community benefit. While new co-operativism remains closely connected at a conceptual level with co-operative values and principles, it refocused attention on four things: the needs of *working* people to build a social solidarity economy (SSE) (De Peuter and Dyer-Witheford, 2010; Laville, 2015; Utting, 2015); the wider benefits to society of an enfranchised workforce engaged in co-operative enterprise (Gonzales, 2010; Ridley-Duff, 2015); online technologies that support co-operative action (Paterson, 2010; Scholz and Schneider, 2016); and links between co-operatives and sustainable development (Gertler, 2004; Wanyama, 2014).

By reintegrating co-operative principles 5, 6 and 7 with 1, 2, 3 and 4 (open and voluntary membership, democratic member control, member economic participation, and autonomy and independence), Jim Brown, author of *Co-operative Capital,* and Freer Spreckley, author of *The Social Audit Toolkit,* defined and developed the concept of SE between 1981 and 1984 at Beechwood College, Leeds, UK, through social auditing courses for members of worker co-operatives. Concurrently with John Elkington's (1978, 2004) corporate work developing the triple bottom line concept, Brown and Spreckley articulated this as SE in early editions of *The Social Audit Toolkit* (subtitled 'a management toolkit for co-operative working').

Such frustrations were not confined to England. Pearce (2003) set out his vision for co-operative communities in Scotland in a book called *Social Enterprise in Anytown*.[2] He too had deep connections to the co-operative movement through revitalizing worker co-operatives (through the Industrial Common Ownership Movement) and designing financial support for them (through Industrial Common Ownership Finance).[3] Later, he participated in the Scottish Co-operative Development Committee. Further south (in London), my own worker co-operative (Computercraft Ltd) joined with other worker-co-operatives (Poptel and Calverts Press) and London-based co-operative development agencies in Hackney, Lambeth, Tower Hamlets and Greenwich to bring about the incorporation of Social Enterprise London Ltd (see Table 9.1). It would take another four years (after the Co-operative Commission reported in 2001) for UK worker-co-operatives to secure board representation at Co-operatives UK.

Table 9.1: Directors and subscribers of Social Enterprise London Ltd, at incorporation

Initial directors	Occupation	Employer
Sipi Hameenaho	Project Co-ordinator	London Co-operative Training
Manuela Sykes	Director	Doddington & Rollo Community Association
Jean Whitehead	Policy Officer	Co-operative Union
Gregory Cohn	Manager	London Co-operative Training
Malcolm Corbett	Sales Director	Soft Solution Ltd (Poptel)
Signatory name	**Subscribing organization**	**Classification**
Anthonia Faponnle	Hackney Co-op Developments Ltd	Co-operative Development Agency
S. M. Kelly	Lambeth CDA	Co-operative Development Agency
Malcolm Corbett	Poptel	Worker co-operative
Rory Ridley-Duff	Computercraft Ltd	Worker co-operative
Robert Smyth	Calverts Press	Worker co-operative
J. Whitehead	The Co-operative Party	Political party
I Saray	Artzone Co-operative Ltd	Worker co-operative
Gregory Cohn	Tower Hamlets CDA	Co-operative Development Agency
Sipi Hameenaho	Greenwich CDA	Co-operative Development Agency

Source: Social Enterprise London Ltd (1998), Memorandum of Association.

Previously published in Ridley-Duff and Southcombe (2012), Appendix A, Table AII.

The objects of Social Enterprise London Ltd were as follows:

(i) To promote the principles and values of the social enterprise economy in Greater London and its environs.

(ii) To promote co-operative solutions for economic and community development.

(iii) To promote social enterprises, in particular co-operatives and common ownerships, social firms, and other organisations and businesses which put into practice the principles of participative democracy, equal opportunities and social justice.

(iv) To promote, develop and support local and regional economic resources and opportunities.

(v) To address social exclusion through economic regeneration.

(vi) To create a regional framework to support and resource development of the social enterprise sector. (Companies House, 1998)

Just as the Rochdale Equitable Pioneers Society had a vision to build links between producers, consumers, housing providers and educators to develop a politics of social transformation, so the pioneers of SE in the UK engaged in a way that made it possible to (re)diversify the co-operative movement and re-enfranchise a wider range of co-operative projects. The first SE agencies did not just support enterprise creation; they promoted the concept through a still-existent academic journal and a degree programme at the University of East London that catalysed other degree programmes that are still going. In short, they gave both an academic and a political voice to a previously disenfranchised group of co-operators.

Given the information in Table 9.1 and the objects of Social Enterprise London Ltd, it is clearly ahistorical to argue that co-operatives and co-operators were not part of the formation of the SE movement within the UK. I would go further, however, and argue that the theoretical and conceptual separation of SE and co-operatives is seriously misleading, given that increasing interest has created more public spaces in which to discuss and develop co-operative business models. Co-operatives are increasingly studied by scholars identifying themselves as either SE or co-operative scholars, and are positioned as key actors in sustainable development policy within the United Nations and B20 business advisory group that makes recommendations to G20 governments (Mills and Davies, 2013; Voinea, 2015).

While the umbilical cord feeding the SSE has been progressively obscured by the rise of neoliberalism (see Teasdale, 2012; Ridley-Duff and

Southcombe, 2012), this does not change history: co-operators registered the most important development agencies (Social Enterprise Partnership, Social Enterprise London, Social Enterprise Coalition), created the first educational courses at the University of East London[4] and edited the first academic journals (*Social Enterprise Journal*, *Journal of Social Entrepreneurship*). The editor of the *Social Enterprise Journal* from 2007 to 2017 previously worked at Divine Chocolate/Twin Trading, a co-operatively owned fair trade producer. The current editor of the *Journal of Social Entrepreneurship* previously worked as a purchaser at the John Lewis Partnership (listed in the global 'Top 300' co-operatives at https://monitor.coop/en). During their academic careers, both worked on and studied fair trade in which 75 per cent of produce is organized through co-operatives (Lacey, 2009).

Revisiting history in this way provides students with a better understanding of the links between several SE subfields. In particular, it is an effective strategy for engaging scholars on the connection between co-operatives and other forms of SE (including the antagonisms between them). In teaching activities, students can investigate and critique how SE in the UK emerged out of: (1) the rejection of state, market and charitable responses to the rise of neoliberal doctrine, and (2) the search by co-operators for something new beyond consumer co-operatives to revitalize and re-enfranchise worker and community co-operatives.

That search for 'something new' informs Strand 2 (see below). While Strand 1 invites students to investigate how those inside the co-operative movement contributed to the development of SE, Strand 2 flips perspective to explore the contribution of those in the wider SSE to the development of the co-operative movement. Using Ostrom's principles of collective action to delve deeper into mutuality, and using ICA principles as a theoretical lens, I now investigate six cases of co-operative practice in growing SEs.

Strand 2: Showcasing platforms for co-operation

Until the 2002 government consultation on the community interest company, the discourse of heroic social entrepreneurs and SE champions highlighted by Ganz *et al.* (2018) had little traction (Ridley-Duff, 2007; Bull, 2015). Even today, its traction remains relatively weak because practitioners show a clear preference for identifying with 'social enterprise', not 'social entrepreneurship' (Dey and Teasdale, 2016). Nevertheless, terminology that distinguishes collective and mutual approaches to SE from more individualized approaches has not established itself successfully (see Spear, 2006; Scott Cato *et al.*, 2008). Strand 2, therefore, places emphasis on helping students to understand mutuality as the route to CSE.

Ridley-Duff and Bull (2016: 7) contend that:

Mutuality implies a bi-directional or network relationship in which parties help, support and supervise each other. This is qualitatively different from the uni-directional relationship between owner-manager and employee in a private enterprise, or the chain of control (philanthropist to trustee [...], trustee to manager, manager to worker, and worker to beneficiary) in a charity. While charity can be present in mutual relations, it is normally framed in law and practice as a financial and managerial one-way relationship in which trustees give and direct while beneficiaries accept and obey. This asymmetry in obligations (i.e. the lack of reciprocal inter-dependence) clearly distinguishes mutuality from charity.

Mutual societies share some of the characteristics of co-operatives (for example, member ownership, community orientation), but – according to Weishaupt (2018) – they are organized to share financial risks, not organize production. Mutuality in financial ventures was established through the case of *Municipal Mutual Insurance Ltd* v. *Hills* (1929–32):

... the cardinal requirement is that all the contributors to the common fund must be entitled to participate in the surplus and that all the participators in the surplus must be contributors to the common fund; in other words, there must be complete identity between the contributors and the participators. If this requirement is satisfied, the particular form which the association takes is immaterial. (HMRC, 2013)

Mutuals, therefore, can be formed using a variety of legal forms when a common fund is created for a given shared purpose. As such, mutuals can be good vehicles for building the co-operative economy where laws recognize the value of permitting them to invest in SE networks, not just property and insurance schemes (see Foote Whyte and King Whyte, 1991; Restakis, 2010). However, mutuality need not be confined to financial risk sharing.

Ostrom's (1990) first five principles for collective action provide a lens through which to examine mutuality. In her work, she extends mutual principles to resource management, governance rights, social reporting and conflict resolution. She observed that sustainability is strengthened where: members have both rights and obligations to maintain shared resources (principle 2); members have governance rights linked to their active use of, or contribution to, a resource (principle 3); the results of resource monitoring are defined by, and reported to, users (not remote government regulators) (principle 4); and members organize low-cost conflict resolution systems that are graduated, equitable and respectful of members' rights and obligations (principle 5).

Six examples of mutuality in the social solidarity economy

These mutual principles will now be used to investigate six cases from the wider SSE: Kiva; Creative Commons; Loomio Co-operative Ltd; FairShares Association Ltd; Kickstarter; and Change.org. The case studies were developed as follows. In the first phase, materials from websites, articles and public documents were gathered together and organized into tables to investigate their commitment to mutuality using Ostrom's (1990) first five principles of collective action (for the tables, see Ridley-Duff and Bull, 2018). Using this information, a second phase of analysis was undertaken by further deconstructing the cases using the ICA's seven co-operative principles as a theoretical lens. In doing so, insights were generated regarding the level of commitment to mutuality as well as the seven co-operative principles.

Kiva (kiva.org) and Creative Commons (creativecommons.org) were established as non-profit associations. They illustrate how mutuality can be practised in charitable organizations. Kiva has a mission to alleviate poverty by connecting lenders and borrowers (entrepreneurs and field partners) through a web platform. It establishes that lending does not have to be based on the choice of gifting money (charity) or charging interest on loans (commerce). Kiva lenders have their money returned, but do not charge interest. Returns are social, not financial. Even so, around $2.5 million is raised *each day* through the web platform to enable individuals and organized networks to allocate funds to field partners who support local projects. Lenders can join kiva.org with an initial capital contribution of $25.

Creative Commons, on the other hand, creates a system for mutualizing intellectual property in a 'commons' by facilitating the legal sharing and distribution of creative works using six open-source, machine-readable licences. This approach challenges the dominance of private sector copyright and patent laws. Authors retain copyright while permitting others to adapt and benefit from replicating their works. Over half of the 1.2 billion works issued with Creative Commons licences have been published using either 'BY' (Attribution) or 'BY-SA' (Attribution-ShareAlike) licences (see https://stateof.creativecommons.org). The 'BY' tag indicates that any derivative works must give an attribution to the author of the original work. The 'SA' tag indicates that derivative works must be shared using the same licence as the original. This effectively prevents privatization of intellectual property (IP) by ensuring that new works have the same Creative Commons licence as the original. Importantly, both licences permit users to benefit commercially from building on existing works, but do so by *sharing* (not transferring) property rights.

Loomio Co-operative Ltd and FairShares Association Ltd are examples of 'new co-operativism' (Vieta, 2010) that illustrate how mutuality can be extended through multi-stakeholder governance. Loomio Co-operative is a New Zealand company that creates safe, secure, searchable websites for democratic discussions and decision-making (see loomio.org). FairShares Association is a UK company that mutualizes IP to support solidarity co-operatives, social enterprise incubators and related knowledge transfer initiatives (see fairshares.coop). Both are registered companies that secure their co-operative identity through the Co-operative Marque[5] rather than their legal form. Although Loomio Co-operative is run as a worker co-operative, it has a multi-stakeholder board that reflects its history of crowdfunding and working with a patent investor. Its open-source software facilitates the making and storing of deliberations and decisions in searchable archives on cloud-based network servers. FairShares Association has founder, labour and user members within its network of academics, educators and consultants. Both co-operatives use Creative Commons to publish IP. Loomio Co-operative publishes its handbook on co-operative management using a Creative Commons licence (see loomio.coop). Similarly, FairShares Association publishes the FairShares Model using a range of Creative Commons licences so it can be adapted and developed by social/blue economy incubators called FairShares Labs (see fairshares.coop/fairshareslabs) and researchers at the FairShares Institute for Cooperative Social Entrepreneurship (fsi.coop). Lastly, both Loomio Co-operative and FairShares Association use loomio.org to promote mutuality in governance. In both cases, any member can propose ideas and initiate a vote without first securing board support. Decisions are made on a one-member, one-vote basis.

Kickstarter and Change.org are both companies that illustrate how mutuality can be organized through benefit corporations (B Corps), a new legal form originating from the USA. Kickstarter's mission is to bring creative projects to life through rewards-based crowdfunding. Change.org expresses its mission as 'empower[ing] people to create the change they want to see'. Kickstarter.com enables site members to raise funds for artistic projects and innovative products. Charity fundraising and private sector financial investment are both barred from the platform – each project is geared towards catalysing direct mutual relations between producers and users based on non-financial (product-based) rewards. Change.org enables site members to petition for social change. Interestingly, their dispute resolution guidelines suggest that members can start *counter*-petitions if they object to another's campaign. The B-Corp legal framework enables organization members to prioritize mission and impact over financial returns, and promote member participation in social change by offering technology for social campaigning free at the point of use. Importantly, the platform does not encourage dependence on charities, foundations, governments or private institutional investors.

Deconstructing the six cases using co-operative principles

Table 9.2 shows how these cases can be meaningfully evaluated using co-operative principles (CPs). All projects offer 'open membership' (CP 1) of their platforms and/or the legal entity that controls them: Kiva.org offers open membership of its investment platform; Creative Commons offers free use of its products; Loomio Co-operative offers free membership of its decision-making platform (and the ability to create new sites); FairShares Association offers free (non-profit) use of its documentation, diagnostic tools and rules generator, plus enhanced commercial rights for members; Kickstarter and Change.org both offer platform membership that is free at the point of use supported by a business model that recovers funds after a successful campaign.

Democratic control (CP 2) is stronger in the non-profit associations and co-operative enterprises that admit members to governing bodies that make strategic decisions. This is less transparent in the B Corps organizations (Kickstarter and Change.org), despite a legal requirement to engage with stakeholders and consider stakeholder interests. However, the products available from the B Corps go furthest in facilitating member-determined allocations of time, energy and money to bring about civic and economic change.

All the platforms catalyse opportunities for economic participation (CP 3) by making it possible to accept capital contributions and offer rewards that create the value that members wish to see. Creative Commons and Kiva ask only for donations towards the costs of maintaining systems for sharing their IP. Loomio Co-operative and FairShares Association both offer ways for members to subscribe capital (either through subscriptions to use the products, or subscriptions to cover the cost of maintaining web resources) alongside shared (member) control over the way surpluses are reinvested. As B Corps, Kickstarter and Change.org can offer shares to members and pay them dividends.

Table 9.2: Deconstructing six SSE cases using ICA principles

Co-operative principle (CP)	Kiva	Creative Commons	Loomio Co-operative	FairShares Association	Kickstarter	Change.org
Open membership (1)	✓ (Product)	✓ (Association) +Open product	✓ (Co-op) +Open product	✓ (Co-op) +Open product	✓ (Product)	✓ (Product)
Democratic member control (2)	At level of use	At level of use +Affiliate network	✓ (Use and board)	✓ (Use and board)	At level of use	At level of use
Member economic participation (3)	✓ (Product)	(Funded by donations)	In capital, surplus and dividends	In capital, surplus and dividends	✓ (Product)	(Funded by purchases)
Autonomy and independence (4)	✓	✓	✓	✓	✓	✓
Member and public education (5)	✓	✓	✓	✓	✓	✓
Inter-co-operation (6)	✓ (Field partners)	✓ (Affiliate network)	✓	✓	In campaigns	In campaigns
Concern for community (7)	✓	✓	✓	✓	✓	✓

The organizations protect their autonomy (CP 4) through carefully crafted legal structures and operational norms. Notably, Kickstarter bars the listing of charity fundraising projects as well as private investment opportunities. The non-profit association status of Kiva and Creative Commons protects them from overzealous regulatory control by either the state or private financial institutions. Similarly, the co-operative structures at Loomio Co-operative and FairShares Association encourage democratic member control that protects them from regulation by the institutions of private investors (CP 2).

There are transparent reporting activities by Kiva, Creative Commons, Kickstarter and Change.org to educate the public about their impacts (CP 5). Kickstarter, Loomio Co-operative and FairShares Association publish educational materials for public benefit (CP 5) using Creative Commons licences that produce a further level of community benefit (CP 7). By offering specific features for members to form subgroups that support collective efforts at social change, Kiva, Loomio Co-operative, FairShares Association and Change.org all promote inter-co-operation (CP 6). Indeed, the observed use of each other's products (such as FairShares Association using loomio.org, and Loomio Co-operative raising funds through crowdfunding, and active use of Creative Commons by FairShares Association and Loomio Co-operative) is further evidence of the way the SSE promotes inter-co-operation through both market and non-market exchange mechanisms (CP 6).

To summarize, Strand 2 invites students to study organizations using Ostrom's design principles for mutuality and the ICA's CPs. These enhance students' understanding of mutuality and co-operation and provide them with a lens through which to judge both formal co-operatives and co-operative practices in the wider SSE. The results do two things: first, they problematize the definition of 'true' (bona fide) co-operatives as they may not need to be constituted under co-operative law provided that they are structured to ensure mutuality; second, co-operative principles can be enacted through any legal form that provides legal defences for mutuality, member control, democratic participation and social trading activity. The six SEs chosen demonstrate how the *infrastructure* of the SSE is developing and challenging neoliberal doctrine through the creation of cultures that support mutuality and the enactment of CPs.

Conclusions: CSE as a challenge to neoliberalism

While none of the six SEs discussed are registered using laws exclusive to co-operatives, they show evidence of commitment to CPs that constitute a coherent challenge to neoliberalism (Table 9.2). This adds to MacPherson's (2015) and Auderbrand *et al.*'s (2017) arguments for co-operative studies in both SE and mainstream management education. For example, by raising $2.5 million a day without paying any interest, Kiva challenges the assumption that you cannot raise money for private and co-operative ventures without offering investors a financial return. By creating a licensing system for the sharing of IP, Creative Commons challenges the assumption that property rights must be transferred by labour providers to capital owners to gain recognition and/or make a living. By creating a decision-making platform that normalizes co-operative democracy, Loomio challenges the idea that efficiency depends on the creation of a management hierarchy. Similarly, by showcasing and offering IP that advances polycentric ownership, governance and management (Ostrom, 2009), the FairShares Model undermines that argument for unitary boards in the UK Corporate Code of Governance (Combined Code). By creating a funding system for artists and creative projects, Kickstarter challenges the notion that creative ideas must be pitched to the 'great and good' or professional investors to get funded. Lastly, by providing platforms that facilitate direct democracy across social movements, Change.org challenges the idea that social change comes only through parliamentary (liberal) democracy.

When all these examples are taken together, they show that the rise of SE creates opportunities in a wide range of university courses to enrich discussions of both the history of co-operatives and their future potential as well as their operating models and organizing principles. However, to take advantage of that opportunity, scholars of co-operatives first need to accept two arguments: that co-operators built important parts of the SE movement and contributed substantively to SE theory; and that co-operative practices within the wider SSE are informing new co-operativism (Vieta, 2010). In this chapter, I have presented evidence to support both arguments.

Strand 1 illustrated how studying the history of SE development in Scotland, the North of England and London exposed the deep connection between co-operators and SE. Furthermore, it shows that co-operators developed CSE through the application of co-operative values and principles absent from mainstream co-operative institutions at that time. Strand 2, on the other hand, deployed Ostrom's (1990) and the ICA's principles to deconstruct six SEs. While none were incorporated under co-operative law, their commitment to co-operative values and principles provides a starting point for studies of new co-operativism (Vieta, 2010; Ridley-Duff, 2015).

There is a need to re-establish the umbilical cord that joins co-operators and co-operatives to the wider field of SE. First, the findings suggest that educators identifying as SE scholars can legitimately introduce the study of co-operatives into curricula to problematize and challenge Ganz *et al.*'s (2018) contention that 'social enterprise is not social change'. Based on the material in this chapter, I argue that SE *is* social change when it is driven by CSE. Second, educators identifying as scholars of co-operation and co-operatives can productively engage with SE by introducing the social innovations of co-operators into curricula. By identifying and studying how they overcame their 'frustrations with the co-operative movement' through social auditing (Spreckley, 2008), solidarity co-operatives (Ridley-Duff, 2015) and platform co-operatives (Scholz and Schneider, 2016), curricula will be enriched. Furthermore, such social innovations show that co-operators challenge, rather than reinforce, neoliberalism. CSE is a commitment to mutuality, member control, democratic governance and trading activities characteristic of new co-operativism that gives more active consideration to the interests of labour, the local community and wider society. It offers a new path for people to reclaim power, infuse their enterprises politically through trading for a social purpose and building resilient alternatives to neoliberalism.

Notes

[1] Cliff Southcombe is now Managing Director of Social Enterprise International Ltd, a partner in the European FairShares Labs for Social and Blue Innovation Project (see www.fairshareslab.org).

[2] See www.socialauditnetwork.org.uk/john-pearce (accessed 12 April 2018).

[3] ICOM (Industrial Common Ownership Movement) produced model rules for worker co-operatives in 1976. Over the next decade, over 1,000 new worker co-operatives formed (Cornforth *et al.*, 1988). ICOF trades today under the name Co-operative and Community Finance.

[4] SEP (Social Enterprise Partnership), SEL (Social Enterprise London), SEC (Social Enterprise Coalition) and UEL (University of East London) offered a BA in Social Enterprise.

[5] See http://identity.coop for information on the Co-operative Marque.

References

Atherton, J., Birchall, J., Mayo, E. and Simon, G. (2011) *Practical Tools for Defining Co-operatives*. Manchester: Co-operatives UK.

Audebrand, L.K., Camus, A. and Michaud, V. (2017) 'A mosquito in the classroom: Using the cooperative business model to foster paradoxical thinking in management education'. *Journal of Management Education*, 41 (2), 216–48.

Balnave, N. and Patmore, G. (2012) 'Rochdale consumer co-operatives in Australia: Decline and survival'. *Business History*, 54 (6), 986–1003.

Borzaga, C. and Defourny, J. (eds) (2001) *The Emergence of Social Enterprise*. London: Routledge.

Bull, M. (2015) 'Shape sorting: Towards defining social enterprise in the UK'. Paper presented at the International Social Innovation Research Conference (ISIRC), York, 6–8 September 2015.

Companies House (1998) *Memorandum of Association for Social Enterprise London, Company Number 03502587*. Online. https://beta.companieshouse. gov.uk/company/03502587/filing-history (accessed 6 January 2018).

Co-operative Commission (2001) *The Co-operative Advantage: Creating a successful family of co-operative businesses*. Manchester: The Co-operative Commission. Online. https://tinyurl.com/y6qd2hnq (accessed 9 March 2019).

Conaty, P. (2014) *Social Co-operatives: A democratic co-production agenda for care services in the UK*. Manchester: Co-operatives UK.

Conaty, P., Bird, A. and Ross, P. (2016) *Not Alone: Trade union and co-operative solutions for self-employed workers*. Manchester: Co-operatives UK.

Co-operatives UK (2018) 'Start a co-op'. Online. www.uk.coop/developing-co-ops/ start-co-operative (accessed 20 March 2018).

Cornforth, C., Thomas, A., Spear, R. and Lewis, J. (1988) *Developing Successful Worker Co-operatives*. London: SAGE Publications.

Defourny, J., Hulgård, L. and Pestoff, V. (eds) (2014) *Social Enterprise and the Third Sector: Changing European landscapes in a comparative perspective*. London: Routledge.

Defourny, J. and Nyssens, M. (2017) 'Fundamentals for an international typology of social enterprise models'. *Voluntas*, 28 (6), 2469–97.

de Peuter, G. and Dyer-Witheford, N. (2010) 'Commons and cooperatives'. *Affinities: A Journal of Radical Theory, Culture, and Action*, 4 (1), 30–56.

Dey, P. and Teasdale, S. (2016) 'The tactical mimicry of social enterprise strategies: Acting "as if" in the everyday life of third sector organizations'. *Organization*, 23 (4), 485–504.

Elkington, J. (1978) 'Business through the looking-glass'. *New Scientist*, 7 September, 692–3. Online. https://t.co/lgj9uhGZ5K (accessed 14 September 2018).

Elkington, J. (2004) 'Enter the triple bottom line'. In Henriques, A. and Richardson, J. (eds) *The Triple Bottom Line: Does it all add up?* London: Earthscan, 1–16.

Foote Whyte, W. and King Whyte, K. (1991) *Making Mondragon: The growth and dynamics of the worker cooperative complex*. 2nd ed. Ithaca, NY: ILR Press.

Ganz, M., Kay, T. and Spicer, J. (2018) 'Social enterprise is not social change'. *Stanford Social Innovation Review*, 16 (2), 59–60.

Gertler, M.E. (2004) 'Synergy and strategic advantage: Cooperatives and sustainable development'. *Journal of Cooperatives*, 18, 32–46.

Gonzales, V. (2010) 'Italian social cooperatives and the development of civic capacity: A case of cooperative renewal?'. *Affinities: A Journal of Radical Theory, Culture, and Action*, 4 (1), 225–51.

HMRC (2013) *Business Income Manual*. BIM24025. Online. www.gov. uk/hmrc-internal-manuals/business-income-manual/bim24025 (accessed 12 February 2019).

Kerlin, J.A. (2013) 'Defining social enterprise across different contexts: A conceptual framework based on institutional factors'. *Nonprofit and Voluntary Sector Quarterly*, 42 (1), 84–108.

Klein, N. (2007) *The Shock Doctrine: The rise of disaster capitalism*. New York: Metropolitan Books.

ICA (International Co-operative Alliance) (2015) *Guidance Notes to the Co-operative Principles*. International Co-operative Alliance. Online. https://tinyurl.com/y6odqr5c (accessed 12 February 2019).

Lacey, S. (2009) *Beyond a Fair Price: The co-operative movement and fair trade* (Co-operative College Paper 14). Manchester: Co-operative College.

Laville, J.-L. (2015) 'Social and solidarity economy in historical perspective'. In Utting, P. (ed.) *Social and Solidarity Economy: Beyond the fringe*. London: Zed Books, 41–56.

MacPherson, I. (2015) 'Mainstreaming some lacunae: Developing co-operative studies as an interdisciplinary, international field of enquiry'. In Woodin, T. (ed.) *Co-operation, Learning and Co-operative Values: Contemporary issues in education*. London: Routledge, 177–94.

Mills, C. and Davies, W. (2013) *Blueprint for a Co-operative Decade*. Brussels: International Co-operative Alliance. Online. https://tinyurl.com/ybt4ul7r (accessed 27 January 2019).

Molina, F. (2012) 'Fagor Electrodomésticos: The multinationalisation of a Basque co-operative, 1955–2010'. *Business History*, 54 (6), 945–63.

Neary, M. and Winn, J. (2017) 'Beyond public and private: A framework for co-operative higher education'. *Open Library of Humanities*, 3 (2), Article 2, 1–36. Online. https://tinyurl.com/y696xxza (accessed 24 January 2019).

Ostrom, E. (1990) *Governing the Commons: The evolution of institutions for collective action*. Cambridge: Cambridge University Press.

Ostrom, E. (2009) 'Beyond markets and states: Polycentric governance of complex economic systems'. Prize Lecture (Nobel Prize in Economics), Stockholm University, 8 December 2009. Online. https://tinyurl.com/y39o93q7 (accessed 2 February 2019).

Ostrom, E., Burger, J., Field, C.B., Norgaard, R.B. and Policansky, D. (1999) 'Revisiting the commons: Local lessons, global challenges'. *Science*, 284 (5412), 278–82.

Paranque, B. and Willmott, H. (2014) 'Cooperatives – saviours or gravediggers of capitalism? Critical performativity and the John Lewis Partnership'. *Organization*, 21 (5), 604–25.

Parigi, V.K., Thomas, K. and Misra, V. (2005) *Social Audit: A toolkit: A guide for performance improvement and outcome measurement*. Hyderabad: Centre for Good Governance. Online. https://tinyurl.com/ydxsew37 (accessed 2 February 2019).

Paterson, A.G. (2010) 'A buzz between rural cooperation and the online swarm'. *Affinities: A Journal of Radical Theory, Culture, and Action*, 4 (1), 83–109.

Pearce, J. (2003) *Social Enterprise in Anytown*. London: Calouste Gulbenkian Foundation.

Peattie, K. and Morley, A. (2008) *Social Enterprises: Diversity and dynamics, contexts and contributions*. Cardiff: BRASS / ESRC / Social Enterprise Coalition.

Restakis, J. (2010) *Humanizing the Economy: Co-operatives in the age of capital.* Gabriola Island, BC: New Society Publishers.

Ridley-Duff, R. (2007) 'Communitarian perspectives on social enterprise'. *Corporate Governance: An International Review*, 15 (2), 382–92.

Ridley-Duff, R. (2015) *The Case for FairShares: A new model for social enterprise development and the strengthening of the social and solidarity economy.* Sheffield: FairShares Association.

Ridley-Duff, R. (2018) 'Diversity, co-operation and the FairShares Model'. Keynote presentation at the UK Society for Co-operative Studies (UKSCS) Annual Conference, Sheffield, 31 August–2 September 2018. Online. www.youtube.com/watch?v=KFX58dfFcsw (accessed 20 October 2018).

Ridley-Duff, R. and Bull, M. (2011) *Understanding Social Enterprise: Theory and practice.* London: SAGE Publications.

Ridley-Duff, R. and Bull, M. (2016) *Understanding Social Enterprise: Theory and practice.* 2nd ed. London: SAGE Publications.

Ridley-Duff, R. and Bull, M. (2018) 'The coming of age of the social solidarity economy'. Paper presented at the Welfare Societies in Transition – 3rd EMES-Polanyi International Seminar, Roskilde, Denmark, 16–17 April 2018.

Ridley-Duff, R. and Southcombe, C. (2012) 'The Social Enterprise Mark: A critical review of its conceptual dimensions'. *Social Enterprise Journal*, 8 (3), 178–200.

Ridley-Duff, R. and Wren, D. (2018) 'Social enterprise, sustainable development and the FairShares model'. *Japanese Journal of Human Welfare Studies*, 11 (1): 23–42.

Ridley-Duff, R., Schmıdtchen, R., Arnold-Schaarschmidt, M., Vuković, S., Klercq, J., Southcombe, C., Trzecınskı, C., Pataki, V., Oparaocha, K., Bedőné Károly, J. and Wren, D. (2018) *Methodology for Creating a FairShares Lab.* Erasmus+ project number 2016-1-DE02-KA204-003397, DOI: 10.13140/RG.2.2.11461.50404.

Scholz, T. and Schneider, N. (eds) (2016) *Ours to Hack and to Own: The rise of platform cooperativism, a new vision for the future of work and a fairer internet.* New York: OR Books.

Scott Cato, M., Arthur, L., Keenoy, T. and Smith, R. (2008) 'Entrepreneurial energy: Associative entrepreneurship in the renewable energy sector in Wales'. *International Journal of Entrepreneurial Behaviour and Research*, 14 (5), 313–29.

Social Enterprise London (1998) *Memorandum of Association, Company Number 03502587.* Online. https://beta.companieshouse.gov.uk/company/03502587/filing-history (accessed 8 March 2019).

Spear, R. (2006) 'Social entrepreneurship: A different model?'. *International Journal of Social Economics*, 33 (5–6), 399–410.

Spreckley, F. (1981) *Social Audit: A management tool for co-operative working.* Leeds: Beechwood College.

Spreckley, F. (2008) *The Social Audit Toolkit* (4th edn). Herefordshire: Local Livelihood.

Teasdale, S. (2012) 'What's in a name? Making sense of social enterprise discourses'. *Public Policy and Administration*, 27 (2), 99–119.

Toms, S. (2012) 'Producer co-operatives and economic efficiency: Evidence from the nineteenth-century cotton textile industry'. *Business History*, 54 (6), 855–82.

Utting, P. (2015) 'Introduction: The challenge of scaling up social and solidarity economy'. In Utting, P. (ed.) *Social and Solidarity Economy: Beyond the fringe.* London: Zed Books, 1–37.

van der Veen, E.W. (2010) 'The new university cooperative: Reclaiming higher education: Prioritizing social justice and ecological sustainability'. *Affinities: A Journal of Radical Theory, Culture, and Action*, 4 (1), 199–204.

Vieta, M. (2010) 'The new cooperativism'. *Affinities: A Journal of Radical Theory, Culture, and Action*, 4 (1), 1–11.

Voinea, A. (2015) 'Pauline Green to step down as International Co-operative Alliance president'. *Co-operative News*, 26 June. Online. https://tinyurl.com/y7bga6kr (accessed 25 January 2019).

Voinea, A. (2016) 'Should co-ops call themselves social enterprises?'. *Co-operative News*, 13 September. Online. https://tinyurl.com/y95an2xg (accessed 25 January 2019).

Wanyama, F.O. (2014) *Cooperatives and the Sustainable Development Goals: A contribution to the post-2015 development debate.* Geneva: International Labour Organization.

Weishaupt, T. (2018) 'Mutuals in China: The case for mutuality type social enterprises and FairShares'. Presentation to Managing People in Times of Social Transformation (MOST School), Hang Seng Management College, 4–6 July 2018.

Wenger, E. (1998) *Communities of Practice: Learning, meaning, and identity.* Cambridge: Cambridge University Press.

Wilson, M., Shaw, L. and Lonergan, G. (2012) *Our Story: Rochdale Pioneers Museum.* Rochdale: Rochdale Pioneers Museum. Online. https://tinyurl.com/yc8rn54z (accessed 27 January 2019).

Chapter 10

Reimagining education policy: Co-operative schools and the social solidarity alternative

Deborah Ralls

Across the globe, social and solidarity economics is gaining in popularity, representing the belief that relationships based on solidarity and co-operation are fundamental components in developing sustainable and inclusive economic activities and policies, rather than individualistic, market-driven approaches serving private interests. However, so far there has been little focus on how social and solidarity approaches to *education* could help to lay the foundations for a viable alternative to market capitalism, and democracy that is defined in terms of individualized consumer choice.

This chapter explores relational forms of democratic engagement and considers both the potential and the challenges for co-operative schools in England in helping to redefine an education system that is fit for a social solidarity economy. Schools are centre stage in the development of a social solidarity economy. They are the key institutions that can foster a democratic culture and allow it to flourish in the future (Audsley *et al.*, 2013). Indeed, Apple (2011: 27–8) advocates that schools have a pivotal role in the production of our identities, with 'lasting effects on the dispositions and values that we do and do not act upon, on who we think we are and on who we think we can become'.

Co-operative opportunities in the English education marketplace

In England, schools and stakeholders have, over the past few decades, been repositioned as 'producers' and 'consumers' (Baquedano-Lopez *et al.*, 2013) within the changing English education landscape of policy reforms. When the first co-operative school was established in 2008, centralization under the then Labour Government concentrated on developing sector-wide education standards, target setting and monitoring (Whitty, 2006).

Marketization efforts were focused on the secondary school system, with the view that there was a need to increase the diversity of schools available and offer greater choice to children and their families (Lupton and Obolenskaya, 2013). Following the election of a Conservative–Liberal Democrat Coalition Government in 2010, the centralization of the English school system rapidly accelerated, further reducing the powers of local government in the management of state school education. The continuation of this direction of travel of the future of English education was clearly articulated in the Coalition Government's White Paper *The Importance of Teaching* in 2010: 'It is our ambition that Academy status should be the norm for all state schools, with schools enjoying direct funding and full independence from central and local bureaucracy' (DfE (Department for Education), 2010: 52).

Since the election of a Conservative Government in 2015, policy has favoured a move towards schools forming multi-academy trusts (MATs), rather than remaining 'as standalone academies' (DfE, 2016: 57). Business language such as 'shareholders' and 'company directors' is used to provide schools with guidance on the governance of a MAT:

> In a multi-academy trust, a single trust is responsible for a number of academies. The MAT consists of the members and the trustees. The members are akin to the shareholders of a company. They have ultimate control over the academy trust, with the ability to appoint some of the trustees and the right to amend the trust's articles of association. (NCTL (National College for Teaching and Leadership), 2014: 4)

Themes of marketization and centralization (Whitty, 2006) have developed apace under the Conservative Government (since 2015), resulting in fundamental changes for the ways in which schools and local authorities operate. A school's identity is increasingly associated with a particular brand or sponsor. Its ability to survive not only depends on the school being viewed as a 'good' or high-performing school but also on its capacity for attracting other schools to its 'brand' – or how far other schools see it as a 'brand fit' for their MAT. The extent of the competition in the English education marketplace is starkly illustrated by figures released by DfE in September 2018, showing that there were 1,133 different sponsors of academy schools in England (DfE, 2018).

Yet, in spite of these developments there are spaces for education institutions to think and act relationally. This has been illustrated by the growth of the co-operative school system in England. Co-operative schools are a particular type of state school that developed mainly in England. In spite of the increasing tendency of English policymakers to view school–stakeholder engagement as an individualistic relationship between producer and consumer, the co-operative school ethos sets out to promote a broader, more relational understanding of civic engagement through co-operative pedagogy, governance models and curriculum. The growth of co-operative schools was rapid and the widespread appeal unprecedented, with the number of co-operative schools expanding from the first co-operative school in 2008 to more than 600 in 2017, although numbers have recently declined. Co-operative schools and their attempts to become more democratic are both complex and differentiated. As with other spheres of co-operative practice, schools are able to interpret the co-operative values and principles flexibly. As a result, individual schools may choose only to focus on one particular area of co-operative education, for example, pedagogy, governance or co-operative approaches to business, and not on others. The very notion of a 'co-operative school' can thus perhaps best be described as a 'hybrid', which has grafted co-operative ideas onto mainstream institutions (Woodin, 2015: 6). There are three main types of co-operative school:

1. *Co-operative foundation trust schools*: In response to the Education and Inspections Act 2006, which enabled a school to own its own assets, employ staff directly and set its own admission arrangements, the Co-operative College developed a co-operative trust model, called a foundation trust. This permitted a school to become a multi-stakeholder co-operative that provided a stakeholder governance model that included parents, carers, staff, learners and the local community (in contrast to a standard trust model). Each trust was an independent co-operative in its own right (Shaw, 2014).

2. *Co-operative academy trust schools*: The adoption of the academy trust model grew apace following the Coalition Government's Academies Act 2010, which meant that all existing state schools could become academy schools, reporting directly to the Department for Education rather than to local education authorities. A similar multi-stakeholder model to that of co-operative foundation trust schools was developed for academies, with a governance structure that included an active role for stakeholder groups. The co-operative academy trust model received government approval in 2011 (Shaw, 2014).

3. *Co-operative Academies Trust schools:* Although similar in their ethos and governance structure, unlike the foundation trust schools and co-operative academy trust schools, the 18 schools (as of March 2019)

in the Co-operative Academies Trust are directly sponsored by the Co-operative Group, and as such are a part of the worldwide co-operative business structure in a way that the other schools are not:

> What makes our Trust unique is that we are sponsored by the Co-operative Group. That close relationship means that we benefit from all of the business expertise that has seen the Co-op grow to one of the most respected, successful businesses in the country (Co-operative Academies Trust, 2018a).

Through their co-operative governance structure and adherence to the international co-operative values, each type of co-operative school looks to develop forms of engagement based on more equal partnerships. Moreover, through the everyday enactment of the international co-operative values (self-help, self-responsibility, democracy, equality, equity and solidarity) in their governance, pedagogy, curriculum and ethos, the co-operative school model could have a profound and lasting effect not only on the way that children and young people see themselves and their roles as citizens but also on how they view society and the economy and the benefits of more collective social solidarity approaches.

Co-operative schools thus have the potential to provide 'counter-narratives' or alternative ways of seeing engagement that challenge unilateral and individualistic approaches to school–stakeholder relationships (Thomson *et al.*, 2012). These narratives offer the opportunity to view school–stakeholder engagement 'otherwise', representing engagement as a shared school and stakeholder approach that could be applied more widely to support the underlying principles of a social solidarity economy. In addition, changes in approaches to local government, namely the increasing number of co-operative councils across the UK, could offer spaces of possibility in which co-operative schools can manoeuvre to enact thicker, more relational forms of engagement with their stakeholders (students, parents/carers and community members), as part of the broader prefigurative change required for the development of a social solidarity vision of education.

Co-operative schools: Building a social solidarity alternative from the bottom up

How can co-operative schools help to forge trustworthy relationships with their stakeholders, in order 'to develop a sense of generalized trust towards the citizenry at large' (Cordelli, 2015: 98)? In terms of understanding what should happen in thick, collective forms of democracy in schools and *how* it should happen, Audsley *et al.* (2013) propose a starting point for identifying democratic decision-making processes: the internal culture of the school. They suggest exploring how the school approaches 'active citizenship', by which they mean 'teamwork, collective decision making and political problem solving' (ibid.: 29). Policymakers should view a school as a 'civic institution' that helps students and other stakeholders to develop 'their ability to participate in public life' (ibid.: 13). They refer to a school that sets out to operate in this way as a 'citizen school', which they define as 'a school that explicitly creates a democratic culture through its role as a civic institution. It does this by enabling young people and other members of the school community to develop their citizenship and their ability to participate in public life' (ibid.: 3). Indeed, Audsley *et al.* (2013) identify co-operative schools as a group of schools that are explicitly setting out to be 'citizen schools', in order to develop 'active citizens' who bear: 'civic responsibility, pride, and ... a sense of agency: a feeling that they can shape the world around them through taking civic action with others' (ibid.: 29).

The notion of 'active citizenship' chimes with the work of Fielding (1999, 2001, 2006, 2010), who envisages student voice as an antidote to what he terms 'high performance schooling'. Rather than student voice being used as 'largely an instrumental undertaking orientated towards increased measurable, organizational performance' (Fielding, 2010: 66), Fielding promotes the idea of student voice as the process of developing more reciprocal relationships among students and between students and staff, relationships that are 'animated and enabled primarily through a communal way of working' (Fielding, 2006: 311). These two-way dialogic encounters between students and teachers create what Fielding refers to as 'spaces for restless encounters between adults and young people in which they are able to re-see and re-engage with each other in creative, holistic and potentially transformational ways' (Fielding, 2010: 61).

The co-operative school governance model was established to counter narratives based on 'functional' or 'instrumental' relationships (Fielding, 2010) that are defined by the specific roles or tasks that a governor has to perform and to offer instead more opportunities for the type of 'restless encounter' advocated by Fielding (ibid.: 61), the intention being that co-operative governance structures would offer the possibility for building relationships that attempt to engage diverse stakeholder voices in 'a more dialogic, reciprocal way of working' (ibid.: 62).

By focusing on building more reciprocal forms of relationships between a school and its stakeholders, a co-operative governance model has the potential to develop a more communal approach to school–stakeholder engagement. In developing such an approach, the importance of communication in establishing the sense of 'a common interest' in education is vital. A co-operative school should, therefore, aim to provide a social environment where learning in and out of school are continually linked by developing a shared understanding of the connections between individuals' diverse social situations and experiences, and the implications of these situations and experiences on an individual's education and life outside the school's four walls (Dewey, 1966).

The implication is that a more reciprocal and communal approach to school–stakeholder engagement necessitates spaces in which to develop relationships that promote the sharing of knowledge based on the recognition that *all* citizens share a common interest in the education and well-being of children and young people. Co-operative governance models based on democratic accountability can provide spaces for such interest to be shared and acknowledged and for education to be developed as a 'collective societal endeavour' (UNESCO, 2015: 83). Indeed, in the absence of such spaces, Dyson (2003) suggests that schools will struggle to gain an understanding of the assets of its stakeholders and will thus be less likely to challenge deficit views of certain communities as 'impoverished'.

Democratic engagement as a collective endeavour: Becoming relational through co-operation

There is an emerging area of research that considers how theories of the relational can be used to support the development of policies and institutional structures that promote social justice and solidarity (McLaughlin and Clarke, 2010; Cordelli, 2015; Donati and Archer, 2015; Burkitt, 2016). Donati and Archer (2015: 15) suggest that:

> Justice and social solidarity require a vision that puts the needs and rights of all members of a community in relation with one another. We discover, in short, that we are all profoundly interdependent. The decisions, choices, and actions of each of us are not purely individual acts, but are arrived at in relation to and with others.

Conceptually, therefore, notions of 'relational' forms of engagement are closely aligned with the mutualization and collectivity promoted by the co-operative movement. A unilateral approach to engagement emphasizes '"power over" others and the capacity to get others to do one's bidding' (Warren *et al.*, 2009: 2213) and could, therefore, be seen as more closely aligned with an individualized and marketized approach to education. A relational approach, in contrast, is defined as a school and its stakeholders getting things done collectively, starting from the point of their 'shared interest in advancing the education and well-being of children' (ibid.: 2213). This latter approach is in line with the values of a co-operative school – and the fundamental principles of the social solidarity economy, pointing to a different power dynamic in school engagement policy and practice. The founding principle of this approach is that 'relationships matter ... engagement, then, should be about creating the relationships that provide a foundation for long-term and sustainable change in schools, not a quick fix to any school's problems' (ibid.: 2248).

Adopting a relational approach to engagement relationships, both in the school context and in wider society, is not to suggest that the progress of the individual should be ignored, but rather to stress the reality of our existence as 'subjects-in-relation' with other people and 'the non-social world', rather than as entirely autonomous beings (Donati and Archer, 2015). Moreover, relational scholars (McLaughlin and Clarke, 2010; Cordelli, 2015; Donati and Archer, 2015; Burkitt, 2016) advocate the notion that agency should be viewed as relational, rather than individual, echoing the beliefs espoused in the international co-operative values and principles:

> ... agency is closer to the definition offered by the OED and is to do with people producing particular effects in the world and on each other through their relational connections and joint actions ... In this relational understanding of agency, individuals are to be thought of as 'interactants' rather than as singular agents or actors. (Burkitt, 2016: 323)

Relational theorists are interested in how our relationships with others are constituted so that they are 'fulfilling rather than alienating' (Donati and Archer, 2015: 15), generating 'relational goods' (or resources) such as interpersonal trust, emotional support, care, special obligations and social influence (Cordelli, 2015). Cordelli (ibid.: 89) argues that relationships need to be viewed as 'socially distributed resources' with 'identifiable institutional social bases' or 'relational distributive structures' that may, or may not, allow for fair distribution of relational resources such as interpersonal trust, emotional support, care, special obligations and social influence, all of which help in turn to build individuals' self-respect. Indeed, without access to these relational resources, Cordelli (ibid.: 98) suggests that behaving co-operatively is extremely difficult: 'it is very unlikely for individuals who lack the experience of trustworthy relationships within their families, friendships, neighborhoods, and voluntary associations to develop a sense of generalized trust towards the citizenry at large, not to mention other cooperative habits'.

While this chapter does not intend to suggest that 'becoming co-operative' offers the only solution for schools attempting to enact more relational forms of engagement, co-operative schools do provide an important experiment in the development of more relational forms and understandings of engagement. Co-operative schools have an explicit focus on building students' understanding of their role as citizens and how they can help build a fairer society (DCSF, 2009), as emphasized by the Co-operative Academies Trust:

> the Trust aims that children and young people and those that work for the Trust understand the benefits of co-operation and how a co-operative approach can make life fairer for all in the modern world, by applying co-operative and ethical values including self-help, self-responsibility, democracy, equality, equity and solidarity. (Co-operative Academies Trust, 2018b)

The development of co-operative schools is thus of key interest for those concerned with democratic practice in schools – and beyond. Scholars have long advocated ways in which democratic values and principles can be applied to school–stakeholder engagement, most famously Dewey (1966). Notions of co-operation are central to Dewey's work. He stated that forms and understandings of, as he termed it, 'human associations' with schools needed to be such that: 'the progress of one member has worth for the experience of other members – it is readily communicable' (Dewey, 1966: 42). Dewey's thinking still resonates with scholars working in the field of education and social justice today, with 'co-operation' cited as being inextricably linked to democratic practice in schools:

> Socially just schools should be safe and welcoming places for the interaction of all their members ... The philosophical principle is that debate, contestation and discussion should be a normal part of the life of the school. Co-operation is a key organizational, curricular and pedagogical concept; there is a strong belief that more will be gained through working together than competing. (Smyth and Wrigley, 2013: 203–4)

Co-operative dilemmas in the English education marketplace

While the co-operative ethos promotes the belief that more can be gained by working together (Smyth and Wrigley, 2013), the realities of constant changes in education policy have had an impact on the ways in which schools sought to position – and reposition – themselves in the education landscape. Within this context, the multi-academy trust (MAT) model has caused a particular dilemma for co-operative schools. In the current political climate, schools can, in effect, choose to be – or not to be – a co-operative school when they join a MAT of existing co-operative schools. This means that if there are two co-operative schools that have formed a small MAT and they need to expand, other schools no longer have to convert to 'become co-operative' when they join the MAT. Moreover, existing co-operative schools can decide 'not to remain co-operative' when they are joined by other non-co-operative schools.

There are anxieties from some schools that the need to 'be co-operative' could be seen as a barrier to expansion, and therefore survival, in the education marketplace. Ironically, 'being co-operative' has been cited by one large ex-co-operative school as being somehow 'less inclusive' in the context of the English education marketplace. This understanding would appear to be causing increasing numbers of schools to say that they have chosen to retain the co-operative values, but not their co-operative school status, or as one school put it: we will be 'co-operative with a small "c"'.

A further change has been in the level of support for schools choosing to convert to become co-operative academies or trust schools. Up until 2017, it was clear that the co-operative conversion process for schools was facilitated by the Co-operative College. However, this specific support in 'becoming co-operative', which offered advice on adopting co-operative governance models, curriculum resources, training for teachers, international links, enterprise projects and school improvement services to help schools embed the co-operative values into all aspects of their work, no longer exists. There is also little evidence of active support for schools from the Schools Co-operative Society (SCS), the organization set up to co-ordinate, support and speak up for co-operative trust schools and co-operative academies across England.

Yet while some of the former most vocal, high profile co-operative academies are no longer operating as 'co-operative' schools, in contrast The Co-operative Group, which established and sponsors the multi-academy trust (MAT) known as the Co-operative Academies Trust, is now the UK's largest corporate sponsor of academies and has expressed an intention to more than treble the number of academies it sponsors to 40 over the next three years (Co-operative Academies Trust, 2018c).

It is interesting to reflect, therefore, that although this latter group of co-operative schools, sponsored by The Co-operative Group, are a highly visible endorsement of the corporate sponsorship model of school academization, their 'branding' has perhaps led them to be able to survive as 'officially' co-operative in a way that other co-operative schools could not. The identities of the Co-operative Academies Trust group of schools are inextricably linked with the co-operative brand and closely connected with the global co-operative movement. The Co-operative Academies Trust schools are, therefore, explicitly 'co-operative' in their marketing to students, parents and communities. As a result, there is perhaps more onus on the 'branded' co-operative schools to enact the co-operative values and principles within and beyond the four walls of the school than is the case for those schools that are attempting to 'be co-operative' without the sponsorship brand of The Co-operative Group.

The declining number of converter co-operative schools and the increasing success of the Co-operative Academies Trust reveal how, in the current context of the English education marketplace, it is hard for a school to 'sell' or promote co-operative values if its 'brand identity' is not viewed as being 'officially' co-operative.

Co-operative places: Spaces for redefining education for a social solidarity economy

Operating in a competitive system based on thin, individualized notions of democracy that are centred on consumer choice has proved difficult for non-sponsored co-operative schools. Yet there are wider possibilities emerging – places that are seeking ways of developing social solidarity approaches to local government, in spite of the capitalist economy in which they operate, through their membership of the Co-operative Councils Innovation Network. Twenty councils in England have become co-operative councils, local authorities that have explicitly stated their intentions to recognize:

> the need to define a new model for local government built on civic leadership, with councils working in equal partnership with local people to shape and strengthen communities. This means a new role for local authorities that replaces traditional models of top down governance and service delivery with local leadership, genuine co-operation, and a new approach built on the founding

> traditions of the co-operative movement: collective action, co-operation, empowerment and enterprise ... We are a network of local authorities who are committed to reforming the way we work through building an equal partnership with local people. (Co-operative Councils' Innovation Network, n.d.)

A high proportion of these councils are operating in areas where communities have, for many years, been identified as 'impoverished' (Dyson, 2003), based on a deficit view that adopts unilateral approaches to professional relationships with local communities: doing to, rather than doing with.

In contrast, thicker, collaborative forms of democratic engagement form the core ethos of the co-operative councils: 'users are more than consumers of services – they are co-creators' (Creasy *et al.*, 2013). Yet much of the discourse in co-operative councils' approaches to education policymaking still focuses on relationship building among professionals, for example, groups of schools collaborating and offering mutual support to ensure improved outcomes (OLCP (Oldham Learning Co-operative Partnership), 2013). While this suggests that co-operative councils are setting out to facilitate more relational forms of engagement between the council and schools, and among schools themselves, the role that stakeholders (students, parents/carers and the local community) have to play in these relationships remains somewhat vague. There is a need to explore the possibilities of co-operative models that support more relational forms of engagement from the bottom up. By promoting a broader, more relational understanding of civic engagement through co-operative pedagogy, governance models, curriculum and ethos in schools, co-operative councils could perhaps provide the initial foundation for the wider prefigurative change required for the development of a social solidarity vision of education.

Building relationships for a social solidarity alternative

In moving towards a social solidarity vision of education we can learn from wider contexts. A 'bottom up' approach towards the establishment of a social solidarity economy has been instigated in Barcelona. The city has developed an 'impetus plan for a social solidarity economy' (SSE). At its heart is the recognition that our understanding of the socio-economic functioning of society, and the active role that we can play in it, is shaped from childhood (Ajuntament de Barcelona, 2016). The plan thus supports a programme of continuing professional development for educators across the city and changes to the curriculum, from primary school through to universities, with the aim to embed SSE values and practices in education institutions and generate 'critical and active citizens' (Ajuntament de Barcelona, 2016: 26).

As Barcelona has recognized, a social solidarity economy should be based on an education system that does more than improve academic outcomes; it demands an explicit commitment to developing pedagogies, curricula and governance structures that nurture a 'consciously democratic community' (Fielding, 2015: 28) from the moment children enter primary school. Developing stronger links between co-operative councils and co-operative schools (and their pedagogy, curriculum and governance) presents an opportunity for policymakers, schools and communities in England to begin to see education otherwise, 'reconciling the purpose and organization of learning as a collective societal endeavour' as a 'common good' (UNESCO, 2015: 83).

However, it cannot be ignored that there remains a particular challenge in the context of the English education marketplace. In the current climate, the dual pressures of expanding academization and the increasing 'withdrawal of the local democratic element of the public sector' (Golding, 2018) suggest that co-operative councils need the support of the Co-operative Academies Trust and its schools if these councils are to become co-operative places from the bottom up. Reimagining education policy for a social-solidarity alternative requires a vision that recognizes the interdependent relationship between education, citizenship and place. Co-operative councils, schools and their stakeholders can come together in a productive way, by actively advocating initiatives that position engagement as a collective endeavour, founded in notions of 'mutuality, a degree of reciprocal influence, and an exchange of views and interests' (Warren and Mapp, 2011: 27). A starting point would be seeking to grow the presence of co-operative schools in co-operative council locations actively. Positioned together in this way, co-operative councils and co-operative schools would no longer be 'bowling alone' (Eaude, 2009; Putnam, 2000) in the face of other, more unilateral engagement policies, but would be inextricably linked components of a 'co-operative place'. Active support for the development of co-operative pedagogy, curriculum and governance structures in schools highlights the importance of relational goods such as interpersonal trust, emotional support, care, special obligations and social influence (Cordelli, 2015), and can provide initial steps towards the broader prefigurative change required for the development of a social solidarity vision of education – and place – as a viable alternative to models of market capitalism and democracy as individualized consumer choice.

References

Ajuntament de Barcelona (2016) *The Impetus Plan for the Social and Solidarity Economy 2016–2019*. Online. http://base.socioeco.org/docs/impetusplan-sse-eng_web.pdf (accessed 12 February 2019).

Apple, M.W. (2011) 'Democratic education in neoliberal and neoconservative times'. *International Studies in Sociology of Education*, 21 (1), 21–31.

Audsley, J., Chitty, C., O'Connell, J., Watson, D. and Wills, J. (2013) *Citizen Schools: Learning to rebuild democracy*. London: Institute for Public Policy Research.

Baquedano-López, P., Alexander, R.A. and Hernandez, S.J. (2013) 'Equity issues in parental and community involvement in schools: What teacher educators need to know'. *Review of Research in Education*, 37 (1), 149–82.

Burkitt, I. (2016) 'Relational agency: Relational sociology, agency and interaction'. *European Journal of Social Theory*, 19 (3), 322–39.

Co-operative Academies Trust (2018a) 'What makes a Co-op Academy different?'. Online. https://tinyurl.com/ycjmqzdj (accessed 25 January 2019).

Co-operative Academies Trust (2018b) 'The Trust and our aims'. Online. https://tinyurl.com/y9wdv4fp (accessed 25 January 2019).

Co-operative Academies Trust (2018c) 'Co-op to turbo charge academy schools plan'. 6 April. Online. https://tinyurl.com/yabt2whs (accessed 25 January 2019).

Co-operative Councils' Innovation Network (n.d.) 'About us'. Online. www.councils.coop/about-us/ (accessed 20 November 2018).

Cordelli, C. (2015) 'Justice as fairness and relational resources'. *Journal of Political Philosophy*, 23 (1), 86–110.

Creasy, S., Reed, S. and Ussher, K. (2013) (eds), *Towards Co-operative Councils: Empowering people to change their lives*. London: Co-operative Councils Network.

DCSF (Department for Children, Schools and Families) (2009) *Co-operative Schools – Making a Difference*. Nottingham: Department for Children, Schools and Families. Online. https://tinyurl.com/y9djlmyc (accessed 28 January 2019).

Dewey, J. (1966 [1916]) *Democracy and Education: An introduction to the philosophy of education*. New York: The Free Press, Collier-Macmillan.

DfE (Department for Education) (2010) *The Importance of Teaching: The Schools White Paper 2010*. London: Department for Education. Online. https://tinyurl.com/ybtg3sxk (accessed 30 January 2019).

DfE (Department for Education) (2016) *Educational Excellence Everywhere*. London: Department for Education. Online. https://tinyurl.com/yc9frp72 (accessed 30 January 2019).

DfE (Department for Education) (2018) 'Academy sponsor contact list'. Online. https://tinyurl.com/y9rgx4qf (accessed 25 January 2019).

Donati, P. and Archer, M.S. (2015) *The Relational Subject*. Cambridge: Cambridge University Press.

Dyson, A. (2003) 'Urban education: Challenges and possibilities'. Inaugural lecture, University of Manchester, 8 December 2003.

Eaude, T. (2009) *Bowling Alone? What can schools do to promote cohesive communities?* London: National Education Trust.

Fielding, M. (1999) 'Radical collegiality: Affirming teaching as an inclusive professional Practice'. *Australian Educational Researcher*, 26 (2), 1–34.

Fielding, M. (2001) 'Students as radical agents of change'. *Journal of Educational Change*, 2 (2), 123–41.

Fielding, M. (2006) 'Leadership, radical student engagement and the necessity of person-centred education'. *International Journal of Leadership in Education*, 9 (4), 299–313.

Fielding, M. (2010) 'The radical potential of student voice: Creating spaces for restless encounters'. *International Journal of Emotional Education*, 2 (1), 61–73.

Fielding, M. (2015) 'Why co-operative schools should oppose competition and what they might do instead'. In Woodin, T. (ed.) *Co-operation, Learning and Co-operative Values: Contemporary issues in education*. London: Routledge, 17–30.

Golding, N. (2018) 'Councils' decline is as much a part of government's legacy as Brexit'. *Local Government Chronicle*, 7 February. Online. https://tinyurl.com/y9ns6gjs (accessed 25 January 2019).

Lupton, R. and Obolenskaya, P. (2013) *Labour's Record on Education: Policy, spending and outcomes 1997–2010* (Social Policy in a Cold Climate Working Paper 3). London: Centre for Analysis of Social Exclusion.

McLaughlin, C. and Clarke, B. (2010) 'Relational matters: A review of the impact of school experience on mental health in early adolescence'. *Educational and Child Psychology*, 27 (1), 91–103.

NCTL (National College for Teaching and Leadership) (2014) *Governance in Multi-Academy Trusts*. Nottingham: National College for Teaching and Leadership. Online. https://tinyurl.com/y7re6lmx (accessed 30 January 2019).

OLCP (Oldham Learning Co-operative Partnership) (2013) *Oldham Learning Co-operative Partnership Conference October 2013 – What Next?* Oldham: Oldham Council. Online. https://tinyurl.com/y9hoajc6 (accessed 30 January 2019).

Putnam, R.D. (2000) *Bowling Alone: The collapse and revival of American community*. New York: Simon and Schuster.

Shaw, L. (2014) *Case Study – A Quiet Revolution: Co-operative schools in the UK*. Online. https://tinyurl.com/y29z7sc5 (accessed 12 March 2019).

Smyth, J. and Wrigley, T. (2013) *Living on the Edge: Rethinking poverty, class and schooling*. New York: Peter Lang Publishing.

Thomson, P., Lingard, B. and Wrigley, T. (2012) 'Ideas for changing educational systems, educational policy and schools'. *Critical Studies in Education*, 53 (1), 1–7.

UNESCO (United Nations Educational, Scientific and Cultural Organization) (2015) *Rethinking Education: Towards a global common good?* Paris: UNESCO Publishing.

Warren, M.R., Hong, S., Rubin, C.L. and Uy, P.S. (2009) 'Beyond the bake sale: A community-based, relational approach to parent engagement in schools'. *Teachers College Record*, 111 (9), 2209–54.

Warren, M.R. and Mapp, K.L. (2011) *A Match on Dry Grass: Community organizing as a catalyst for school reform*. New York: Oxford University Press.

Whitty, G. (2006) 'Teacher professionalism in a new era'. General Teaching Council for Northern Ireland (GTCNI) Annual Lecture, Queens University, Belfast, March 2006.

Woodin, T. (2015) *Co-operation, Learning and Co-operative values: Contemporary issues in education*. London: Routledge.

Chapter 11

The co-operative university now!

Mike Neary and Joss Winn

> What we want and seek to obtain is a co-operative journey that will end in a co-operative university. (Rae, 1909: 29, quoted in Woodin, 2017: 34)

This chapter narrates the recent efforts of a growing number of people, including ourselves, to create a co-operative university in England. In doing so, we situate these efforts within the broader political and economic climate of UK higher education and in light of both historical and recent developments in the co-operative movement. Recognizing that the idea of creating a co-operative university in the UK is one that has been written about for over a century, we found ourselves asking, 'why now?'

Before now

Throughout this chapter, we point to the role of the Co-operative College, Manchester, in supporting, and more recently leading, efforts to develop a co-operative university. During the course of our research in the College's archives, we found that this desire for co-operative higher education extends back to the mid-nineteenth century.

The earliest references we could find to a co-operative university or co-operative higher education dates to 1872, with Nicholas Balline, an advocate of co-operatives in Russia, who saw the establishment of a co-operative university as a way to further 'propaganda' about the co-operative movement (Twigg, 1924: 17). The idea that education is integral to the promotion of a more co-operative society has been shared throughout the history of the co-operative movement and is instilled in the current principle of 'education, training and information'.[1] Co-operators were also urging closer relations with the University Extension Scheme, which began in 1873 with support from 'various co-operative stores ... both financially and supplying meeting rooms, and continued to do so for years afterwards' (Twigg, 1924: 18–19). At the Stratford Congress in 1904, Edward Owen Greening made a plea in his inaugural address for a co-operative university, as did W.R. Rae in 1909 in his presidential address at the Newcastle Congress quoted at the start of this chapter.

By 1913, there is a sense of rapid social change and a need for the co-operative movement to understand itself and its historical conditions. A pamphlet written by Thomas Anderson, the chairman of York Education Committee, expresses a sense of urgency, stating that, 'If nothing is done to change present conditions we shall sink back into barbarism from which there seems no escape ... Our real weapon of defence is knowledge, and that knowledge must come from some highly developed centre directing the movement on right line' (Anderson, 1913: 10). A co-operative college was seen as a way to fulfil the need for research, teaching and training of its members and for leadership of the movement (ibid.: 7–9).

A year later, we find that money once contributed by co-operatives to fund their libraries was no longer required as the state was increasingly providing public facilities. In a pamphlet entitled *A Co-operative College*, an (anonymous) author argues that 'co-operative funds can now be well applied for the extension of facilities for the higher education of co-operators in other ways, and, in particular, for education in liberal subjects ... for the realization of the co-operative ideal' (Anonymous, 1914: 3). This emphasis on a liberal curriculum recurs throughout these early publications. The same author writes that, 'In short, the college should create a burning desire for social justice, inspire a willingness to work for it, and provide the knowledge how best to attain it ... Our aim should be to provide education in its widest sense: an education for the highest purposes of life' (ibid.: 5). Indeed, in this and later publications, we find that the Co-operative College fulfils this aim by offering a broad curriculum of education in the social sciences, economics and humanities.

In the same 1914 pamphlet, the first 'Objects of a Co-operative College' were published, clearly setting out the ambition for co-operative higher education. Two of the three Objects were:

> To complete the scheme of Co-operative Education by providing a centre for higher education in the specialised subjects required for the full equipment of the co-operator and for the further development of efficiency in the Co-operative Movement ... To undertake investigation and research calculated to aid the general development and progress of Co-operation and stimulate the application of co-operative principles in the solution of social problems. (ibid.: 13)

This brief, foundational statement indicates that by this time, the vision for co-operative higher education was broader than propaganda for the movement and extended to education and research that served wider social objectives. Early co-operators also recognized the need to combine research and teaching, envisioning the College to be 'a centre for enquiry and investigation' where 'teaching should never be divorced from learning and enquiry' (ibid.: 15).

However, despite the establishment of the College in 1919, there appears to have been no further development towards a co-operative university until 1936, when the College published 'A ten-year plan for co-operative education', which included among its six points that of 'Strengthening the Co-operative College and its Work, with a view to the ultimate establishment of a Co-operative University with constituent colleges in various parts of the country' (Co-operative Union, 1936: 11–12). It is likely that the Second World War interrupted such a development, yet in 1944 the vision of a co-operative university was being refined and articulated in a retrospective Co-operative College brochure (Co-operative Union, 1944). The publication offers a history of the College during this period and states that, 'This central British Co-operative College could become the nucleus of a Co-operative University of Great Britain, with a number of affiliated sectional and regional Colleges of Co-operative Institutes, as the demand arises.'

It is not our intention here to write a history of the Co-operative College, nor have we investigated post-war archival literature, yet what we hope to have shown is that the explicit idea of a co-operative university has existed within the co-operative movement for over 140 years and that the Co-operative College has, since its original conception, had the objective of becoming a centre for higher education: a federated co-operative university. This is evident in the way that early co-operators referred to the College as a centre that combines both research and teaching, that offers a wide curriculum across the scholarly disciplines and that makes a contribution to a democratic society as well as equipping students with the knowledge and skills needed in the (co-operative) workplace. These aspirations remain the same today.

Now: 2009–18

The preceding section shows that we are writing at a specific moment in the history of an idea and an institution: the idea of co-operative higher education and the establishment of a co-operative university in the UK. At *this* moment, we are increasingly confident that a co-operative university will be created in England within the next five years due to activities happening right *now*. Unlike previous work in this area that we have written about (Neary and Winn, 2017a, 2017b, 2017c; Neary *et al.*, 2018), which discusses discrete research projects, this chapter is an attempt to understand the historical moment in which we are working. By narrating this process we aim to reflect on the momentum being built for a co-operative university. At the same time, other scholars are also beginning to undertake research into co-operative higher education (Woodin, 2017, 2018) and it is increasingly attracting commentary in the press.[2]

The decade between 2009 and 2018 has been one of significant reform in the English higher education sector. In November 2009, the Labour Government announced the 'Independent Review of Higher Education Funding and Student Finance' (the 'Browne Review'). Among its recommendations, the Browne Review (Browne, 2010) made the case for removing the cap on tuition fees altogether and proposed a revised loan system to support this radical move. The new Conservative–Liberal Democrat Coalition Government responded by introducing a maximum fee of £9,000 per year from 2012/13, and at the same time removing most of the direct funding provided to universities. Students attending English universities now graduate with an average debt of over £50,000 incurred by their university education, double the figure before the changes in 2012 (Belfield *et al.*, 2017: 2). In anticipation of this scenario, students were quick to respond to the Browne Review. Between the publication of the report in October 2010 and the parliamentary vote on tuition fees two months later, students staged a series of protests and occupations across the country. We attended some of those events, including an occupation at our own university.

Students' and academics' demands for democratic governance of universities

Although the rise in tuition fees and the removal of core funding for teaching was a focal point for the protests, students and academics were aware of the wider implications of the new funding system. The principle of converting direct public funding of universities to private debt, and the concomitant conversion of the student into a consumer of higher education, had both ontological and epistemological ramifications. Students were clearly positioned as consumers in the marketization of higher education, prior to becoming learners (Consumer Rights Act 2015; see UK Parliament, 2015).

In 2015, we reviewed the websites of over 35 student occupations that had taken place in the previous five years[3] and found that students were increasingly seeing the issues they were protesting against as a matter of a 'democratic deficit' (McGettigan, 2014) in higher education. Among the list of demands students were issuing from their occupation of university spaces was a demand for greater democratic participation in the running of their institutions. For example, an occupation of University College London in 2010 included the following:

> We demand an increase in the number of students on the council. These students should be directly elected through UCLU [Students' Union UCL]. We assert that all staff of UCL have an equal right to take part in the decision making process of the university. We therefore demand that UCL includes non-academic staff on the council. ... Regarding the academic board, we wish to re-implement genuine democracy through an increase in student representation and the re-introduction of elected Deans.[4]

In Edinburgh in 2011, students demanded that 'Universities should be democratically organised: directly controlled by staff and students.'[5] And in Manchester in 2015, students demanded:

> a student–staff body, directly elected by students and academic and non-academic staff, responsible for making all managerial decisions of the institution. The university is nothing but the sum of its parts. Students and workers are at the essence of this institution and thus should have direct and democratic control.[6]

Most recently, a two-week strike that took place in March 2018 over changes to one of the main university pension schemes (Universities Superannuation Scheme, USS) provides a similar form of data – only this time published by academics who, although protesting about their pensions, understood the broader implications of what was happening to their work and lives. A USSbrief (a set of papers written by university staff and students) published during the strike notes that 'The industrial dispute has brought a certain unruly democracy crashing into higher education, opening up spaces to discuss the effects of recent trends' and that 'As many of the USSbriefs have shown, the processes prompted by these values have up to now escaped democratic oversight, remaining concealed within obscure reports or beyond the remit of FOI [Freedom of Information] requests' (Pearce, 2018: 1–2). It is noteworthy, too, that during the period of the strike, there were 26 student-led occupations acting in solidarity with the University and College Union (UCU) strike. The author of USSbriefs20 stated that:

In all these examples, we saw students draw explicit connections between their struggles and those of staff members via such broader concerns as the democratic accountability of academic institutions and, of course, the marketisation and commodification of education. (Davison, 2018: 3)

In April 2018, the National Campaign Against Fees and Cuts (NCAFC) coalition of students and workers reflected on the efforts of striking academics, writing that:

From the beginning of this dispute you consistently argued that 'this is about more than pensions'; if this strike is won, students and staff will be in a much better position to roll back the marketisation of education, form an end to tuition fees, casualisation, the gender pay gap, and outsourcing, to the democratisation of our institutions. Together we have shown that #WeAreTheUniversity, that together workers and students run the show, and together if necessary we can shut it down: we have shaken higher education to the bone.[7]

This evidence testifies to the anger and anxiety among many students and academics caused by the Browne Review. These views and experiences are not shared by all across the higher education sector, but have given rise to a significant energy to create alternatives within and against the current system.

Similar motivations and challenges are shared by many of the recent initiatives to create co-operative forms of higher education.[8] We have personal experience of this, too, having been founding members of the Social Science Centre, Lincoln (SSC)[9] in 2010 (Neary and Winn, 2017c). Unknown to us at that time, scholars and members of the UK co-operative movement were also discussing the need and potential for a co-operative university (Juby, 2011; Ridley-Duff, 2011) and in the past eight years the knowledge, energy and aspirations of people working and studying within the higher education and co-operative sectors in the UK and elsewhere have led to concrete plans to establish a federated co-operative university in the UK, co-ordinated by the Co-operative College. The RED Learning Co-operative encapsulates the issues raised by the co-operative university:

The RED Learning Co-operative has emerged from the tradition of radical trade union education. This tradition takes as its starting point, that critical and engaged study is an integral part of how the labour movement, and other allied social movements, can face the challenges of the current political landscape, as well as grasp the opportunities that are emerging. Our approach has been a response to the neoliberalisation of education and the narrow instrumentalist focus around employability which is currently dominating the HE [higher education] landscape, and shaping the relationship of academics and tutors with HE students.

The education we offer is based on principles of working collaboratively to develop critically reflective, radical education. We aim to provide research, training and education that responds to the needs and interests of the learners and research partners, and in which the relationship with students and research participants is at the core of the educational and research experience. The constituency of RED Learning Co-operative are, therefore, those who see the need for education to go beyond the skills training of mainstream education, and provide a space for engaged dialogue and learning. We have started our educational co-operative by building a base of training courses and through these, our relationships with trade unions.

However, there have been significant challenges faced in the process of setting up an HE Co-operative. At a relatively superficial (but hugely important) level these have been practical – finding the time to meet together as a group, getting access to money to fund initial start-up costs, and managing the initial workload of training between us, and earning a minimal income for individual members at the same time as coming together as a group of workers in a more co-operative financial arrangement.

At another level, the challenges have also concerned the processes of validation and accreditation. As experienced educationalists we are familiar with, and able to undertake, benchmarking exercises, and we are confident that our courses offer appropriate levels of educational achievement. After level 5 it is significantly more expensive and difficult to validate and accredit courses as this constitutes a full under-graduate qualification. This poses a serious financial challenge for small co-operatives, without funding, to undertake this process, and we therefore will struggle to offer fully validated alternatives to mainstream HE. This is a clear illustration of the way that gaining academic 'legitimacy' has been effectively restricted to established and funded institutions, excluding those who want to challenge this model of HE institutions.

Finally, it is important to recognise the challenges of finding the space to develop our own ways of working, and establishing the values and principles that lie at the heart of what we do. As a group of teachers and researchers who worked together in a mainstream institutional HE context, we were – in that context – able to work together co-operatively, and collegially. However, finding a new set of practices outside of the familiar hierarchies and routines is difficult. We are increasingly conscious of the need to recognise, name and challenge collectively the hidden hierarchies between us, and the inevitable clashes of values and principles that come to the fore when not shrouded by institutionalised norms and practices. (Personal communication, 8 July 2018)

As we can see, there are a number of challenges for small co-operatives such as RED to confront and not all such projects can be sustained. Reflecting recently on his involvement in creating co-operative higher education since 2013, Joel Lazarus from the Bristol Learning Co-op[10] also sees the process as both challenging and educational but offers a broader perspective on what is currently happening:

Over the years, most of the embryonic projects folded. Some remained. At the time, I couldn't see the bigger picture. I saw the end of a project as failure. I couldn't see how failure was just part of a collective, emergent learning process being experienced by a UK-wide community of praxis and how, through its praxis, through its constant prototyping, through its imagination, this community was contributing the vital foundations – the people, the energy, the ideas – to the movement to establish a co-operative university. (Personal communication, 11 June 2018)

Inside the co-operative university

The co-operative university is being created as we write in November 2018. Next, we want to record what that has recently entailed before reflecting on how we got here. In 2017, there were a series of significant initiatives that have helped legitimize and accelerate efforts towards creating a co-operative university. The first was the hosting of a round-table event at the Co-operative College in January 2017 to discuss establishing a co-operative university.

Members of the round-table event included representatives from Students for Cooperation,[11] researchers of co-operatives, and representatives of Vaughan College, RED and the Social Science Centre, Manchester. This was the first time such a group had come together to discuss co-operative higher education and was recognized as a historic moment, there being unanimous support to create a co-operative university in England. The group was tasked with drafting a proposal to be put to the Co-operative College trustees to formally establish a Co-operative University Working Group (CUWG).

The CUWG was established in April 2017. Its purpose was to take a twin-track approach to exploring (a) a federated co-operative university model and (b) how the Co-operative College might work towards acquiring degree-awarding powers as a secondary co-operative. In October 2017, the CUWG presented 'A Feasibility Study to Acquire Degree Awarding Powers (in the light of the Higher Education and Research Act)' (Ramos-Arroyo, 2017) to the Co-operative College's board of trustees, who accepted the report's recommendations to create an Academic Board at the College and to explore the feasibility of 'a federated co-operative university and all of its possibilities'. This was the second such report commissioned by the College, the first being *Realising the Co-operative University* (Cook, 2013), a landmark study that helped establish the potential for a co-operative university in the UK. Informed by the work of the CUWG, the Co-operative Party included a section on co-operative higher education in its Education Policy 2017.[12]

In November 2017, the CUWG hosted a dedicated 'Making the co-operative university' conference [13] attended by over 90 delegates. An outcome of the conference was for the CUWG to establish a Co-operative Higher Education Network (CHEN) and a Co-operative University Forum (CUF). The CHEN is a general-purpose mailing list with a focus on co-operative higher education. The CUF is hosted by the Co-operative University Working Group and acts as an advisory group to help support the development of a co-operative university linked to the Co-operative College.

In December 2017, representatives from the CUF met with the Higher Education Funding Council for England (HEFCE) to discuss the College's plans to establish a co-operative university. In January 2018, representatives from the CUF met with the Quality Assurance Agency (QAA) to discuss the aspirations of the College, the timeline for higher education accreditation and the support available from the QAA. These discussions were encouraging and provided the CUF with sufficient direction about the expectations of the new regulator, the Office for Students (OfS), and the timescales involved. The task was to work towards obtaining degree-awarding powers so that a degree programme could be run from September 2019. This required that the College first register with the OfS in April 2018 and submit its application in August 2018. To achieve this, three expert round tables were organized. In preparation for the round tables, members of the CUF were invited to contribute their views on the themes of governance, accreditation and funding for the Co-operative University. These online discussions confirmed for us that the vision among those involved was quite consistent and coherent and that the co-operative values and principles provided a common language for the discussion of what we are trying to achieve.

Governance

The round table on governance was attended by student and academic representatives from the CUF, as well as by the College's chair of trustees, an invited member of the Committee of University Chairs (CUC, the oversight body of governance in the higher education sector) and a legal expert from Co-operatives UK. It took place just weeks after the College had announced at its annual conference that it had formally registered with the new regulator, and that plans for acquiring degree-awarding powers and developing a model for a future Co-operative University were on track. The aim of the first meeting was to develop a model of democratic governance that was federated, with member co-operatives undertaking research and delivering educational programmes that were accredited by the university, which acted as an 'apex body' or secondary co-operative, similar to the way that the University of Mondragon operates (Wright *et al.*, 2011; Neary *et al.*, 2018). This model of governance would need to comply with the values, principles and regulations of co-operatives, as well as the Higher Education Code of Governance (CUC, 2018). The outcome of the day was both a sense of compatibility between co-operative governance and the Higher Education Code of Governance. It provided sufficient information for Co-operatives UK to draft a document that outlined the features of the governance model in terms of membership, organizational culture, financial management and the operation of the board. Given the Co-operative College's now integral role in the formation of a co-operative university, it was clear that adoption of the model would have to be gradual, allowing it time to modify its own constitutional arrangements. The College would initially run one or more degree programmes under its current form of governance, while developing the federated model over a three-year period, by which time it would hope to be in a position to validate and award the degree programmes of other co-operatives and work towards gaining university title.

Pedagogy, curriculum and assessment

The next round table was held a month later. Those present established a baseline of understanding for teaching practice, conceived as a form of radical epistemology. The group understood 'radical epistemology' to mean that teaching is a key component in the production of knowledge for the benefit of the commonwealth. An appreciation of this baseline provided the framework within which the main themes (pedagogy, curriculum and assessment) for the day were discussed. These main themes were brought together with the understanding of radical epistemology as 'a demanding common task' based on a shared vision and learning by doing. In this model, everyone approaches the task from a different starting point, skills and experience, yet all develop a mastery of a shared set of mental and manual tools, used in different ways. The round table concluded with an exercise in mapping the main themes to the regulator's concerns of student retention, employability and engagement. We all agreed that not only did the way in which we conceptualized our themes match with these imperatives, but they even transcended them: not simply student engagement but co-operative membership involving democratic ownership and control of the university; not simply student retention but commitment and a sense of belonging to the co-operative, and not simply employability but the reorganization of employment that supports the interests of workers rather than capital.

Finance

The final round table was held in July 2018. Attendees included experts in co-operative finance and higher education funding. Throughout the past decade of discussions about co-operative higher education, we have found that the most difficult questions were those relating to the business model of a co-operative university. In one sense, this is not surprising because, as discussed earlier, the impact of the tuition fee rise and the new loan system that followed the Browne Review meant that many of us were committed to restoring free, public, higher education, yet had identified with co-operative values and principles, which emphasized self-help, member economic participation and autonomy from the state. Co-operatives are owned and run by members rather than by public organizations, and typically rely on investment from the members rather than the state. The contradiction between public and private organizations has been apparent to us for some time (Neary and Winn, 2017b) and increasingly, in our own work, we have privileged the need for democratic member control over creating a publicly funded institution. Most of the participants at the round table favoured a model of charging student fees along with maintenance loans to take advantage of the government funding available, with the knowledge that repayment rates would be low. Participants discussed ways in which monies could be returned to the students through bursaries, wages and even a dividend on their fees, now seen as an investment, at the end of their period of studies and/or annually. The financial relationship between the Co-operative College and the network of federated co-operatives was discussed at length, but without arriving at any final conclusions.

Next steps

Each of the round-table events provided critical and practical guidance that informed the Co-operative College's application for degree-awarding powers, recognizing that this was the necessary first step towards creating a federated co-operative university. A key and ongoing concern for the project is whether prospective higher education students want to come to the Co-operative College (HE).

Following the round-table meetings, a writing group was established to complete the Office for Students' *Access and Participation Plan*. The group met for three days in July 2018 at the Co-operative College. The *Access and Participation Plan* had to show how providers will promote access to their degree programmes for students who have found it difficult to access higher education in ways that improve student success and social mobility.[14] The meeting provided the opportunity for those present to clearly express the aims and ambitions of the Co-operative College (HE) in writing. The approach to this activity was to set out the aims and ambitions of the Co-operative College (HE) in ways that challenged the basis of the questions that were being asked, while at the same time showing how enhanced provision, based on the OfS's planning imperatives, could be provided by the College's co-operative, collegiate and collective approach.

Why now?

Having offered our narrative of the development of the idea of co-operative higher education and the creation of a co-operative university in England, we now want to return to the question that was provoked by our reading of the archival documents from the early history of the Co-operative College: Given that the idea of a co-operative university is over a century old, why is it happening only now? While acknowledging the agency of individuals, we argue that it is a confluence of changes in both the higher education and co-operative sectors that has only recently reached a point whereby it was felt among students and academics that a co-operative alternative was needed in the higher education sector and that the co-operative sector had an adequate response to this need.

Contrary to common complaints about the effective privatization of UK higher education since the 1980s, Shattock (2008) argues that the higher education sector has moved from being explicitly 'self-governed' to one that is now 'state governed', and subsequently 'the formation of higher education policy therefore needs to be reinterpreted as an adjunct of public policy, rather than as something intrinsic to higher education' (ibid.: 185–6). Exogenously driven policy initiatives over the past three decades have weakened the control that academics had over the running of their institutions and made way for the implementation of New Public Management reforms in the higher education sector.

Although this development would suggest a concurrent strengthening of both governance and leadership within the university sector, the effect has been 'to reduce the role of governance and greatly enhance that of leadership and management' (Shattock, 2013: 219). This is due to the volatility of funding to the sector in the first decade of the century and the implicit threats, which have reinforced hierarchies and encouraged centralization of decision-making. University governing bodies are, Shattock argues, too far removed from university strategy to contribute effectively and we thus have the paradox that at a time when the higher education environment has come to replicate private sector conditions in its market orientation more than at any time since the First World War, the private sector company governance model seems to be the least appropriate (Shattock, 2013: 222).

Earlier in this chapter, we have shown what impact these changes in higher education policy have had on students and academics and the way in which some have responded by occupying their institutions and striking, demanding greater democracy and accountability in their universities. While these acts of resistance are both understandable and necessary, the most recent change in higher education legislation (Higher Education and Research Act 2017; see UK Parliament, 2017) appears to have offered a historically unique opportunity for the introduction of co-operative governance and leadership in higher education. In fact, the publications leading up to the Higher Education and Research Act 2017 explicitly encouraged 'challenger institutions' as a way to further the marketization of the sector (and potentially widen participation), stimulate efficiencies and raise the quality of provision to paying students (BIS (Department for Business, Innovation and Skills), 2016).

Since 2018, the higher education sector has never been more open to new entrants yet it has never been more subject to state regulation and control. Within this difficult regulatory environment, those of us working on the co-operative university are drawing on developments within co-operative governance over the past few decades, in particular the multi-stakeholder model, which offer a way of reconciling the diverse interests of a university community. As a historically new form of institutional governance, the multi-stakeholder model appears to be compatible with traditional collegial structures (Cook, 2013) and speaks to many of the concerns raised over increased corporate governance structures and hierarchical management of universities (Bacon, 2014; Shattock, 2013). It also has much to commend for more radical, popular and community-based forms of education, which are already identifying with the 'new co-operativism' for the 'social-solidarity economy' (Vieta, 2010).

Ridley-Duff and Bull's work (2014) provides a useful account of the development of the multi-stakeholder co-operative model that has become aligned with the new co-operativism. Their research examines 'the historical shifts that have led to the emergence of a social and solidarity economy, and how those shifts were expressed in the UK during its formative years' (ibid.: 2). The multi-stakeholder (also referred to as the 'solidarity' or 'social') co-operative model overcomes the single-member models of worker or consumer co-operatives and recognizes that both workers and consumers, as well as other supporting individuals and organizations, might each wish to share the responsibility of owning and running the co-operative. Such a model has its historical roots in Spanish co-operatives during the 1960s, where workers and consumers wanted to integrate shared ownership and governance as an expression of solidarity (Ridley-Duff and Bull, 2014). By the 1990s, multi-stakeholder models were thriving elsewhere in Europe with political and legal support and recognition, yet the UK instead shifted towards a US model of social entrepreneurship, which was more broadly defined to accommodate the charity and voluntary sectors.

The multi-stakeholder co-operative model is relatively new as a form of corporate governance; most universities were created before it was introduced into the UK in 2009, but it is now a credible model of governance when existing public and private models of higher education governance have arguably failed. In the UK, the multi-stakeholder model of co-operative governance has only been formally supported by Co-operatives UK since 2012 and was only internationally endorsed by the co-operative movement in 2011 (CICOPA, 2011). Yet, in our view, for the first time in recent university history, a model of institutional ownership and control exists that is adequate for a post-1968[15] university, one that helps overcome the unnecessary antagonism between the interests of academics and students. This co-operative model of ownership and governance has matured exactly at a time when both students and academics are aware that the idea of 'public higher education' has disintegrated; when corporate governance is weak and executive decision-making is being strengthened; and at a time when entry into the higher education sector has been encouraged by the same legislation.

Then, now and the future

We have set out an account showing how the co-operative university is being created, as part of a historical process, focusing on the contemporary context: the now. It is important at the end of this account to recognize the co-operative movement's interest not only in history and the now but also in the future. For the early co-operators like George Jacob Holyoake (1817–1906), the co-operative enterprise was a moment of transition towards a more enlarged and comprehensive version of co-operativism, as a type of association based on absolute equality where all goods and land would be held in common along with the end of wage slavery (Gurney, 1988). Explicit then in the co-operative movement is the ambition not simply to replicate forms of corporation that can subsist on terms established by the financial and state sectors, nor simply to create more socialized models of governance like the multi-stakeholder approach, but to create a new commonwealth as the basis for a co-operative future. This is a continuing story.

Notes

[1] The original Objects of the Rochdale Pioneers (1844) state: 'That as soon as practicable the Society shall proceed to arrange the powers of production, distribution, education and government, or in other words, to establish a self-supporting home colony of united interests, or assist other societies in establishing such colonies.' The 'Rochdale Principles' (1937) refer to the 'promotion of education', later revised by the International Co-operative Alliance (1966) to become 'Education of members and public in cooperative principles'. The most recent ICA Principles (1995) include principle five: education, training and information.

[2] A bibliography can be found at http://josswinn.org/2013/11/21/co-operative-universities-a-bibliography (accessed 1 November 2018).

[3] http://josswinn.org/2015/05/21/student-demands-for-democratic-control-over-universities (accessed 1 November 2018).

[4] https://ucloccupation.wordpress.com/demands (accessed 1 November 2018).

[5] https://edinunianticuts.wordpress.com/2011/11/27/our-demands-2 (accessed 1 November 2018).

[6] https://freeeducationmcr.wordpress.com/2015/05/14/demands-from-the-occupation-to-university-management (accessed 1 November 2018).

[7] http://anticuts.com/2018/04/13/students-stand-in-solidarity-with-no-vote (accessed 1 November 2018).

[8] Other initiatives currently also exist, such as the Social Science Centre (in Lincoln and Manchester), Leicester Vaughan College, the Centre for Human Ecology (Glasgow), the Feral Art College (Hull) and Bristol Learning Co-op. Outside the UK, we are aware of the Cooperative Institute for Transnational Studies (Greece), the People's University of Social Solidarity Economy (Greece), UniCoop (Mexico), Florida Universitaria (Spain) and Mondragon University (Spain). The two examples from Spain are both well-established worker co-operatives with decades of experience as providers of higher education. The Vice-Rector of Mondragon University, Jon Altuna, has been hugely supportive of establishing a co-operative university in England and a regular contributor to discussions.

[9] http://socialsciencecentre.org.uk (accessed 1 November 2018).

[10] http://bristollearningcoop.org.uk (accessed 1 November 2018).

[11] www.students.coop (accessed 1 November 2018).

[12] https://party.coop/publication/instilling-co-operation-into-learning (accessed 1 November 2018).

[13] www.timeshighereducation.com/blog/working-towards-cooperative-university-uk (accessed 1 November 2018).

[14] *Access and Participation Plan 2019–2020*. https://tinyurl.com/y3dc8xxd (accessed 1 November 2018).

[15] 1968 was a historic year when students and others demonstrated across the world (Ross, 2002; Cockburn and Blackburn, 1969).

References

Anderson, T. (1913) *A Co-operative College: The next step in our educational development*. Manchester: Co-operative Union.

Anonymous (1914) *A Co-operative College*. Manchester: Co-operative Union.

Bacon, E. (2014) *Neo-Collegiality: Restoring academic engagement in the managerial university* (Stimulus Paper). London: Leadership Foundation for Higher Education. Online. https://tinyurl.com/jtt97uc (accessed 30 January 2019).

BIS (Department for Business, Innovation and Skills) (2016) *Success as a Knowledge Economy: Teaching excellence, social mobility and student choice*. London: Department for Business, Innovation and Skills. Online. https://tinyurl.com/ybs973ep (accessed 30 January 2019).

Belfield, C., Britton, J., Dearden, L. and van der Erve, L. (2017) *Higher Education Funding in England: Past, present and options for the future* (IFS Briefing Note BN211). London: Institute for Fiscal Studies. Online. www.ifs.org.uk/uploads/BN211.pdf (accessed 30 January 2019).

Browne, J. (2010) *Securing a Sustainable Future for Higher Education: An independent review of higher education funding and student finance*. London: Department for Business, Innovation and Skills. Online. https://tinyurl.com/y7vrl7s8 (accessed 30 January 2019).

CICOPA (2011) 'World Standard of Social Cooperatives'. Online. https://tinyurl.com/yb3qddwv (accessed 30 January 2019).

Cockburn, A. and Blackburn, R. (eds) (1969) *Student Power: Problems, diagnosis, action*. Harmondsworth: Penguin Books Ltd.

Cook, D. (2013) *Realising the Co-operative University: A consultancy report for the Co-operative College*. Manchester: Co-operative College. Online. https://tinyurl.com/y929axq9 (accessed 30 January 2019).

Co-operative Union (1936) *The Co-operative Educator,* January. Manchester: The Co-operative Union Ltd.

Co-operative Union (1944) *The British Co-operative College 1919–1944:* Through knowledge to service. Manchester: The Co-operative Union Ltd.

CUC (Committee of University Chairs) (2018) *The Higher Education Code of Governance.* Bristol: Committee of University Chairs. Online. https://tinyurl.com/ydy926jf (accessed 30 January 2019).

Davison, D. (2018) 'From 2010 to 2018: Some observations about occupations'. *USS Briefs*, 20, 1–4. Online. https://tinyurl.com/y9r2kdvr (accessed 30 January 2019).

Gurney, P. (1988) 'George Jacob Holyoake: Socialism, association and co-operation in nineteenth-century England'. In Yeo, S. (ed.) *New Views of Co-operation.* London: Routledge, 52–72.

Juby, P. (2011) 'A co-operative university?'. Presentation at the UK Society for Co-operative Studies (UKSCS) Annual Conference, 3–4 September 2011. Online. https://tinyurl.com/y7x9qzbq (accessed 1 February 2019).

McGettigan, A. (2014) 'Financialising the university'. *Arena Magazine*, 128, 39–41. Online. https://arena.org.au/financialising-the-university/ (accessed 1 November 2018).

Neary, M., Valenzuela-Fuentes, K. and Winn, J. (2018) *Co-operative Leadership for Higher Education.* London: Leadership Foundation for Higher Education.

Neary, M. and Winn, J. (2017a) 'There is an alternative: A report on an action research project to develop a framework for co-operative higher education'. *Learning and Teaching: The International Journal of Higher Education in the Social Sciences*, 10 (1), 87–105.

Neary, M. and Winn, J. (2017b) 'Beyond public and private: A framework for co-operative higher education'. *Open Library of Humanities*, 3 (2), Article 2, 1–36. Online. https://olh.openlibhums.org/articles/10.16995/olh.195/ (accessed 24 January 2019).

Neary, M. and Winn, J. (2017c) 'The Social Science Centre, Lincoln: The theory and practice of a radical idea'. *Roars Transactions: A Journal on Research Policy and Evaluation*, 5 (1), 1–12.

Pearce, W. (2018) 'How to constitute a Joint Expert Panel'. *USS Briefs*, 19, 1–3. Online. https://tinyurl.com/yatut3o4 (accessed 30 January 2019).

Ramos-Arroyo, E. (2017) 'A Feasibility Study to Acquire Degree Awarding Powers (in the Light of the Higher Education and Research Act)'. Unpublished MBA thesis, UCL Institute of Education.

Ridley-Duff, R. (2011) *Co-operative University and Business School: Developing an institutional and educational offer* (Discussion Document Draft 3). Manchester: UK Society for Co-operative Studies. Online. https://tinyurl.com/yavmxorf (accessed 30 January 2019).

Ridley-Duff, R. and Bull, M. (2014) 'Solidarity co-operatives: An embedded historical communitarian pluralist approach to social enterprise development?'. Keynote presentation at the Social Innovation and Entrepreneurship Research Colloquium, RMIT University, Melbourne, 26–28 November 2014. Online. http://shura.shu.ac.uk/9890/ (accessed 1 November 2018).

Ross, K. (2002) *May '68 and its Afterlives.* Chicago: University of Chicago Press.

Shattock, M. (2008) 'The change from private to public governance of British higher education: Its consequences for higher education policy making 1980–2006'. *Higher Education Quarterly*, 62 (3), 181–203.

Shattock, M. (2013) 'University governance, leadership and management in a decade of diversification and uncertainty'. *Higher Education Quarterly*, 67 (3), 217–33.

Twigg, H.J. (1924) *An Outline History of Co-operative Education*. Manchester: Co-operative Union.

UK Parliament (2015) 'Consumer Rights Act 2015'. Online. https://tinyurl.com/ohuacyo (accessed 30 January 2019).

UK Parliament (2017) 'Higher Education and Research Act 2017'. Online. https://tinyurl.com/y8julfme (accessed 30 January 2019).

Vieta, M. (2010) 'The new cooperativism'. *Affinities: A Journal of Radical Theory, Culture, and Action*, 4 (1), 1–11.

Woodin, T. (2017) 'Co-operation, leadership and learning: Fred Hall and the Co-operative College before 1939'. In Hall, R. and Winn, J. (eds) *Mass Intellectuality and Democratic Leadership in Higher Education*. London: Bloomsbury Academic, 27–40.

Woodin, T. (2018) 'Co-operative approaches to leading and learning: Ideas for democratic innovation from the UK and beyond'. In Gornall, L., Thomas, B. and Sweetman, L. (eds) *Exploring Consensual Leadership in Higher Education: Co-operation, collaboration and partnership*. London: Bloomsbury Academic, 71–88.

Wright, S., Greenwood, D. and Boden, R. (2011) 'Report on a field visit to Mondragón University: A cooperative experience/experiment'. *Learning and Teaching*, 4 (3), 38–56.

Index

Index